William Cowper, John Bruce

Poetical Works

Vol. 2

William Cowper, John Bruce

Poetical Works
Vol. 2

ISBN/EAN: 9783337778538

Printed in Europe, USA, Canada, Australia, Japan

Cover: Foto ©Thomas Meinert / pixelio.de

More available books at **www.hansebooks.com**

THE POETICAL WORKS OF

WILLIAM COWPER

WITH NOTES AND A MEMOIR

BY JOHN BRUCE

VOLUME II

LONDON

BELL AND DALDY, FLEET STREET

1865

CONTENTS.

VOL. II.

vi   CONTENTS.

T H E

T A S K,

A

P O E M,

I N S I X B O O K S.

By WILLIAM COWPER,

OF THE INNER TEMPLE, ESQ.

Fit furculus arbor.
ANONYM.

To which are added,

BY THE SAME AUTHOR,

An EPISTLE to JOSEPH HILL, Efq. TIROCINIUM, or a REVIEW of SCHOOLS, and the HISTORY of JOHN GILPIN.

———————

LONDON:
PRINTED FOR J. JOHNSON, N° 72, ST. PAUL'S CHURCH-YARD:
1785.

[*Copy of the title-page of Cowper's second publication.*]

THE TASK.   BOOK I.

THE SOFA.

ARGUMENT.

HISTORICAL deduction of seats, from the Stool to the Sofa.
A schoolboy's ramble. A walk in the country. The scene
described. Rural sounds as well as sights delightful. A-
nother walk. Mistake concerning the charms of solitude
corrected. Colonnades commended. Alcove, and the view
from it. The wilderness. The grove. The thresher. The
necessity and the benefits of exercise. The works of Nature
superior to, and in some instances inimitable by, Art. The
wearisomeness of what is commonly called a life of pleasure.
Change of scene sometimes expedient. A common described,
and the character of crazy Kate introduced.* Gipsies. The
blessings of civilized life. That state most favourable to
virtue. The South Sea islanders compassionated, but chiefly
Omai. His present state of mind supposed. Civilized life
friendly to virtue, but not great cities. Great cities, and
London in particular, allowed their due praise, but censured.
Fête champêtre. The book concludes with a reflection on the
effects of dissipation and effeminacy upon our public measures.

* "Upon it," was originally added here. It was omitted
from the edition of 1787, and from subsequent editions, but
has been restored by Southey.

ADVERTISEMENT.

HE history of the following production is briefly this : A lady, fond of blank verse, demanded a poem of that kind from the Author, and gave him the SOFA for a subject. He obeyed; and having much leisure, connected another subject with it ; and pursuing the train of thought to which his situation and turn of mind led him, brought forth at length, instead of the trifle which he at first intended, a serious affair—a Volume.

In the poem on the subject of Education, he would be, very sorry to stand suspected of having aimed his censure at any particular school. His objections are such as naturally apply themselves to schools in general. If there were not, as for the most part there is, wilful neglect in those who manage them, and an omission even of such discipline as they are susceptible of, the objects are yet too numerous for minute attention ; and the aching hearts of ten thousand parents, mourning under the bitterest of all disappointments, attest the truth of the allegation. His quarrel, therefore, is with the mischief at large, and not with any particular instance of it.

THE TASK.* BOOK I.

THE SOFA.

SING the Sofa. I who lately sang
Truth, Hope, and Charity, and touched
   with awe
The solemn chords, and with a trem-
   bling hand,
Escaped with pain from that adventurous flight,
Now seek repose upon an humbler theme;   5

* The Task was begun to be written in the summer, probably near the Midsummer, of 1783; it was finished, revised,
and transcribed, in the autumn of 1784; and was offered
to Johnson for publication about the end of October in that
year. The printing began immediately after the acceptance
of the volume, but the last proof was not returned until near
the end of May 1785. In the meantime, Cowper had written Tirocinium, which was added to the volume, and Johnson
had first declined, and afterwards consented to add, John
Gilpin. The volume was published early in July 1785, with
the title-page of which we have given a copy. Southey indeed has printed (Cowper's Works, ix. vii.) a copy of what
seems to be a title-page with the date of 1784, but we have
not been able to find a copy of the published book with anything of the kind. Probably what Southey has given was a
title-page designed when the first portion of the work went to
press, which was in 1784, but afterwards cancelled when the
printing ran on into the following year, and other poems were
added to the volume.

The theme though humble, yet august and proud
The occasion—for the Fair commands the song.
  Time was, when clothing, sumptuous or for use,
Save their own painted skins, our sires had none.
As yet black breeches were not, satin smooth,   10
Or velvet soft, or plush with shaggy pile;
The hardy chief, upon the rugged rock
Washed by the sea, or on the gravelly bank
Thrown up by wintry torrents roaring loud,
Fearless of wrong, reposed his weary strength.   15
Those barbarous ages past, succeeded next
The birthday of Invention; weak at first,
Dull in design, and clumsy to perform.
Joint-stools were then created; on three legs
Upborne they stood. Three legs upholding firm   20
A massy slab, in fashion square or round.
On such a STOOL immortal Alfred sat,
And swayed the sceptre of his infant realms;
And such in ancient halls and mansions drear
May still be seen; but perforated sore,   25
And drilled in holes, the solid oak is found,
By worms voracious eating through and through.
  At length a generation more refined
Improved the simple plan; made three legs four,
Gave them a twisted form vermicular,   30
And o'er the seat, with plenteous wadding stuffed,
Induced a splendid cover, green and blue,
Yellow and red, of tapestry richly wrought
And woven close, or needlework sublime.
There might ye see the peony spread wide,   35
The full-blown rose, the shepherd and his lass,
Lapdog and lambkin with black, staring eyes,
And parrots with twin cherries in their beak.

Now came the cane from India, smooth and bright
With Nature's varnish ; severed into stripes   40
That interlaced each other, these supplied
Of texture firm a lattice-work, that braced
The new machine, and it became a CHAIR.
But restless was the Chair ; the back erect
Distressed the weary loins that felt no ease ;   45
The slippery seat betrayed the sliding part
That pressed it, and the feet hung dangling down,
Anxious in vain to find the distant floor.
These for the rich : the rest, whom Fate had placed
In modest mediocrity, content   50
With base materials, sat on well-tanned hides,
Obdurate and unyielding, glassy smooth,
With here and there a tuft of crimson yarn,
Or scarlet crewel, in the cushion fixed ;
If cushion might be called, what harder seemed   55
Than the firm oak of which the frame was formed.
No want of timber then was felt or feared
In Albion's happy isle. The lumber* stood
Ponderous, and fixed by its own massy weight.
But elbows still were wanting ; these, some say,   60
An alderman of Cripplegate contrived,
And some ascribe the invention to a priest
Burly and big, and studious of his ease.
But rude at first, and not with easy slope
Receding wide, they pressed against the ribs,   65
And bruised the side, and, elevated high,
Taught the raised shoulders to invade the ears.

* " Umber ;" Eds. 1785, 1786, 1787, 1788, 1793, 1795,
1798, 1799, 1800. " Lumber ;" Eds. 1803, 1805, 1806(2),
1808, 1810, 1812, 1817, 1825, Grimshawe, Southey, Dale,
and Bell.

Long time elapsed or e'er our rugged sires
Complained, though incommodiously pent in,
And ill at ease behind. The ladies first   70
'Gan murmur, as became the softer sex.
Ingenious Fancy, never better pleased
Than when employed to accommodate the fair,
Heard the sweet moan with pity, and devised
The soft SETTEE; one elbow at each end,   75
And in the midst an elbow, it received,
United yet divided, twain at once;
So sit two kings of Brentford on one throne,*
And so two citizens who take the air,
Close packed and smiling, in a chaise and one.   80
But relaxation of the languid frame,
By soft recumbency of outstretched limbs,
Was bliss reserved for happier days;—so slow
The growth of what is excellent, so hard
To attain perfection in this nether world.   85
Thus first Necessity invented Stools,
Convenience next suggested Elbow Chairs,
And Luxury the accomplished SOFA last.
The nurse sleeps sweetly, hired to watch the sick
Whom snoring she disturbs. As sweetly he   90
Who quits the coachbox at the midnight hour
To sleep within the carriage more secure,
His legs depending at the open door.

* The two Kings of Brentford owe their celebrity, if not
their existence, to the Rehearsal by the Duke of Buckingham,
in which they were prominent characters. They were represented as entering upon the stage hand in hand, and sitting
on one throne. Smelling at one nosegay, which is also popu-
larly reckoned among their attributes, was probably part of
the action of the play, but is not mentioned in the printed
book; this was pointed out in Notes and Queries, 1st S. iv. 369.

Sweet sleep enjoys the curate in his desk,
The tedious rector drawling o'er his head,   95
And sweet the clerk below. But neither sleep
Of lazy nurse who snores the sick man dead,
Nor his who quits the box at midnight hour
To slumber in the carriage more secure,
Nor sleep enjoyed by curate in his desk,   100
Nor yet the dozings of the clerk, are sweet,
Compared with the repose the Sofa yields.
    Oh! may I live exempted (while I live
Guiltless of pampered appetite obscene)
From pangs arthritic that infest the toe   105
Of libertine excess. The Sofa suits
The gouty limb, 'tis true; but gouty limb,
Though on a Sofa, may I never feel:
For I have loved the rural walk through lanes
Of grassy swarth, close cropped by nibbling sheep, 110
And skirted thick with intertexture firm
Of thorny boughs: have loved the rural walk
O'er hills, through valleys, and by river's brink,
E'er since, a truant boy, I passed my bounds,
To enjoy a ramble on the banks of Thames;   115
And still remember, nor without regret,
Of hours that sorrow since has much endeared,
How oft, my slice of pocket-store consumed,
Still hungering, pennyless, and far from home,
I fed on scarlet hips and stony haws,   120
Or blushing crabs, or berries that emboss
The bramble, black as jet, or sloes austere.
Hard fare! but such as boyish appetite
Disdains not, nor the palate, undepraved
By culinary arts, unsavoury deems.   125
No Sofa then awaited my return,

Nor Sofa then I needed.   Youth repairs
His wasted spirits quickly, by long toil
Incurring short fatigue : and though our years,
As life declines, speed rapidly away,   130
And not a year but pilfers as he goes
Some youthful grace that age would gladly keep,
A tooth or auburn lock, and by degrees
Their length and colour from the locks they spare ;
The elastic spring of an unwearied foot   135
That mounts the stile with ease, or leaps the fence,
That play of lungs, inhaling and again
Respiring freely the fresh air, that makes
Swift pace or steep ascent no toil to me,
Mine have not pilfered yet ; nor yet impaired   140
My relish of fair prospect ; scenes that soothed
Or charmed me young, no longer young, I find
Still soothing, and of power to charm me still.
And witness, dear companion of my walks,
Whose arm this twentieth winter* I perceive   145

* In this charming introduction of Mrs. Unwin, effected
with so much grace and ease, Cowper gives the date of
their first acquaintance, as well as the period of the year in
which the lines were written.   His chronology has been
called in question.   He removed from St. Alban's to Hun-
tingdon on the 22nd of June 1765.   In a few weeks afterwards
he formed the intimacy which gave a colour to his whole future
life.   The twentieth winter of his acquaintance with Mrs.
Unwin was therefore that of 1784, whilst this part of the Task
was written in the summer of 1783.   The point is scarcely
worthy of notice.   In the exercise of a poetical prevision he
might surely have spoken without blame as from the time of
his anticipated publication, but the passage is probably literally
accurate.   Hayley satisfied himself that it was added in the
course of a revisal, in the early winter of 1784, and Cowper
writing to Hill in the November of that year, as if fresh from
the insertion of this very passage, alludes to Mrs. Unwin as
the companion he had had " these twenty years."

Fast locked in mine, with pleasure such as Love,
Confirmed by long experience of thy worth
And well tried virtues, could alone inspire—
Witness a joy that thou hast doubled long.
Thou knowest my praise of Nature most sincere, 150
And that my raptures are not conjured up
To serve occasions of poetic pomp,
But genuine, and art partner of them all.
How oft upon yon Eminence* our pace
Has slackened to a pause, and we have borne 155
The ruffling wind, scarce conscious that it blew,
While Admiration, feeding at the eye,
And still unsated, dwelt upon the scene.
Thence with what pleasure have we just discerned
The distant plough slow-moving, and beside 160
His labouring team that swerved not from the track,
The sturdy swain diminished to a boy!
Here Ouse, slow-winding through a level plain
Of spacious meads with cattle sprinkled o'er,
Conducts the eye along his sinuous course 165
Delighted. There, fast rooted in their bank,
Stand, never overlooked, our favourite elms,
That screen the herdsman's solitary hut; †

* With one trifling exception, the following lines contain
a literally accurate description of the leading objects which
meet the eye on a walk westward by a pathway over fields
from Olney to Weston. After the lapse of eighty years
every spot gives evidence to the minute faithfulness of the
delineation of the poet. A very gradual and gentle ascent
leads to the Eminence here commemorated. Its height is not
considerable, but every one that visits it will find his pace
" slacken to a pause" in order to enjoy the view, not only of
the pleasant valley of the Ouse, but that more distant " beyond
and overthwart the stream."

† This passage is the one exception to Cowper's accuracy
in description which we have just noted. The elms are pop-

While far beyond, and overthwart the stream,
That, as with molten glass, inlays the vale,   170
The sloping land recedes into the clouds;
Displaying, on its varied side, the grace
Of hedge-row beauties numberless, square tower,*
Tall spire,† from which the sound of cheerful bells
Just undulates upon the listening ear,   175
Groves, heaths, and smoking villages, remote.
Scenes must be beautiful which, daily viewed,
Please daily, and whose novelty survives
Long knowledge and the scrutiny of years.
Praise justly due to those that I describe.   ⌜180
    Nor rural sights alone, but rural sounds,
Exhilarate the spirit, and restore
The tone of languid Nature. Mighty winds
That sweep the skirt of some far-spreading wood
Of ancient growth, make music not unlike   185
The dash of Ocean on his winding shore,
And lull the spirit while they fill the mind,
Unnumbered branches waving in the blast,
And all their leaves fast fluttering, all at once.
Nor less composure waits upon the roar   190
Of distant floods, or on the softer voice
Of neighbouring fountain, or of rills that slip
Through the cleft rock, and, chiming as they fall

lars, and "the herdsman's solitary hut" is a boat-house. The
trees stand, in a cluster, apart, by the side of the Ouse, conspicuous when observed from certain directions, but when
seen at a distance, and mixed up with the surrounding
landscape, as from Cowper's Eminence, very easily mistaken.
    * Of the Church of Clifton Reynes, about a mile from Olney
to the East.
    † Of Olney Church; a beautiful object and conspicuous in
every direction.

Upon loose pebbles, lose themselves at length
In matted grass, that with a livelier green   195
Betrays the secret of their silent course.
Nature inanimate employs sweet sounds,
But animated Nature sweeter still,
To soothe and satisfy the human ear.
Ten thousand warblers cheer the day, and one   200
The livelong night: nor these alone, whose notes
Nice-fingered Art must emulate in vain,
But cawing rooks, and kites that swim sublime
In still repeated circles, screaming loud,
The jay, the pie, and even the boding owl   205
That hails the rising moon, have charms for me.
Sounds inharmonious in themselves and harsh,
Yet heard in scenes where peace for ever reigns,
And only there, please highly for their sake.
. Peace to the artist whose ingenious thought   210
Devised the Weatherhouse,* that useful toy!
Fearless of humid air and gathering rains,
Forth steps the man—an emblem of myself!
More delicate his timorous mate retires.
When Winter soaks the fields, and female feet   215
Too weak to struggle with tenacious clay,
Or ford the rivulets, are best at home,
The task of new discoveries falls on me.
At such a season, and with such a charge,

* This cheap substitute for a barometer is not yet entirely obsolete. It had many forms. That described by Cowper was one of the most elaborate. In others, the man appeared with an umbrella over his head, and very frequently he was represented as a monk with a cowl, which was gradually lowered or thrown back, according to the state of the weather. In Cowper's time these barometrical toys were common, especially in country places, and among simple people were viewed with some amazement.

16 THE TASK. B. I.

Once went I forth, and found, till then unknown, 220
A cottage, whither oft we since repair:
'Tis perched upon the green hill top, but close
Environed with a ring of branching elms
That overhang the thatch, itself unseen
Peeps at the vale below; so thick beset 225
With foliage of such dark redundant growth,
I called the low-roofed lodge the Peasant's Nest.*
And hidden as it is, and far remote
From such unpleasing sounds as haunt the ear
In village or in town, the bay of curs 230
Incessant, clinking hammers, grinding wheels,
And infants clamorous whether pleased or pained,
Oft have I wished the peaceful covert mine.
Here, I have said, at least I should possess
The poet's treasure, silence, and indulge 235
The dreams of fancy, tranquil and secure.
Vain thought! the dweller in that still retreat
Dearly obtains the refuge it affords.
Its elevated site forbids the wretch
To drink sweet waters of the crystal well; 240
He dips his bowl into the weedy ditch,
And, heavy laden, brings his beverage home,
Far fetched and little worth; nor seldom waits,
Dependant on the baker's punctual call,
To hear his creaking panniers at the door, 245
Angry and sad, and his last crust consumed.
So farewell envy of the Peasant's Nest!

* The Peasant's Nest exists, but the thatched roof has given way to tiles, many of the surrounding trees have been cut down, and the whole place has been altered and enlarged. It stands on the northern side of Weston park, and although not so entirely embowered as when Cowper described it, still " peeps at the vale below."

If Solitude make scant the means of life,
Society for me! Thou seeming sweet,
Be still a pleasing object in my view, 250
My visit still, but never mine abode.
    Not distant far, a length of Colonnade*
Invites us. Monument of ancient taste,
Now scorned, but worthy of a better fate.
Our fathers knew the value of a screen 255
From sultry suns, and in their shaded walks,
And long protracted bowers, enjoyed at noon
The gloom and coolness of declining day.
We bear our shades about us; self-deprived
Of other screen, the thin umbrella spread, 260
And range an Indian waste without a tree.
Thanks to Benevolus†—he spares me yet
These chestnuts ranged in corresponding lines,
And though himself so polished, still reprieves
The obsolete prolixity of shade. 265
    Descending now (but cautious, lest too fast)
A sudden steep upon a Rustic Bridge,
We pass a gulf in which the willows dip
Their pendant boughs, stooping as if to drink.
Hence, ankle-deep in moss and flowery thyme, 270
We mount again, and feel at every step
Our foot half sunk in hillocks green and soft,
Raised by the mole, the miner of the soil.
He, not unlike the great ones of mankind,
Disfigures Earth, and, plotting in the dark, 275

* The Colonnade, the Rustic Bridge, and the Wilderness,
yet attest the accuracy of Cowper's description. The Alcove
has been rebuilt since his time, and the other objects alluded
to are more or less changed, but all are easily recognizable.
    † John Courtenay Throckmorton, Esq. of Weston Under-
wood. (C. 1785.)

Toils much to earn a monumental pile,
That may record the mischiefs he has done.
  The summit gained, behold the proud Alcove
That crowns it! yet not all its pride secures
The grand retreat from injuries impressed   280
By rural carvers, who with knives deface
The panels, leaving an obscure, rude name,
In characters uncouth, and spelt amiss.
So strong the zeal to immortalize himself
Beats in the breast of man, that even a few,   285
Few transient years, won from the abyss abhorred
Of blank oblivion, seem a glorious prize,
And even to a clown.—Now roves the eye,
And posted on this speculative height,
Exults in its command. The sheepfold here   290
Pours out its fleecy tenants o'er the glebe.
At first, progressive as a stream, they seek
The middle field; but scattered by degrees,
Each to his choice, soon whiten all the land.   294
There from the sunburnt hayfield homeward creeps
The loaded wain, while lightened of its charge,
The wain that meets it passes swiftly by,
The boorish driver leaning o'er his team
Vociferous, and impatient of delay.
Nor less attractive is the woodland scene,   300
Diversified with trees of every growth,
Alike yet various. Here the grey smooth trunks
Of ash, or lime, or beech, distinctly shine,
Within the twilight of their distant shades;
There, lost behind a rising ground, the wood   305
Seems sunk, and shortened to its topmost boughs.
No tree in all the grove but has its charms,
Though each its hue peculiar; paler some,

And of a wannish grey; the willow such,
And poplar that with silver lines his leaf,   310
And ash far-stretching his umbrageous arm;
Of deeper green the elm; and deeper still,
Lord of the woods, the long-surviving oak.
Some glossy-leaved, and shining in the sun,
The maple, and the beech of oily nuts   315
Prolific, and the lime at dewy eve
Diffusing odours: nor unnoted pass
The sycamore, capricious in attire,
Now green, now tawny, and ere autumn yet   319
Have changed the woods, in scarlet honours bright.
O'er these, but far beyond, a spacious map
Of hill and valley interposed between,
The Ouse, dividing the well-watered land,
Now glitters in the sun, and now retires,
As bashful, yet impatient to be seen.   325
    Hence the declivity is sharp and short,
And such the reascent; between them weeps
A little Naiad her impoverished urn
All summer long, which winter fills again.
The folded gates would bar my progress now,   330
But that the lord* of this enclosed demesne,
Communicative of the good he owns,
Admits me to a share: the guiltless eye
Commits no wrong, nor wastes what it enjoys.
Refreshing change! where now the blazing sun?
By short transition we have lost his glare,   336
And stepped at once into a cooler clime.
Ye fallen avenues! once more I mourn
Your fate unmerited, once more rejoice
That yet a remnant of your race survives.   340

* See the foregoing note.

How airy and how light the graceful arch,
Yet awful as the consecrated roof
Re-echoing pious anthems! while beneath
The chequered earth seems restless as a flood }
Brushed by the wind. So sportive is the light 345
Shot through the boughs, it dances as they dance,
Shadow and sunshine intermingling quick,
And darkening and enlightening, as the leaves
Play wanton, every moment, every spot.
    And now, with nerves new braced and spirits
        cheered,   350
We tread the Wilderness, whose well-rolled walks,
With curvature of slow and easy sweep—
Deception innocent—give ample space
To narrow bounds. The Grove receives us next;
Between the upright shafts of whose tall elms 355
We may discern the thresher at his task.
Thump after thump resounds the constant flail,
That seems to swing uncertain, and yet falls
Full on the destined ear. Wide flies the chaff,
The rustling straw sends up a frequent mist 360
Of atoms, sparkling in the noonday beam.
Come hither, ye that press your beds of down
And sleep not; see him sweating o'er his bread
Before he eats it.—'Tis the primal curse,
But softened into mercy; made the pledge 365
Of cheerful days, and nights without a groan.
    By ceaseless action all that is subsists.
Constant rotation of the unwearied wheel
That Nature rides upon, maintains her health,
Her beauty, her fertility. She dreads 370
An instant's pause, and lives but while she moves;
Its own revolvency upholds the world.

Winds from all quarters agitate the air,
And fit the limpid element for use,
Else noxious: oceans, rivers, lakes, and streams, 375.
All feel the freshening impulse, and are cleansed
By restless undulation; even the oak
Thrives by the rude concussion of the storm;
He seems indeed indignant, and to feel
The impression of the blast with proud disdain,
Frowning as if in his unconscious arm 381
He held the thunder. But the monarch owes
His firm stability to what he scorns,
More fixed below, the more disturbed above.
The law by which all creatures else are bound, 385
Binds man, the lord of all. Himself derives
No mean advantage from a kindred cause,
From strenuous toil his hours of sweetest ease.
The sedentary stretch their lazy length
When Custom bids, but no refreshment find, 390
For none they need: the languid eye, the cheek
Deserted of its bloom, the flaccid, shrunk,
And withered muscle, and the vapid soul,
Reproach their owner with that love of rest
To which he forfeits even the rest he loves. 395
Not such the alert and active. Measure life
By its true worth, the comforts it affords,
And theirs alone seems worthy of the name.
Good health, and, its associate in the most,
Good temper; spirits prompt to undertake, 400
And not soon spent, though in an arduous task;
The powers of fancy and strong thought are theirs;
Even age itself seems privileged in them
With clear exemption from its own defects.
A sparkling eye beneath a wrinkled front 405

The veteran shows, and gracing a grey beard
With youthful smiles, descends toward the grave
Sprightly, and old almost without decay.
    Like a coy maiden, Ease, when courted most,
Farthest retires—an idol, at whose shrine   410
Who oftenest sacrifice are favoured least.
The love of Nature, and the scenes she draws,
Is Nature's dictate.   Strange! there should be
        found,
Who, self-imprisoned in their proud saloons,
Renounce the odours of the open field   415
For the unscented fictions of the loom;
Who, satisfied with only pencilled scenes,
Prefer to the performance of a God
The inferior wonders of an artist's hand.
Lovely indeed the mimic works of Art;   420
But Nature's works far lovelier.   I admire,
None more admires, the painter's magic skill,
Who shows me that which I shall never see,
Conveys a distant country into mine,
And throws Italian light on English walls.   425
But imitative strokes can do no more
Than please the eye—sweet Nature every sense.
The air salubrious of her lofty hills,
The cheering fragrance of her dewy vales,
And music of her woods—no works of man   430
May rival these; these all bespeak a power
Peculiar, and exclusively her own.
Beneath the open sky she spreads the feast;
'Tis free to all—'tis every day renewed;
Who scorns it, starves deservedly at home.   435
He does not scorn it, who, imprisoned long
In some unwholesome dungeon, and a prey

To sallow sickness, which the vapours, dank
And clammy, of his dark abode have bred,
Escapes at last to liberty and light.   440
His cheek recovers soon its healthful hue,
His eye relumines its extinguished fires,
He walks, he leaps, he runs—is winged with joy,
And riots in the sweets of every breeze.
He does not scorn it, who has long endured   445
A fever's agonies, and fed on drugs ;
Nor yet the mariner, his blood inflamed
With acrid salts, his very heart athirst
To gaze at Nature in her green array ;
Upon the ship's tall side he stands, possessed   450
With visions prompted by intense desire ;
Fair fields appear below, such as he left
Far distant, such as he would die to find—
He seeks them headlong, and is seen no more.*

   The spleen is seldom felt where Flora reigns ; 455
The lowering eye, the petulance, the frown,
And sullen sadness, that o'ershade, distort,
And mar the face of Beauty, when no cause
For such immeasurable woe appears,

* Swift's description of the fatal illusion which deceives the sufferers under a calenture may well be paralleled with that of Cowper's :—

   So, by a calenture misled,
     The mariner with rapture sees,
   On the smooth ocean's azure bed,
     Enamelled fields and verdant trees.

   With eager haste he longs to rove
     In that fantastic scene, and thinks
   It must be some enchanted grove ;
     And in he leaps, and down he sinks.
        South Sea Project. Works, Ed. Scott,
           vol. xiv. p. 148.

These Flora banishes, and gives the fair   460
Sweet smiles, and bloom less transient than her own.
It is the constant revolution, stale
And tasteless, of the same repeated joys,
That palls and satiates, and makes languid life
A pedler's pack, that bows the bearer down.   465
Health suffers, and the spirits ebb; the heart
Recoils from its own choice—at the full feast
Is famished—finds no music in the song,
No smartness in the jest, and wonders why.
Yet thousands still desire to journey on,   470
Though halt, and weary of the path they tread.
The paralytic, who can hold her cards
But cannot play them, borrows a friend's hand
To deal and shuffle, to divide and sort
Her mingled suits and sequences, and sits,   475
Spectatress both and spectacle, a sad
And silent cipher, while her proxy plays.
Others are dragged into the crowded room
Between supporters; and, once seated, sit,
Through downright inability to rise,   480
Till the stout bearers lift the corpse again.
These speak a loud memento. Yet even these
Themselves love life, and cling to it, as he
That overhangs a torrent, to a twig.
They love it, and yet loathe it; fear to die,   485
Yet scorn the purposes for which they live.
Then wherefore not renounce them? No—the dread,
The slavish dread of solitude, that breeds
Reflection and remorse, the fear of shame,
And their inveterate habits, all forbid.   490
    Whom call we gay? That honour has been long
The boast of mere pretenders to the name.

The innocent are gay—the lark is gay,
That dries his feathers, saturate with dew,
Beneath the rosy cloud, while yet the beams 495
Of dayspring overshoot his humble nest.
The peasant too, a witness of his song,
Himself a songster, is as gay as he.
But save me from the gaiety of those
Whose headaches nail them to a noonday bed; 500
And save me too from theirs whose haggard eyes
Flash desperation, and betray their pangs
For property stripped off by cruel chance;
From gaiety that fills the bones with pain,
The mouth with blasphemy, the heart with woe. 505
     The Earth was made so various, that the mind
Of desultory man, studious of change,
And pleased with novelty, might be indulged.
Prospects, however lovely, may be seen
Till half their beauties fade; the weary sight, 510
Too well acquainted with their smiles, slides off
Fastidious, seeking less familiar scenes.
Then snug enclosures in the sheltered vale,
Where frequent hedges intercept the eye,
Delight us, happy to renounce awhile, 515
Not senseless of its charms, what still we love,
That such short absence may endear it more.
Then forests, or the savage rock, may please,
That hides the seamew in his hollow clefts
Above the reach of man: his hoary head, 520
Conspicuous many a league, the mariner,
Bound homeward, and in hope already there,
Greets with three cheers exulting. At his waist
A girdle of half-withered shrubs he shows,
And at his feet the baffled billows die. 525

The common, overgrown with fern, and rough
With prickly gorse,* that shapeless and deformed,†
And dangerous to the touch, has yet its bloom,
And decks itself with ornaments of gold,
Yields no unpleasing ramble ; there the turf   530
Smells fresh, and, rich in odoriferous herbs
And fungous fruits of earth, regales the sense
With luxury of unexpected sweets.
   There often wanders one, whom better days
Saw better clad, in cloak of satin trimmed   535
With lace, and hat with splendid riband bound.
A serving-maid was she, and fell in love
With one who left her, went to sea, and died.
Her Fancy followed him through foaming waves
To distant shores, and she would sit and weep   540
At what a sailor suffers ; Fancy too,
Delusive most where warmest wishes are,
Would oft anticipate his glad return,
And dream of transports she was not to know.
She heard the doleful tidings of his death—   545
And never smiled again ! and now she roams
The dreary waste ; there spends the livelong day,
And there, unless when Charity forbids,
The livelong night.   A tattered apron hides,
Worn as a cloak, and hardly hides, a gown   550
More tattered still ; and both but ill conceal
A bosom heaved with never ceasing sighs.
She begs an idle pin of all she meets,

---

* "Goss ;" Eds. 1785, 1786 ; altered to " gorse" in 1787,
which has been followed in all subsequent editions, except
Southey's, which has retained the first reading.
   † " Deform ;" Eds. 1785, 1786, Southey.   " Deformed ;"
Ed. 1787, and all subsequent editions, except Southey's.

And hoards them in her sleeve; but needful food, 555
Though pressed with hunger oft, or comelier clothes,
Though pinched with cold, asks never.—Kate is
    crazed!
    I see a column of slow-rising smoke
O'ertop the lofty wood that skirts the wild.
A vagabond and useless tribe there eat
Their miserable meal. A kettle, slung 560
Between two poles upon a stick transverse,
Receives the morsel—flesh obscene of dog,
Or vermin, or at best of cock purloined
From his accustomed perch. Hard-faring race!
They pick their fuel out of every hedge, 565
Which, kindled with dry leaves, just saves un-
    quenched
The spark of life. The sportive wind blows wide
Their fluttering rags, and shows a tawny skin,
The vellum of the pedigree they claim.
Great skill have they in palmistry, and more 570
To conjure clean away the gold they touch,
Conveying worthless dross into its place;
Loud when they beg, dumb only when they steal.
Strange! that a creature rational, and cast
In human mould, should brutalize by choice 575
His nature, and though capable of arts
By which the world might profit, and himself,
Self-banished from society, prefer
Such squalid sloth to honourable toil!
Yet even these, though, feigning sickness oft, 580
They swathe the forehead, drag the limping limb,
And vex their flesh with artificial sores,
Can change their whine into a mirthful note
When safe occasion offers; and with dance,

And music of the bladder and the bag,   585
Beguile their woes, and make the woods resound.
Such health and gaiety of heart enjoy
The houseless rovers of the sylvan world ;
And breathing wholesome air, and wandering much,
Need other physic none to heal the effects   590
Of loathsome diet, penury, and cold.
 Blest he, though undistinguished from the crowd
By wealth or dignity, who dwells secure,
Where man, by nature fierce, has laid aside
His fierceness, having learnt, though slow to learn,
The manners and the arts of civil life.   595
His wants, indeed, are many; but supply
Is obvious, placed within the easy reach
Of temperate wishes and industrious hands.
Here virtue thrives as in her proper soil ;   600
Not rude and surly, and beset with thorns,
And terrible to sight, as when she springs,
(If e'er she spring spontaneous) in remote
And barbarous climes, where violence prevails,
And strength is lord of all ; but gentle, kind, 605
By culture tamed, by liberty refreshed,
And all her fruits by radiant truth matured.
War and the chase engross the savage whole ;
War followed for revenge, or to supplant
The envied tenants of some happier spot,   610
The chase for sustenance, precarious trust!
His hard condition with severe constraint
Binds all his faculties, forbids all growth
Of wisdom, proves a school in which he learns
Sly circumvention, unrelenting hate,   615
Mean self-attachment, and scarce aught beside.
Thus fare the shivering natives of the north,

And thus the rangers of the western world
Where it advances far into the deep,
Towards the Antarctic. Even the favoured isles 620
So lately found,* although the constant sun
Cheer all their seasons with a grateful smile,
Can boast but little virtue; and inert
Through plenty, lose in morals what they gain
In manners—victims of luxurious ease. 625
These therefore I can pity, placed remote
From all that Science traces, Art invents,
Or Inspiration teaches; and enclosed
In boundless oceans, never to be passed
By navigators uninformed as they, 630
Or ploughed perhaps by British bark again.
But far beyond the rest, and with most cause,
Thee, gentle savage!† whom no love of thee
Or thine, but curiosity, perhaps,
Or else vain-glory, prompted us to draw 635
Forth from thy native bowers, to show thee here
With what superior skill we can abuse
The gifts of Providence, and squander life.
The dream is past; and thou hast found again

* The Society and Friendly Islands recently discovered in
the Pacific by Captain Cook.

† Omai, a native of Otaheite, brought to England in 1774,
in one of the ships under the command of Captain Cook on his
second voyage. He was kindly received by George III, and
many persons of distinction vied in affording him entertainment, and exciting his amazement at the wonders of civiliza-
tion. Loaded with presents, he was taken back to his native
land by Captain Cook on his third voyage, and died there a
few years afterwards. Cowper's anticipations of his unhap-
piness after his return home were, it is to be feared, realized,
and the disposition of some of his presents was the occasion
after his death of a bloody war between two native tribes.

Thy cocoas and bananas, palms and yams,   640
And homestall thatched with leaves.   But hast
   thou found
Their former charms?   And having seen our state,
Our palaces, our ladies, and our pomp
Of equipage, our gardens, and our sports,
And heard our music; are thy simple friends,   645
Thy simple fare, and all thy plain delights
As dear to thee as once?   And have thy joys
Lost nothing by comparison with ours?
Rude as thou art (for we returned thee rude
And ignorant, except of outward show)   650
I cannot think thee yet so dull of heart
And spiritless, as never to regret
Sweets tasted here, and left as soon as known.
Methinks I see thee straying on the beach,
And asking of the surge that bathes thy foot,   655
If ever it has washed our distant shore.
I see thee weep, and thine are honest tears,
A patriot's for his country : thou art sad
At thought of her forlorn and abject state,
From which no power of thine can raise her up.   660
Thus Fancy paints thee, and though apt to err,
Perhaps errs little when she paints thee thus.
She tells me, too, that duly every morn
Thou climbest the mountain top, with eager eye
Exploring far and wide the watery waste   665
For sight of ship from England.   Every speck
Seen in the dim horizon, turns thee pale
With conflict of contending hopes and fears.
But comes at last the dull and dusky eve,
And sends thee to thy cabin, well prepared   670
To dream all night of what the day denied.

Alas! expect it not. We found no bait
To tempt us in thy country. Doing good,
Disinterested good, is not our trade.
We travel far, 'tis true, but not for naught;   675
And must be bribed to compass earth again
By other hopes and richer fruits than yours.
   But though true worth and virtue, in the mild
And genial soil of cultivated life
Thrive most, and may perhaps thrive only there, 680
Yet not in cities oft: in proud, and gay,
And gain-devoted cities. Thither flow,
As to a common and most noisome sewer,
The dregs and feculence of every land.
In cities foul example on most minds   685
Begets its likeness. Rank abundance breeds,
In gross and pampered cities, sloth, and lust,
And wantonness, and gluttonous excess.
In cities, vice is hidden with most ease,
Or seen with least reproach; and virtue, taught 690
By frequent lapse, can hope no triumph there
Beyond the achievement of successful flight.
I do confess them nurseries of the arts,
In which they flourish most; where, in the beams
Of warm encouragement, and in the eye   695
Of public note, they reach their perfect size.
Such London is, by taste and wealth proclaimed
The fairest capital of all the world,
By riot and incontinence the worst.
There touched by Reynolds,* a dull blank becomes

---

* When these lines were written Sir Joshua had, for many
years, stood, worthily, at the head of the English School of
Pictorial Art. Born in 1723, he continued to paint until
1789.

A lucid mirror, in which Nature sees   701
All her reflected features.   Bacon there
Gives more than female beauty to a stone,
And Chatham's eloquence to marble lips.*
Nor-does the chisel occupy alone   705
Tho powers of sculpture, but the style as much ;
Each province of her art her equal care.
With nice incision of her guided steel   ✓
She ploughs a brazen field, and clothes a soil
So sterile with what charms soe'er she will,   710
The richest scenery and tho loveliest forms.
Where finds Philosophy her eagle eye,
With which she gazes at yon burning disk
Undazzled, and detects and counts his spots?
In London.   Where her implements exact,   715
With which she calculates, computes, and scans
All distance, motion, magnitude, and now
Measures an atom, and now girds a world ?
In London.   Where has commerce such a mart,
So rich, so thronged, so drained, and so supplied,   720
As London, opulent, enlarged, and still
Increasing London ? Babylon of old
Not more the glory of the earth than sho,
A more accomplished world's chief glory now.
      She has her praise.   Now mark a spot or two, 725
That so much beauty would do well to purge ;
And show this queen of cities, that so fair

* Bacon had recently finished the monument to Chatham
which stands in the north transept of Westminster Abbey.
He was delighted with Cowper's praise, and acknowledged
his feelings in a characteristic letter which was communi-
cated by Upcott to Southey. Bacon, both in his opinions
and in his genius, was a man after Cowper's own heart.

May yet be foul; so witty, yet not wise.
It is not seemly, nor of good report,
That she is slack in discipline ; more prompt   730
To avenge than to prevent the breach of law ;
That she is rigid in denouncing death
On petty robbers, and indulges life
And liberty, and oft-times honour too,
To peculators of the public gold;   735
That thieves at home must hang, but he that puts
Into his overgorged and bloated purse
The wealth of Indian provinces, escapes.
Nor is it well, nor can it come to good,
That, through profane and infidel contempt   740
Of holy writ, she has presumed to annul
And abrogate, as roundly as she may,
The total ordinance and will of God ;
Advancing Fashion to the post of Truth,
And centering all authority in modes   745
And customs of her own, till sabbath-rites
Have dwindled into unrespected forms,
And knees and hassocks are well nigh divorced.
  God made the country, and man made the town.
What wonder then that health and virtue, gifts   750
That can alone make sweet the bitter draught
That life holds out to all, should most abound
And least be threatened in the fields and groves ?
Possess ye, therefore, ye who, borne about
In chariots and sedans, know no fatigue   755
But that of idleness, and taste no scenes
But such as Art contrives, possess ye still
Your element ; there only ye can shine,*

* " Only ye can shine," Eds. 1785, 6, 7, 8, Southey, Bell;
" only can ye shine," Ed. 1793, and subsequent editions except those before mentioned.

There only minds like yours can do no harm.
Our groves were planted to console at noon   760
The pensive wanderer in their shades.   At eve
The moonbeam, sliding softly in between
The sleeping leaves, is all the light they wish,
Birds warbling all the music.   We can spare
The splendour of your lamps; they but eclipse 765
Our softer satellite.   Your songs confound
Our more harmonious notes: the thrush departs
Scared, and the offended nightingale is mute.
There is a public mischief in your mirth;
It plagues your country.   Folly such as yours 770
Graced with a sword, and worthier of a fan,
Has made, what enemies could ne'er have done,
Our arch of empire, steadfast but for you,
A mutilated structure, soon to fall.

THE TASK. BOOK II.

THE TIME-PIECE.

ARGUMENT.

REFLECTIONS suggested by the conclusion of the former book. Peace among the nations recommended on the ground of their common fellowship in sorrow. Prodigies enumerated. Sicilian earthquakes. Man rendered obnoxious to these calamities by sin. God the agent in them. The philosophy that stops at secondary causes reproved. Our own late miscarriages accounted for. Satirical notice taken of our trips to Fontainebleau. But the pulpit, not satire, the proper engine of reformation. The Reverend Advertiser of engraved sermons. Petit-maître parson. The good preacher. Picture of a theatrical clerical coxcomb. Story tellers and jesters in the pulpit reproved. Apostrophe to popular applause. Retailers of ancient philosophy expostulated with. Sum of the whole matter. Effects of sacerdotal mismanagement on the laity. Their folly and extravagance. The mischiefs of profusion. Profusion itself, with all its consequent evils, ascribed, as to its principal cause, to the want of discipline in the universities.

THE TASK. BOOK II.

THE TIME-PIECE.

H for a lodge in some vast wilderness,
Some boundless contiguity of shade,
Where rumour of oppression and deceit,
Of unsuccessful or successful war,
Might never reach me more ! My ear is pained, 5
My soul is sick, with every day's report
Of wrong and outrage with which earth is filled.
There is no flesh in man's obdurate heart,
It does not feel for man.   The natural bond
Of brotherhood is severed as the flax   10
That falls asunder at the touch of fire.
He finds his fellow guilty of a skin
Not coloured like his own, and having power
To enforce the wrong, for such a worthy cause
Dooms and devotes him as his lawful prey.   15
Lands intersected by a narrow frith
Abhor each other.   Mountains interposed
Make enemies of nations who had else
Like kindred drops been mingled into one.
Thus man devotes his brother, and destroys;   20
And worse than all, and most to be deplored,
As human nature's broadest, foulest blot,

Chains him, and tasks him, and exacts his sweat
With stripes, that Mercy, with a bleeding heart,
Weeps when she sees inflicted on a beast.   25
Then what is man ? And what man, seeing this
And having human feelings, does not blush,
And hang his head, to think himself a man ?
I would not have a slave to till my ground,
To carry me, to fan me while I sleep,   30
And tremble when I wake, for all the wealth
That sinews bought and sold have ever earned.
No: dear as freedom is, and in my heart's
Just estimation prized above all price,
I had much rather be myself the slave,   35
And wear the bonds, than fasten them on him.
We have no slaves at home :—Then why abroad ?
And they themselves once ferried o'er the wave
That parts us, are emancipate and loosed.
Slaves cannot breathe in England; if their lungs
Receive our air, that moment they are free ;   41
They touch our country, and their shackles fall.*
That's noble, and bespeaks a nation proud
And jealous of the blessing.   Spread it then,
And let it circulate through every vein   45
Of all your empire; that where Britain's power

* These noble lines must have greatly aided the result at
which they aimed. The case of Somerset, in which the judges
determined that " Slaves cannot breathe in England," occurred in 1772. In May 1787, nearly two years after the
publication of " The Task," the Society for the Suppression
of the Slave Trade was instituted. On the 9th of May, 1788,
the first motion against the slave trade was made in the
House of Commons. It was abolished on the 25th of March,
1807 ; slavery ceased on the 1st of August, 1834 ; and the
1st of August, 1838, was the day of final and complete
emancipation.

Is felt, mankind may feel her mercy too.
Sure there is need of social intercourse,
Benevolence, and peace, and mutual aid,
Between the nations, in a world that seems   50
To toll the deathbell of its own decease,
And by the voice of all its elements
To preach the general doom.* When were the winds
Let slip with such a warrant to destroy?
When did the waves so haughtily o'erleap   55
Their ancient barriers, deluging the dry?
Fires from beneath, and meteors† from above
Portentous, unexampled, unexplained,
Have kindled beacons in the skies, and the old
And crazy earth has had her shaking fits   60
More frequent, and foregone her usual rest.
Is it a time to wrangle, when the props
And pillars of our planet seem to fail,
And Nature,‡ with a dim and sickly eye,
To wait the close of all? But grant her end   65
More distant, and that prophecy demands
A longer respite, unaccomplished yet;
Still they are frowning signals, and bespeak
Displeasure in his breast who smites the earth
Or heals it, makes it languish or rejoice.   70
And 'tis but seemly, that where all deserve

---

* Alluding to the late calamities in Jamaica.—(C. 1785.)
† August 18, 1783.—(C.) A description of these singular
meteoric lights may be read in the "Annual Register" for
1783, p. 214]. Many of the facts stated seem to indicate an
unusually bright display of the Northern Lights.
‡ Alluding to the fog that covered both Europe and Asia
during the whole summer of 1783.—(C.) There are several
allusions to this unusual accompaniment of summer in Cowper's
letters; see especially those to Newton of 13th and 17th of
June, 1783.

And stand exposed by common peccancy
To what no few have felt, there should be peace,
And brethren in calamity should love.
   Alas for Sicily! rude fragments now   75
Lie scattered where the shapely column stood.
Her palaces are dust. In all her streets
The voice of singing and the sprightly chord
Are silent. Revelry, and dance, and show,
Suffer a syncope and solemn pause,   80
While God performs, upon the trembling stage
Of his own works, his dreadful part alone.
How does the earth receive him?—with what signs
Of gratulation and delight, her King?
Pours she not all her choicest fruits abroad,   85
Her sweetest flowers, her aromatic gums,
Disclosing Paradise where'er He treads?—
She quakes at his approach. Her hollow womb,
Conceiving thunders, through a thousand deeps
And fiery caverns, roars beneath his foot.   90
The hills move lightly, and the mountains smoke,
For He has touched them. From the extremest point
Of elevation down into the abyss,
His wrath is busy, and his frown is felt.
The rocks fall headlong, and the valleys rise,   95
The rivers die into offensive pools,
And, charged with putrid verdure, breathe a gross
And mortal nuisance into all the air.
What solid was, by transformation strange,
Grows fluid; and the fixed and rooted earth,   100
Tormented into billows, heaves and swells,
Or with vortiginous and hideous whirl
Sucks down its prey insatiable. Immense
The tumult and the overthrow, the pangs

And agonies of human and of brute 105
Multitudes, fugitive on every side,
And fugitive in vain. The sylvan scene
Migrates uplifted, and, with all its soil,
Alighting in far distant fields, finds out
A new possessor, and survives the change. 110
Ocean has caught the frenzy, and upwrought
To an enormous and o'erbearing height,
Not by a mighty wind, but by that voice
Which winds and waves obey, invades the shore
Resistless. Never such a sudden flood, 115
Upridged so high, and sent on such a charge,
Possessed an inland scene. Where now the throng
That pressed the beach, and hasty to depart
Looked to the sea for safety? They are gone,
Gone with the refluent wave into the deep— 120
A prince with half his people!* Ancient towers,

* The frightful earthquake, or rather succession of earthquakes, which took place in Calabria and Sicily in February,
1783, is still remembered with astonishment and horror. The
particular incident to which Cowper here alludes occurred
at Scylla. The first shocks of the earthquake having almost
destroyed the town, the aged Prince of the place persuaded a
great number of the surviving inhabitants that they would
be safer at sea than on shore among the ruined buildings.
On the evening of the 5th of February he and they betook
themselves to the supposed shelter of a large fleet of fishing-
boats, whilst others sought safety on a level plain slightly
elevated above the sea. In the night a great mass, suddenly
torn from Mount Jaci, overwhelmed the multitude upon the
plain, whilst the sea, rising many feet above its ordinary
level, rolled foaming over them. In a moment "the refluent
wave" retreated, and then again rushed back with greater
violence, dashing the swamped boats upon the beach, and
sweeping the wrecks of many of them far inland. Prince
and people were involved in universal ruin. The numbers
killed were stated to be from 1500 to 2500; more corpses

And roofs embattled high, the gloomy scenes
Where beauty oft and lettered worth consume
Life in the unproductive shades of death,
Fall prone; the pale inhabitants come forth, 125
And happy in their unforeseen release
From all the rigours of restraint, enjoy
The terrors of the day that sets them free.
Who then that has thee, would not hold thee fast,
Freedom! whom they that lose thee so regret, 130
That even a judgment, making way for thee,
Seems, in their eyes, a mercy, for thy sake.
  Such evil Sin hath wrought, and such a flame
Kindled in Heaven, that it burns down to earth,
And in the furious inquest that it makes 135
On God's behalf, lays waste his fairest works.
The very elements, though each be meant
The minister of man, to serve his wants,
Conspire against him. With his breath, he draws
A plague into his blood; and cannot use 140
Life's necessary means, but he must die.
Storms rise to o'erwhelm him; or if stormy winds
Rise not, the waters of the deep shall rise,
And needing none assistance of the storm,
Shall roll themselves ashore, and reach him there.
The earth shall shake him out of all his holds, 146
Or make his house his grave: nor so content,
Shall counterfeit the motions of the flood,
And drown him in her dry and dusty gulfs.
What then? Were they the wicked above all, 150
And we the righteous, whose fast-anchored isle

were thrown upon the beach on the following day than there
remained people alive to bury them.—See LYELL's *Principles
of Geology*, p. 488, ed. 1853.

Moved not, while theirs was rocked like a light skiff,
The sport of every wave? No: none are clear,
And none than we more guilty. But where all
Stand chargeable with guilt, and to the shafts   155
Of wrath obnoxious, God may choose his mark;
May punish, if he please, the less, to warn
The more malignant. If he spared not them,
Tremble and be amazed at thine escape,
Far guiltier England! lest he spare not thee.   160
  Happy the man who sees a God employed
In all the good and ill that chequer life!
Resolving all events, with their effects
And manifold results, into the will
And arbitration wise of the Supreme.   165
Did not his eye rule all things, and intend
The least of our concerns, (since from the least
The greatest oft originate) could Chance
Find place in his dominion, or dispose
One lawless particle to thwart his plan,   170
Then God might be surprised, and unforeseen
Contingence might alarm him, and disturb   .
The smooth and equal course of his affairs.
This truth, Philosophy, though eagle-eyed
In Nature's tendencies, oft overlooks;   175
And having found his instrument, forgets
Or disregards, or more presumptuous still,
Denies the power that wields it. God proclaims
His hot displeasure against foolish men
That live an atheist life; involves the Heaven   180
In tempests; quits his grasp upon the winds,
And gives them all their fury; bids a plague   .
Kindle a fiery boil upon the skin,
And putrify the breath of blooming Health.

He calls for Famine, and the meagre fiend   185
Blows mildew from between his shrivelled lips,
And taints the golden ear. He springs his mines,
And desolates a nation at a blast.
Forth steps the spruce philosopher, and tells
Of homogeneal and discordant springs   190
And principles; of causes, how they work
By necessary laws their sure effects;
Of action and reaction. He has found
The source of the disease that Nature feels,
And bids the world take heart and banish fear. 195
Thou fool! Will thy discovery of the cause
Suspend the effect, or heal it? Has not God
Still wrought by means since first He made the world?
And did He not of old employ his means
To drown it? What is his creation less   200
Than a capacious reservoir of means
Formed for his use, and ready at his will?
Go, dress thine eyes with eyesalve; ask of him,
Or ask of whomsoever he has taught,   204
And learn, though late, the genuine cause of all.
    England, with all thy faults, I love thee still,
My country! and while yet a nook is left
Where English minds and manners may be found,
Shall be constrained to love thee. Though thy clime
Be fickle, and thy year, most part, deformed   210
With dripping rains, or withered by a frost,
I would not yet exchange thy sullen skies,
And fields without a flower, for warmer France
With all her vines; nor for Ausonia's* groves

* Ausonia, the country of the Ausones, a people descended
from Auson, a son of Ulysses and Calypso, but here and elsewhere used as a synonyme for Italy.

Of golden fruitage, and her myrtle bowers. 215
To shake thy senate, and from heights sublime
Of patriot eloquence to flash down fire
Upon thy foes, was never meant my task;
But I can feel thy fortunes, and partake
Thy joys and sorrows, with as true a heart 220
As any thunderer there.   And I can feel
Thy follies too; and with a just disdain
Frown at effeminates, whose very looks
Reflect dishonour on the land I love.
How, in the name of soldiership and sense, 225
Should England prosper, when such things, as smooth
And tender as a girl, all essenced o'er
With odours, and as profligate as sweet;
Who sell their laurel for a myrtle wreath,
And love when they should fight; when such as
        these 230
Presume to lay their hand upon the ark
Of her magnificent and awful cause?
Time was, when it was praise and boast enough ·
In every clime, and travel where we might,
That we were born her children.   Praise enough
To fill the ambition of a private man, 235
That Chatham's language was his mother tongue,
And Wolfe's great name compatriot with his own.
Farewell those honours, and farewell with them
The hope of such hereafter! They have fallen, 240
Each in his field of glory; one in arms,
And one in council.   Wolfe, upon the lap
Of smiling Victory that moment won,
And Chatham, heart-sick of his country's shame.
They made us many soldiers.   Chatham, still 245
Consulting England's happiness at home,

Secured it by an unforgiving frown,
If any wronged her.   Wolfe, where'er he fought,
Put so much of his heart into his act,
That his example had a magnet's force,   250
And all were swift to follow whom all loved.
Those suns are set.   Oh, rise some other such!
Or all that we have left, is empty talk
Of old achievements, and despair of new.

    Now hoist the sail, and let the streamers float
Upon the wanton breezes.   Strew the deck   256
With lavender, and sprinkle liquid sweets,
That no rude savour maritime invade
The nose of nice nobility.   Breathe soft,
Ye clarionets, and softer still, ye flutes,   260
That winds and waters, lulled by magic sounds,
May bear us smoothly to the Gallic shore.
True, we have lost an empire—let it pass.
True, we may thank the perfidy of France,
That picked the jewel out of England's crown,   265
With all the cunning of an envious shrew.
And let that pass—'twas but a trick of state.
A brave man knows no malice, but at once
Forgets in peace the injuries of war,
And gives his direst foe a friend's embrace.   270
And shamed as we have been, to the very beard
Braved and defied, and in our own sea proved
Too weak for those decisive blows that once
Ensured us mastery there, we yet retain
Some small preeminence ; we justly boast   275
At least superior jockeyship, and claim
The honours of the turf as all our own.
Go then, well worthy of the praise ye seek,
And show the shame ye might conceal at home,

In foreign eyes!—be grooms, and win the plate, 280
Where once your noble fathers won a crown!—
'Tis generous to communicate your skill
To those that need it. Folly is soon learned,
And under such preceptors, who can fail? ·
   There is a pleasure in poetic pains   285
Which only poets know. The shifts and turns,
The expedients and inventions multiform,
To which the mind resorts, in chase of terms
Though apt, yet coy, and difficult to win—
To arrest the fleeting images that fill   290
The mirror of the mind, and hold them fast,
And force them sit, till he has pencilled off
A faithful likeness of the forms he views;
Then to dispose his copies with such art
That each may find its most propitious light,   295
And shine by situation, hardly less
Than by the labour and the skill it cost;
Are occupations of the poet's mind
So pleasing, and that steal away the thought
With such address from themes of sad import,   300
That lost in his own musings, happy man!
He feels the anxieties of life, denied
Their wonted entertainment, all retire.
Such joys has he that sings. But ah! not such,
Or seldom such, the hearers of his song.   305
Fastidious, or else listless, or perhaps
Aware of nothing arduous in a task
They never undertook, they little note
His dangers or escapes, and haply find
Their least amusement where he found the most.
But is amusement all? Studious of song,   311
And yet ambitious not to sing in vain,

I would not trifle merely, though the world
Be loudest in their praise who do no more.
Yet what can satire, whether grave or gay?   315
It may correct a foible, may chastise
The freaks of fashion, regulate the dress,
Retrench a swordblade, or displace a patch;
But where are its sublimer trophies found?
What vice has it subdued? whose heart reclaimed
By rigour? or whom laughed into reform?   321
Alas! Leviathan is not so tamed;
Laughed at, he laughs again; and stricken hard,
Turns to the stroke his adamantine scales,
That fear no discipline of human hands.   325
    The pulpit, therefore, (and I name it filled
With solemn awe, that bids me well beware
With what intent I touch that holy thing)—
The pulpit (when the satirist has at last,
Strutting and vapouring in an empty school,   330
Spent all his force, and made no proselyte)—
I say the pulpit (in the sober use
Of its legitimate, peculiar powers)
Must stand acknowledged, while the world shall stand,
The most important and effectual guard,   335
Support, and ornament of Virtue's cause.
There stands the messenger of truth; there stands
The legate of the skies!—His theme divine,
His office sacred, his credentials clear.
By him, the violated law speaks out   340
Its thunders; and by him, in strains as sweet
As angels use, the Gospel whispers peace.
He stablishes the strong, restores the weak,
Reclaims the wanderer, binds the broken heart,
And armed himself in panoply complete   345

Of heavenly temper, furnishes with arms
Bright as his own, and trains by every rule
Of holy discipline, to glorious war,
The sacramental host of God's elect.
Are all such teachers? Would to Heaven all were!
But hark—the Doctor's voice!—fast wedged be-
    tween   351
Two empirics he stands, and with swoln cheeks
Inspires the News, his trumpet.*   Keener far
Than all invective is his bold harangue,
While, through that public organ of report,   355
He hails the clergy, and defying shame,
Announces to the world his own and theirs.
He teaches those to read, whom schools dismissed,
And colleges, untaught; sells accent, tone,
And emphasis in score, and gives to prayer   360
The *adagio* and *andante* it demands.
He grinds divinity of other days
Down into modern use; transforms old print
To zigzag manuscript, and cheats the eyes
Of gallery critics by a thousand arts.   365
Are there who purchase of the Doctor's ware?

---

* An old pencil note in Mr. Gough's copy of the edition
of 1785, intimates that " Dr. Trusler " was the reverend
advertiser here alluded to. This person, successively medical
man, or probably chemist, clergyman, author, and bookseller,
occupied a conspicuous position in the literature of Cowper's
time. His books were principally compilations from standard
works of his day, such as Cook's Voyages and Blackstone's
Commentaries. One of his most successful projects was
that alluded to by Cowper at the close of this paragraph—
abridging the sermons of eminent divines, and printing the
abridgments in a manuscript character for the use of clergy-
men in the pulpit. Assisted by the *prestige* of a degree of
LL.D. his publications were eminently popular, and brought
him a considerable fortune. He died in 1820.

Oh name it not in Gath! it cannot be,
That grave and learned clerks should need such aid.
He doubtless is in sport, and does but droll,
Assuming thus a rank unknown before—   370
Grand caterer and dry nurse of the church!
    I venerate the man whose heart is warm,
Whose hands are pure, whose doctrine and whose life
Coincident, exhibit lucid proof
That he is honest in the sacred cause.   375
To such I render more than mere respect,
Whose actions say that they respect themselves.
But loose in morals, and in manners vain,
In conversation frivolous, in dress
Extreme, at once rapacious and profuse;   380
Frequent in Park with lady at his side,
Ambling and prattling scandal as he goes;
But rare at home, and never at his books,
Or with his pen, save when he scrawls a card;
Constant at routs, familiar with a round   385
Of ladyships, a stranger to the poor;
Ambitious of preferment for its gold,
And well prepared, by ignorance and sloth,
By infidelity and love o' the world,*
To make God's work a sinecure; a slave   390
To his own pleasures and his patron's pride:—
From such apostles, O ye mitred heads
Preserve the church! and lay not careless hands
On skulls that cannot teach, and will not learn.
    Would I describe a preacher, such as Paul,   395
Were he on earth, would hear, approve, and own,

· * "Love o' th' world;" Eds. 1785, 1786. "Love of
world;" Ed. 1787, and subsequent editions, except Southey's.
"Love of the world;" Southey.

Paul should himself direct me.   I would trace
His master-strokes, and draw from his design.
I would express him simple, grave, sincere;
In doctrine uncorrupt; in language plain,   400
And plain in manner; decent, solemn, chaste
And natural in gesture; much impressed
Himself, as conscious of his awful charge,
And anxious mainly that the flock he feeds
May feel it too; affectionate in look,   405
And tender in address, as well becomes
A messenger of grace to guilty men.
Behold the picture!—Is it like?—Like whom?
The things that mount the rostrum with a skip,
And then skip down again; pronounce a text;   410
Cry—hem! and reading what they never wrote
Just fifteen minutes, huddle up their work,
And with a well-bred whisper close the scene!
      In man or woman, but far most in man,
And most of all in man that ministers   415
And serves the altar, in my soul I loathe
All affectation.   'Tis my perfect scorn;
Object of my implacable disgust.
What!—will a man play tricks, will he indulge
A silly fond conceit of his fair form   420
And just proportion, fashionable mien
And pretty face, in presence of his God? ·
Or will he seek to dazzle me with tropes,
As with the diamond on his lily hand,
And play his brilliant parts before my eyes,   425
When I am hungry for the bread of life?
He mocks his Maker, prostitutes and shames
His noble office, and, instead of truth,
Displaying his own beauty, starves his flock!

Therefore, avaunt all attitude, and stare,   430
And start theatric, practised at the glass!
I seek divine simplicity in him
Who handles things divine; and all beside,*
Though learned with labour, and though much
          admired
By curious eyes and judgments ill informed,   435
To me is odious as the nasal twang
Heard at conventicle,† where worthy men,
Misled by custom, strain celestial themes
Through the pressed nostril, spectacle-bestrid.
    Some, decent in demeanour while they preach,
That task performed, relapse into themselves,   441
And having spoken wisely, at the close
Grow wanton, and give proof to every eye,
Whoe'er was edified, themselves were not!
Forth comes the pocket mirror.—First we stroke
An eyebrow, next compose a straggling lock,   446
Then, with an air most gracefully performed,
Fall back into our seat, extend an arm,
And lay it at its ease with gentle care,
With handkerchief in hand depending low: 450
The better hand, more busy, gives the nose
Its bergamot, or aids the indebted eye
With opera glass to watch the moving scene,
And recognise the slow retiring fair.—
Now this is fulsome; and offends me more   455
Than in a churchman slovenly neglect

* "Beside;" Eds. 1785, 1786, 1787, 1788, Southey, Bell.
"Besides;" Eds. 1793, 1794, and subsequent editions, except
Southey and Bell.
    † "At conventicle heard;" Eds. 1785, 1786. "Heard
at conventicle;" Eds. 1787, 1788, 1793, 1794, 1799, and
subsequent editions.

And rustic coarseness would. A* heavenly mind
May be indifferent to her house of clay,
And slight the hovel as beneath her care;
But how a body so fantastic, trim, 460
And quaint in its deportment and attire,
Can lodge a* heavenly mind—demands a doubt.
   He that negotiates between God and man,
As God's ambassador, the grand concerns
Of judgment and of mercy, should beware 465
Of lightness in his speech. 'Tis pitiful
To court a grin, when you should woo a soul;
To break a jest, when pity would inspire
Pathetic exhortation; and to address
The skittish fancy with facetious tales, 470
When sent with God's commission to the heart.
So did not Paul. Direct me to a quip
Or merry turn in all he ever wrote,
And I consent you take it for your text,
Your only one, till sides and benches fail. 475
No: he was serious in a serious cause,
And understood too well the weighty terms
That he had ta'en in charge. He would not stoop
To conquer those by jocular exploits,
Whom Truth and Soberness assailed in vain. 480
   O Popular Applause! what heart of man
Is proof against thy sweet seducing charms?
The wisest and the best feel urgent need
Of all their caution in thy gentlest gales;
But swelled into a gust—who then, alas! 485
With all his canvas set, and inexpert,

   * In both the passages referred to the article " An " was
used until the edition of 1808, except in edition 1798. From
1808, " a " has been printed in all editions, except Southey's.

And therefore heedless, can withstand thy power?
Praise from the rivelled lips of toothless, bald
Decrepitude, and in the looks of lean
And craving Poverty, and in the bow   490
Respectful of the smutched artificer,
Is oft too welcome, and may much disturb
The bias of the purpose.   How much more,
Poured forth by Beauty splendid and polite,
In language soft as Adoration breathes!   495
Ah spare your idol! think him human still;
Charms he may have, but he has frailties too;
Dote not too much, nor spoil what ye admire.
    All truth is from the sempiternal source
Of Light Divine. But Egypt, Greece, and Rome 500
Drew from the stream below. More favoured, we
Drink, when we choose it, at the fountain head.
To them it flowed much mingled and defiled
With hurtful error, prejudice, and dreams
Illusive of philosophy, so called,   505
But falsely.   Sages after sages strove
In vain to filter off a crystal draught
Pure from the lees, which often more enhanced
The thirst than slaked it, and not seldom bred
Intoxication and delirium wild.   510
In vain they pushed inquiry to the birth
And spring-time of the world; asked, Whence is
        man?
Why formed at all?   And wherefore as he is?
Where must he find his Maker?   With what rites
Adore him?   Will he hear, accept, and bless?   515
Or does he sit regardless of his works?
Has man within him an immortal seed?
Or does the tomb take all?   If he survive

His ashes, where, and in what weal or woe?
Knots worthy of solution, which alone   520
A Deity could solve.   Their answers, vague
And all at random, fabulous and dark,
Left them as dark themselves.   Their rules of life,
Defective and unsanctioned, proved too weak
To bind the roving appetite, and lead   525
Blind nature to a God not yet revealed.
'Tis Revelation satisfies all doubts,
Explains all mysteries, except her own,
And so illuminates the path of life,
That fools discover it, and stray no more.   530
Now tell me, dignified and sapient sir,
My man of morals, nurtured in the shades
Of Academus, is this false or true?
Is Christ the abler teacher, or the schools?
If Christ, then why resort at every turn   535
To Athens or to Rome, for wisdom short
Of man's occasions, when in him reside
Grace, knowledge, comfort—an unfathomed store?
How oft, when Paul has served us with a text,
Has Epictetus, Plato, Tully, preached!   540
Men that, if now alive, would sit content
And humble learners of a Saviour's worth,
Preach it who might.   Such was their love of
       truth,
Their thirst of knowledge, and their candour too!
And thus it is.   The pastor, either vain   545
By nature, or by flattery made so, taught
To gaze at his own splendour, and to exalt
Absurdly, not his office, but himself;
Or unenlightened, and too proud to learn;
Or vicious, and not therefore apt to teach;   550

Perverting often, by the stress of lewd
And loose example, whom he should instruct;
Exposes, and holds up to broad disgrace,
The noblest function, and discredits much
The brightest truths that man has ever seen. . 555
For ghostly counsel, if it either fall
Below the exigence, or be not backed
With show of love, at least with hopeful proof
Of some sincerity, on the giver's part;
Or be dishonoured, in the exterior form   560
And mode of its conveyance, by such tricks
As move derision, or by foppish airs
And histrionic mummery, that let down
The pulpit to the level of the stage,
Drops from the lips a disregarded thing.   565
The weak perhaps are moved, but are not taught,
While prejudice in men of stronger minds
Takes deeper root, confirmed by what they see.
A relaxation of Religion's hold
Upon the roving and untutored heart   570
Soon follows, and the curb of conscience snapped,
The laity run wild.—But do they now?
Note their extravagance, and be convinced.
     As nations ignorant of God contrive
A wooden one, so we, no longer taught   575
By monitors that mother church supplies,
Now make our own.   Posterity will ask
(If e'er posterity see verse of mine)
Some fifty or a hundred lustrums hence,
What was a Monitor in George's days?   580
My very gentle reader yet unborn,
Of whom I needs must augur better things,
Since Heaven would sure grow weary of a world

Productive only of a race like ours,*
A Monitor is wood—plank shaven thin.   585
We wear it at our backs.   There, closely braced
And neatly fitted, it compresses hard
The prominent and most unsightly bones,
And binds the shoulders flat.   We prove its use
Sovereign, and most effectual, to secure   590
A form not now gymnastic as of yore,
From rickets and distortion, else our lot.
But thus admonished, we can walk erect—
One proof at least of manhood ! while the friend
Sticks close, a Mentor worthy of his charge.†   595
Our habits, costlier than Lucullus wore,
And by caprice as multiplied as his,
Just please us while the passion is at full,
But change with every moon.   The sycophant
Who ‡ waits to dress us, arbitrates their date; 600
Surveys his fair reversion with keen eye ;
Finds one ill made, another obsolete ;
This fits not nicely, that is ill conceived ;
And making prize of all that he condemns,
With our expenditure defrays his own.   605
Variety's the very spice of life,
That gives it all its flavour.   We have run
Through every change that Fancy, at the loom
Exhausted, has had genius to supply ;

* " Like us;" Eds. 1785, 1786, Southey.   " Like ours;"
Ed. 1787, and subsequent editions, except Southey's.
  † The monitor, or back-board, long ago discarded by men,
remained in use in girls' schools until within the last few
years, perhaps is even still known in some of those establish-
ments.
  ‡ " That;" Eds. 1785, 1786, Southey.   " Who;" Ed.
1787, and subsequent editions, except Southey's.

And studious of mutation still, discard   610
A real elegance, a little used,
For monstrous novelty and strange disguise.
We sacrifice to dress, till household joys
And comforts cease.   Dress drains our cellar dry,
And keeps our larder lean; puts out our fires,   615
And introduces hunger, frost, and woe,
Where peace and hospitality might reign.
What man that lives, and that knows how to live,
Would fail to exhibit at the public shows
A form as splendid as the proudest there,   620
Though Appetite raise outcries at the cost?
A man o' the town dines late, but soon enough,
With reasonable forecast and dispatch,
To insure a side-box station at half price.
You think, perhaps, so delicate his dress,   625
His daily fare as delicate.   Alas!
He picks clean teeth, and, busy as he seems
With an old tavern quill, is hungry yet.
The Rout is Folly's circle, which she draws
With magic wand.   So potent is the spell,   630
That none, decoyed into that fatal ring,
Unless by Heaven's peculiar grace, escape.
There we grow early grey, but never wise;
There form connexions, but* acquire no friend;
Solicit pleasure, hopeless of success;   635
Waste youth in occupations only fit
For second childhood; and devote old age
To sports which only childhood could excuse.
There they are happiest who dissemble best
Their weariness; and they the most polite   640

* "And;" Eds. 1785, 1786, Southey. "But;" Ed. 1787,
and subsequent editions, except Southey's.

Who squander time and treasure with a smile,
Though at their own destruction. She that asks
Her dear five hundred friends, contemns them all,
And hates their coming. They (what can they less?)
Make just reprisals, and with cringe and shrug, 645
And bow obsequious, hide their hate of her.
All catch the frenzy, downward from her Grace,
Whose flambeaux flash against the morning skies,
And gild our chamber ceilings as they pass,
To her who, frugal only that her thrift   650
May feed* excesses she can ill afford,
Is hackneyed home unlackeyed; who, in haste
Alighting, turns the key in her own door,
And, at the watchman's lantern borrowing light,
Finds a cold bed her only comfort left.   655
Wives beggar husbands, husbands starve their wives,
On Fortune's velvet altar offering up
Their last poor pittance—Fortune, most severe
Of goddesses yet known, and costlier far
Than all that held their routs in Juno's† heaven !
So fare we in this prison-house, the world;   661
And 'tis a fearful spectacle to see
So many maniacs dancing in their chains.
They gaze upon the links that hold them fast,
With eyes of anguish, execrate their lot,   665
Then shake them in despair, and dance again.
    Now basket up the family of plagues
That waste our vitals; peculation, sale
Of honour, perjury, corruption, frauds

---

* The beautiful little edition of 1799 (printed by Bensley)
has here "feel," instead of "feed."
    † "Heathen heaven;" Eds. 1785, 1786, Southey. "Juno's
heaven;" Ed. 1787, and subsequent editions, except
Southey's.

By forgery, by subterfuge of law,   670
By tricks and lies as numerous and as keen
As the necessities their authors feel;
Then cast them, closely bundled, every brat
At the right door. Profusion is the* sire.
Profusion unrestrained, with all that's base 675
In character has littered all the land,   .
And bred, within the memory of no few,
A priesthood such as Baal's was of old,
A people such as never was till now.
It is a hungry vice;—it eats up all   680
That gives society its beauty, strength,
Convenience, and security, and use;
Makes men mere vermin, worthy to be trapped
And gibbeted, as fast as catchpole-claws
Can seize the slippery prey, unties the knot 685
Of union, and converts the sacred band
That holds mankind together, to a scourge.
Profusion, deluging a state with lusts
Of grossest nature and of worst effects,
Prepares it for its ruin; hardens, blinds, 690
And warps the consciences of public men,
Till they can laugh at virtue, mock the fools
That trust them, and in the end disclose a face
That would have shocked Credulity herself,
Unmasked, vouchsafing this their sole excuse— 695
Since all alike are selfish, why not they?
This does Profusion, and the accursed cause
Of such deep mischief has itself a cause.
  In colleges and halls, in ancient days,
When learning, virtue, piety, and truth 700

---

* " Its sire;" Eds. 1785, 1786, Southey. " The sire;"
Ed. 1787, and subsequent editions, except Southey's.

Were precious, and inculcated with care,
There dwelt a sage called Discipline. His head,
Not yet by time completely silvered o'er,
Bespoke him past the bounds of freakish youth,
But strong for service still, and unimpaired. 705
His eye was meek and gentle, and a smile
Played on his lips, and in his speech was heard
Paternal sweetness, dignity, and love.
The occupation dearest to his heart
Was to encourage goodness. He would stroke 710
The head of modest and ingenuous worth
That blushed at its own praise; and press the youth
Close to his side that pleased him. Learning grew
Beneath his care, a thriving vigorous plant;
The mind was well-informed, the passions held 715
Subordinate, and diligence was choice.
If e'er it chanced, as sometimes chance it must,
That one among so many overleaped
The limits of control, his gentle eye
Grew stern, and darted a severe rebuke; 720
His frown was full of terror, and his voice
Shook the delinquent with such fits of awe
As left him not, till penitence had won
Lost favour back again, and closed the breach.
But Discipline, a faithful servant long, 725
Declined at length into the vale of years;
A palsy struck his arm, his sparkling eye
Was quenched in rheums of age, his voice, un-
          strung,
Grew tremulous, and moved derision more
Than reverence, in perverse rebellious youth. 730
So colleges and halls neglected much
Their good old friend, and Discipline at length,

O'erlooked and unemployed, fell sick, and died.
Then Study languished, Emulation slept,
And Virtue fled.   The schools became a scene   735
Of solemn farce, where Ignorance in stilts,
His cap well-lined with logic not his own,
With parrot tongue performed the scholar's part,
Proceeding soon a graduated dunce.
Then compromise had place, and scrutiny   740
Became stone blind; precedence went in truck,
And he was competent whose purse was so.
A dissolution of all bonds ensued;
The curbs invented for the mulish mouth
Of headstrong youth were broken; bars and bolts
Grew rusty by disuse; and massy gates   745
Forgot their office, opening with a touch;
Till gowns at length are found mere masquerade,
The tasselled cap and the spruce band a jest,
A mockery of the world!   What need of these   750
For gamesters, jockeys, brothellers impure,
Spendthrifts, and booted sportsmen, oftener seen
With belted waist and pointers at their heels
Than in the bounds of duty?   What was learned,
If aught was learned in childhood, is forgot;   755
And such expense as pinches parents blue,
And mortifies the liberal hand of love,
Is squandered in pursuit of idle sports
And vicious pleasures; buys the boy a name
That sits a stigma on his father's house,   760
And cleaves through life inseparably close
To him that wears it.   What can after-games
Of riper joys, and commerce with the world,
The lewd vain world that must receive him soon,
Add to such erudition, thus acquired   765
Where science and where virtue are professed?

They may confirm his habits, rivet fast
His folly, but to spoil him is a task
That bids defiance to the united powers
Of fashion, dissipation, taverns, stews.　　　770
Now blame we most the nurslings, or the nurse?
The children, crooked, and twisted, and deformed
Through want of care; or her whose winking eye
And slumbering oscitancy mars the brood?
The nurse, no doubt.　Regardless of her charge,
She needs herself correction; needs to learn　776
That it is dangerous sporting with the world,
With things so sacred as a nation's trust,
The nurture of her youth, her dearest pledge.

　　All are not such.　I had a brother once—　780
Peace to the memory of a man of worth,
A man of letters, and of manners too!
Of manners sweet as Virtue always wears,
When gay Goodnature dresses her in smiles.
He graced a college,* in which order yet　785
Was sacred, and was honoured, loved, and wept
By more than one, themselves conspicuous there.
Some minds are tempered happily, and mixed
With such ingredients of good sense and taste
Of what is excellent in man, they thirst　790
With such a zeal to be what they approve,
That no restraints can circumscribe them more
Than they themselves by choice, for wisdom's sake.
Nor can example hurt them: what they see
Of vice in others but enhancing more　795
The charms of virtue in their just esteem.
If such escape contagion, and emerge.
Pure, from so foul a pool, to shine abroad,

* Benet College, Cambridge.—(C.) It is now better known
as Corpus Christi.

And give the world their talents and themselves,
Small thanks to those whose negligence or sloth
Exposed their inexperience to the snare,   801
And left them to an undirected choice.
    See then the quiver broken and decayed,
In which are kept our arrows! Rusting there
In wild disorder, and unfit for use,   805
What wonder, if discharged into the world,
They shame their shooters with a random flight,
Their points obtuse, and feathers drunk with wine!
Well may the Church wage unsuccessful war,
With such artillery armed. Vice parries wide   810
The undreaded volley with a sword of straw,
And stands an impudent and fearless mark.
    Have we not tracked the felon home, and found
His birth-place and his dam? The country mourns,
Mourns because every plague that can infest   815
Society, and that saps and worms the base
Of the edifice that policy has raised,
Swarms in all quarters; meets the eye, the ear,
And suffocates the breath at every turn.
Profusion breeds them; and the cause itself   820
Of that calamitous mischief has been found:
Found too where most offensive, in the skirts
Of the robed pedagogue! Else let the arraigned
Stand up unconscious, and refute the charge.
So when the Jewish leader stretched his arm,   825
And waved his rod divine, a race obscene,
Spawned in the muddy beds of Nile, came forth,
Polluting Egypt: gardens, fields, and plains
Were covered with the pest; the streets were filled;
The croaking nuisance lurked in every nook;   830
Nor palaces, nor even chambers, 'scaped;
And the land stank—so numerous was the fry.

THE TASK.   BOOK III.

THE GARDEN.

ARGUMENT.

THE TASK. BOOK III.

THE GARDEN.

S one who long in thickets and in brakes
Entangled, winds now this way and now
that
His devious course uncertain, seeking
home ;
Or having long in miry ways been foiled
And sore discomfited, from slough to slough   5
Plunging, and half despairing of escape ;
If chance at length he find a greensward smooth
And faithful to the foot, his spirits rise,
He cherups brisk his ear-erecting steed,
And winds his way with pleasure and with ease ;
So I, designing other themes, and called   11
To adorn the Sofa with eulogium due,
To tell its slumbers, and to paint its dreams,
Have rambled wide.   In country, city, seat
Of academic fame (howe'er deserved)   15
Long held, and scarcely disengaged at last.
But now with pleasant pace a cleanlier road
I mean to tread.   I feel myself at large,
Courageous, and refreshed for future toil,
If toil await me, or if dangers new.   20

Since pulpits fail, and sounding boards reflect
Most part an empty ineffectual sound,
What chance that I, to fame so little known,
Nor conversant with men or manners much,
Should speak to purpose, or with better hope   25
Crack the satiric thong? 'Twere wiser far
For me, enamoured of sequestered scenes,
And charmed with rural beauty, to repose ·
Where chance may throw me, beneath elm or vine,
My languid limbs, when summer scars the plains,
Or when rough winter rages, on the soft   31
And sheltered Sofa, while the nitrous air
Feeds a blue flame, and makes a cheerful hearth;
There, undisturbed by Folly, and apprised
How great the danger of disturbing her,   35
To muse in silence, or at least confine
Remarks that gall so many, to the few
My partners in retreat.   Disgust concealed
Is oft-times proof of wisdom, when the fault
Is obstinate, and cure beyond our reach.   40
    Domestic Happiness, thou only bliss
Of Paradise that has survived the fall!
Though few now taste thee unimpaired and pure,
Or tasting long enjoy thee; too infirm,
Or too incautious, to preserve thy sweets   45
Unmixed with drops of bitter, which Neglect
Or Temper sheds into thy crystal cup.
Thou art the nurse of Virtue.   In thine arms
She smiles, appearing, as in truth she is,
Heaven-born, and destined to the skies again.   50
Thou art not known where Pleasure is adored,
That reeling goddess with the zoneless waist
And wandering eyes, still leaning on the arm

Of Novelty, her fickle, frail support;
For thou art meek and constant, hating change,   55
And finding in the calm of truth-tried love
Joys that her stormy raptures never yield.
Forsaking thee, what shipwreck have we made
Of honour, dignity, and fair renown!
Till prostitution elbows us aside   60
In all our crowded streets; and senates seem
Convened for purposes of empire less
Than to release the adultress from her bond.
The adultress! what a theme for angry verse!
What provocation to the indignant heart,   65
That feels for injured love! but I disdain
The nauseous task to paint her as she is,
Cruel, abandoned, glorying in her shame!
No:—let her pass, and charioted along
In guilty splendour, shake the public ways;   70
The frequency of crimes has washed them white,
And verse of mine shall never brand the wretch,
Whom matrons now, of character unsmirched
And chaste themselves, are not ashamed to own.
Virtue and vice had boundaries in old time,   75
Not to be passed: and she that had renounced
Her sex's honour, was renounced herself
By all that prized it; not for prudery's sake,
But dignity's, resentful of the wrong.
'Twas hard perhaps on here and there a waif   80
Desirous to return, and not received,
But was a wholesome rigour in the main,
And taught the unblemished to preserve with care
That purity, whose loss was loss of all.
Men too were nice in honour in those days,   85
And judged offenders well. Then he that sharped,

And pocketed a prize by fraud obtained,
Was marked and shunned as odious. He that sold
His country, or was slack when she required
His every nerve in action and at stretch,   90
Paid with the blood that he had basely spared,
The price of his default. But now—yes, now,
We are become so candid and so fair,
So liberal in construction, and so rich
In Christian charity, (good-natured age!)*   95
That they are safe, sinners of either sex,
Transgress what laws they may. Well-dressed,
          well-bred,
Well-equipaged, is ticket good enough
To pass us readily through every door.
Hypocrisy, detest her as we may,   100
(And no man's hatred ever wronged her yet)
May claim this merit still—that she admits
The worth of what she mimics with such care,
And thus gives Virtue indirect applause;
But she has burned her mask, not needed here,   105
Where Vice has such allowance, that her shifts
And specious semblances have lost their use.

   I was a stricken deer that left the herd
Long since: with many an arrow deep infixed
My panting side was charged, when I withdrew   110
To seek a tranquil death in distant shades.
There was I found by One who had himself
Been hurt by the archers. In his side He bore,
And in his hands and feet, the cruel scars.

   * "In christian charity, a good-natured age!" was the
reading of the first four editions. The line was altered as it
stands in our text in Ed. 1793, and that reading has been
adopted by subsequent Editors, except Southey, who restored
the original reading.

With gentle force soliciting the darts, 115
He drew them forth, and healed, and bade me live.
Since then, with few associates, in remote
And silent woods I wander, far from those
My former partners of my peopled scene ;
With few associates, and not wishing more. 120
Here much I ruminate, as much I may,
With other views of men and manners now
Than once, and others of a life to come.
I see that all are wanderers, gone astray
Each in his own delusions ; they are lost 125
In chase of fancied happiness, still wooed
And never won.   Dream after dream ensues,
And still they dream that they shall still succeed,
And still are disappointed.   Rings the world
With the vain stir.   I sum up half mankind, 130
And add two-thirds of the remaining half,*
And find the total of their hopes and fears
Dreams, empty dreams.   The million flit as gay
As if created only like the fly
That spreads his motley wings in the eye of noon,
To sport their season, and be seen no more. 136
The rest are sober dreamers, grave and wise,
And pregnant with discoveries new and rare.
Some write a narrative of wars and feats
Of heroes little known, and call the rant 140
A history : describe the man, of whom
His own coevals took but little note,
And paint his person, character and views,
As they had known him from his mother's womb.

---

* " Remainder-half;" Eds. 1785, 1786, and Southey.
" Remaining half;" Ed. 1787, and subsequent editions, except Southey's.

They disentangle from the puzzled skein,   145
In which obscurity has wrapped them up,
The threads of politic and shrewd design
That ran through all his purposes, and charge
His mind with meanings that he never had,
Or having, kept concealed. Some drill and bore 150
The solid earth, and from the strata there
Extract a register, by which we learn,
That He who made it, and revealed its date
To Moses, was mistaken in its age.
Some, more acute and more industrious still,   155
Contrive creation; travel nature up
To the sharp peak of her sublimest height,
And tell us whence the stars; why some are fixed,
And planetary some; what gave them first
Rotation; from what fountain flowed their light. 160
Great contest follows, and much learnèd dust
Involves the combatants; each claiming Truth,
And Truth disclaiming both; and thus they spend
The little wick of life's poor shallow lamp,
In playing tricks with Nature, giving laws   165
To distant worlds, and trifling in their own.
Is't not a pity now, that tickling rheums
Should ever tease the lungs and blear the sight
Of oracles like these? Great pity too,
That having wielded th' elements, and built   170
A thousand systems, each in his own way,
They should go out in fume, and be forgot?
Ah! what is life thus spent? and what are they
But frantic who thus spend it all for smoke?—
Eternity for bubbles proves at last   175
A senseless bargain. When I see such games
Played by the creatures of a Power who swears

That He will judge the earth, and call the fool
To a sharp reckoning that has lived in vain ;
And when I weigh this seeming wisdom well,   180
And prove it in the infallible result
So hollow and so false—I feel my heart
Dissolve in pity, and account the learn'd,
If this be learning, most of all deceived.
Great crimes alarm the Conscience, but it sleeps   185
While thoughtful man is plausibly amused.
" Defend me therefore, Common Sense," say I,
" From reveries so airy, from the toil
Of dropping buckets into empty wells,
And growing old in drawing nothing up!"   190
    " 'Twere well," says one sage, erudite, profound,
Terribly arched and aquiline his nose,
And overbuilt with most impending brows,
" 'Twere well, could you permit the world to live
As the world pleases.   What's the world to you ?"
Much.   I was born of woman, and drew milk   196
As sweet as charity from human breasts.
I think, articulate, I laugh and weep,
And exercise all functions of a man.
How then should I and any man that lives   200
Be strangers to each other ?   Pierce my vein,
Take of the crimson stream meandering there,
And catechise it well; apply thy* glass,
Search it, and prove now if it be not blood
Congenial with thine own ; and if it be,   205
What edge of subtlety canst thou suppose
Keen enough, wise and skilful as thou art,

* " Your;" Eds. 1785, 1786, 1787, 1788, Southey, Bell.
" Thy;" Ed. 1794, and subsequent editions, except Southey's
and Bell's.

To cut the link of brotherhood, by which
One common Maker bound me to the kind?
True, I am no proficient, I confess,   210
In arts like yours.   I cannot call the swift
And perilous lightnings from the angry clouds,
And bid them hide themselves in earth * beneath;
I cannot analyse the air, nor catch
The parallax of yonder luminous point   215
That seems half quenched in the immense abyss;
Such powers I boast not—neither can I rest
A silent witness of the headlong rage,
Or heedless folly, by which thousands die,
Bone of my bone, and kindred souls to mine.   220
    God never meant that man should scale the
        Heavens
By strides of human wisdom.   In his works,
Though wondrous, He commands us, in his word,
To seek him rather where his mercy shines.
The mind indeed, enlightened from above,   225
Views him in all; ascribes to the grand cause
The grand effect; acknowledges with joy
His manner, and with rapture tastes his style.
But never yet did philosophic tube,
That brings the planets home into the eye   230
Of Observation, and discovers, else
Not visible, his family of worlds,
Discover him that rules them; such a veil
Hangs over mortal eyes, blind from the birth,
And dark in things divine.   Full often too   235
Our wayward intellect, the more we learn

* In th' earth;" Eds. 1785, 1786. " In the earth;"
Southey. " In earth;" Ed. 1787, and subsequent editions,
except Southey's.

Of Nature, overlooks her author more;
From instrumental causes proud to draw
Conclusion retrograde, and mad mistake.
But if his word once teach us, shoot a ray   240
Through all the heart's dark chambers, and reveal
Truths undiscerned but by that holy light,
Then all is plain.   Philosophy baptized
In the pure fountain of eternal love
Has eyes indeed; and viewing all she sees   245
As meant to indicate a God to man,
Gives him his praise, and forfeits not her own.
Learning has borne such fruit in other days
On all her branches.   Piety has found
Friends in the friends of science, and true prayer 250
Has flowed from lips wet with Castalian dews.
Such was thy wisdom, Newton, childlike sage!
Sagacious reader of the works of God,
And in his word sagacious.   Such too thine,
Milton, whose genius had angelic wings,   255
And fed on manna.   And such thine, in whom
Our British Themis gloried with just cause,
Immortal Hale! for deep discernment praised,
And sound integrity, not more than famed
For sanctity of manners undefiled.   260
    All flesh is grass, and all its glory fades
Like the fair flower dishevelled in the wind;
Riches have wings, and grandeur is a dream.
The man we celebrate must find a tomb,
And we that worship him, ignoble graves.   265
Nothing is proof against the general curse
Of vanity, that seizes all below.
The only amaranthine flower on earth
Is virtue; the only lasting treasure, truth.

But what is truth? 'Twas Pilate's question put 270
To Truth itself, that deigned him no reply.
And wherefore? Will not God impart his light
To them that ask it?—Freely.—'Tis his joy,
His glory, and his nature to impart;
But to the proud, uncandid, insincere, 275
Or negligent inquirer, not a spark.
What's that which brings contempt upon a book,
And him who* writes it, though the style be neat,
The method clear, and argument exact?
That makes a minister in holy things 280
The joy of many, and the dread of more,
His name a theme for praise and for reproach?—
That, while it gives us worth in God's account,
Depreciates and undoes us in our own?
What pearl is it that rich men cannot buy, 285
That learning is too proud to gather up,
But which the poor, and the despised of all,
Seek and obtain, and often find unsought?
Tell me—and I will tell thee what is Truth.

    Oh friendly to the best pursuits of man, 290
Friendly to thought, to.virtue, and to peace,
Domestic life in rural leisure† passed!
Few know thy value, and few taste thy sweets,
Though many boast thy favours, and affect
To understand and choose thee for their own. 295
But foolish man foregoes his proper bliss,
Even as his first progenitor, and quits,
Though placed in Paradise, (for earth has still

   * " That;" Eds. 1785, 1786, Southey. " Who;" Ed.
1787, and subsequent editions, except Southey's.
   † " Leisure;" all Eds. down to 1806. " Pleasure;" Eds.
1808, 1810, 1812, and 1817; " Leisure;" Eds. 1821, 1825,
and Southey. " Pleasure;" Grimshawe, Dale, and Bell.

Some traces of her youthful beauty left)
Substantial happiness for transient joy.　300
Scenes formed for contemplation, and to nurse
The growing seeds of wisdom; that suggest,
By every pleasing image they present,
Reflections such as meliorate the heart,
Compose the passions, and exalt the mind;　305
Scenes such as these, 'tis his supreme delight
To fill with riot, and defile with blood.
Should some contagion, kind to the poor brutes
We persecute, annihilate the tribes
That draw the sportsman over hill and dale　310
Fearless, and rapt away from all his cares;
Should never game-fowl hatch her eggs again,
Nor baited hook deceive the fish's eye;
Could pageantry and dance, and feast and song,
Be quelled in all our summer-months' retreats;*
How many self-deluded nymphs and swains,　316
Who dream they have a taste for fields and groves,
Would find them hideous nurseries of the spleen,
And crowd the roads, impatient for the town!
They love the country, and none else, who seek　320
For their own sake its silence and its shade;—
Delights which who would leave, that has a heart
Susceptible of pity, or a mind
Cultured and capable of sober thought—
For all the savage din of the swift pack,　325
And clamours of the field? Detested sport,
That owes its pleasures to another's pain,

* "Summer-month retreats;" Eds. 1785, 1786, Southey.
"Summer-months retreat;" 1787, 1788. Summer-months'
retreat;" Eds. 1793, 1794, 1798, 1799, 1800, 1803, 1806,
Grimshawe. "Summer-months' retreats;" Eds. 1815, 1817,
1825, Dale, Bell. "Summer-mouth's retreat;" Ed. 1805.

That feeds upon the sobs and dying shrieks
Of harmless Nature, dumb, but yet endued
With eloquence that agonies inspire,   330
Of silent tears and heart-distending sighs!
Vain tears, alas! and sighs that never find
A corresponding tone in jovial souls.
Well—one at least is safe.   One sheltered hare
Has never heard the sanguinary yell   335
Of cruel man, exulting in her woes.
Innocent partner of my peaceful home,
Whom ten long years' experience of my care
Has made at last familiar; she has lost
Much of her vigilant instinctive dread,   340
Not needful here, beneath a roof like mine.
Yes—thou may'st eat thy bread, and lick the hand
That feeds thee; thou may'st frolic on the floor
At evening, and at night retire secure
To thy straw couch, and slumber unalarmed;   345
For I have gained thy confidence, have pledged
All that is human in me, to protect
Thine unsuspecting gratitude and love.
If I survive thee, I will dig thy grave;
And when I place thee in it, sighing say,   350
I knew at least one hare that had a friend.*

How various his employments whom the world
Calls idle, and who justly, in return,
Esteems that busy world an idler too!
Friends, books, a garden, and perhaps his pen, 355
Delightful industry enjoyed at home,
And Nature in her cultivated trim
Dressed to his taste, inviting him abroad—
Can he want occupation who has these?

* See the note at the end of this volume.—(C.)

Will he be idle who has much to enjoy? 360
Me, therefore, studious of laborious ease,
Not slothful; happy to deceive the time
Not waste it, and aware that human life
Is but a loan, to be repaid with use,
When He shall call his debtors to account 365
From whom are all our blessings, business finds
Even here: while sedulous I seek to improve,
At least neglect not, or leave unemployed,
The mind He gave me; driving it, though slack
Too oft, and much impeded in its work 370
By causes not to be divulged in vain,
To its just point—the service of mankind.
He that attends to his interior self;
That has a heart, and keeps it; has a mind
That hungers, and supplies it; and who seeks 375
A social, not a dissipated life,
Has business; feels himself engaged to achieve
No unimportant, though a silent task.
A life all turbulence and noise may seem
To him that leads it, wise, and to be praised; 380
But wisdom is a pearl with most success
Sought in still water, and beneath clear skies.
He that is ever occupied in storms,
Or dives not for it, or brings up instead,
Vainly industrious, a disgraceful prize. 385
      The morning finds the self-sequestered man
Fresh for his task, intend what task he may.
Whether inclement seasons recommend
His warm but simple home, where he enjoys,
With her who shares his pleasures and his heart, 390
Sweet converse, sipping calm the fragrant lymph
Which neatly she prepares; then to his book

Well-chosen, and not sullenly perused
In selfish silence, but imparted oft,
As aught occurs that she may smile to hear,   395
Or turn to nourishment, digested well.
Or if the garden with its many cares,
All well repaid, demand him, he attends
The welcome call, conscious how much the hand
Of lubbard Labour needs his watchful eye,   400
Oft loitering lazily if not o'erseen,
Or misapplying his unskilful strength.
Nor does he govern only, or direct,
But much performs himself.   No works, indeed,
That ask robust, tough sinews, bred to toil,   405
Servile employ; but such as may amuse
Not tire, demanding rather skill than force.
Proud of his well-spread walls, he views his trees,
That meet (no barren interval between)
With pleasure more than even their fruits afford, 410
Which, save himself who trains them, none can feel;
These therefore are his own peculiar charge,
No meaner hand may discipline the shoots,
None but his steel approach them.   What is weak,
Distempered, or has lost prolific powers,   415
Impaired by age, his unrelenting hand
Dooms to the knife; nor does he spare the soft
And succulent, that feeds its giant growth
But barren, at the expense of neighbouring twigs
Less ostentatious, and yet studded thick   420
With hopeful gems.   The rest, no portion left
That may disgrace his art, or disappoint
Large expectation, he disposes neat
At measured distances, that air and sun
Admitted freely, may afford their aid,   425

And ventilate and warm the swelling buds.
Hence Summer has her riches, Autumn hence,
And hence even Winter fills his withered hand
With blushing fruits, and plenty not his own.*
Fair recompense of labour well bestowed,   430
And wise precaution, which a clime so rude
Makes needful† still; whose Spring is but the child
Of churlish Winter, in her froward moods
Discovering much the temper of her sire.
For oft, as if in her the stream of mild   435
Maternal nature had reversed its course,
She brings her infants forth with many smiles,
But, once delivered, kills them with a frown.
He, therefore, timely warned, himself supplies
Her want of care, screening and keeping warm 440
The plenteous bloom, that no rough blast may sweep
His garlands from the boughs.   Again, as oft
As the sun peeps, and vernal airs breathe mild,
The fence withdrawn, he gives them every beam,
And spreads his hopes before the blaze of day. 445
   To raise the prickly and green-coated gourd,
So grateful to the palate, and when rare
So coveted, else base and disesteemed—
Food for the vulgar merely—is an art
That toiling ages have but just matured,   450
And at this moment unassayed in song.
Yet gnats have had, and frogs and mice, long since,
Their eulogy; those sang the Mantuan bard,
And these the Grecian, in ennobling strains;
And in thy numbers, Philips, shines for aye   455

* Miraturque novos fructus [frondes] et non sua poma.—
Virg.—(C.) [Georg. II. 82.]
† The edition of 1799 alone has " needed."

The solitary Shilling.*   Pardon then,
Ye sage dispensers of poetic fame,
The ambition of one meaner far, whose powers,
Presuming an attempt not less sublime,
Pant for the praise of dressing to the taste   ,   460
Of critic appetite, no sordid fare,
A cucumber, while costly yet and scarce.
   The stable yields a stercoraceous † heap,
Impregnated with quick fermenting salts,
And potent to resist the freezing blast;   465
For ere the beech and elm have cast their leaf
Deciduous,‡ when now November dark
Checks vegetation in the torpid plant
Exposed to his cold breath, the task begins.
Warily therefore, and with prudent heed,   470
He seeks a favoured spot; that where he builds
The agglomerated pile, his frame may front
The sun's meridian disk, and at the back
Enjoy close shelter, wall, or reeds, or hedge
Impervious to the wind.   First he bids spread 475
Dry fern or littered hay, that may imbibe
The ascending damps; then leisurely impose,   ,
And lightly, shaking it with agile hand
From the full fork, the saturated straw.
What longest binds the closest, forms secure   480

   * The allusions to the *Culex* and *Batrachomyomachia*, poems
attributed to Virgil and Homer, need no comment. Philips's
burlesque of the Splendid Shilling was first published in 1703,
before the author was out of his teens.
   † " Stercorarious;" Eds. 1785, 1786, and Southey. " Stercoraceous;" Ed. 1787, and subsequent editions, except
Southey's.
   ‡ "Deciduous, and when;" Eds. 1785, 1786, and Southey.
" Deciduous, when;" Ed. 1787, and subsequent editions,
except Southey's and Dale's.

The shapely side, that as it rises takes,
By just degrees, an overhanging breadth,
Sheltering the base with its projected eaves.
The uplifted frame, compact at every joint,
And overlaid with clear translucent glass,   435
He settles next upon the sloping mount,
Whose sharp declivity shoots off secure
From the dashed pane the deluge as it falls :
He shuts it close, and the first labour ends.
Thrice must the voluble and restless earth   490
Spin round upon her axle, ere the warmth,
Slow gathering in the midst, through the square mass
Diffused, attain the surface ; when, behold !
A pestilent and most corrosive steam,
Like a gross fog Bœotian, rising fast,   495
And fast condensed upon the dewy sash,
Asks egress ; which obtained, the overcharged
And drenched conservatory breathes abroad,
In volumes wheeling slow, the vapour dank,
And purified, rejoices to have lost   500
Its foul inhabitant.   But to assuage
The impatient fervour which it first conceives
Within its reeking bosom, threatening death
To his young hopes, requires discreet delay.
Experience, slow preceptress, teaching oft   505
The way to glory by miscarriage foul,
Must prompt him, and admonish how to catch
The auspicious moment, when the tempered heat
Friendly to vital motion, may afford
Soft fomentation,* and invite the seed.   510

* " Fomentation ;" Eds. 1785, 1787, and subsequent editions, except Southey's and Bell's. " Fermentation ;" Eds.
1786, Southey, Bell.

The seed, selected wisely, plump, and smooth,
And glossy, he commits to pots of size
Diminutive, well filled with well-prepared
And fruitful soil, that has been treasured long,
And drunk no moisture from the dripping clouds.
These on the warm and genial earth that hides 516
The smoking manure, and overspreads it all,
He places lightly, and as time subdues
The rage of fermentation, plunges deep,
In the soft medium, till they stand immersed. 520
Then rise the tender germs, upstarting quick
And spreading wide their spongy lobes, at first
Pale, wan, and livid, but assuming soon,
If fanned by balmy and nutritious air, 524
Strained through the friendly mats, a vivid green.
Two leaves produced, two rough indented leaves,
Cautious he pinches from the second stalk
A pimple that portends a future sprout,
And interdicts its growth.　Thence straight succeed
The branches, sturdy to his utmost wish, 530
Prolific all, and harbingers of more.
The crowded roots demand enlargement now,
And transplantation in an ampler space.
Indulged in what they wish, they soon supply
Large foliage, overshadowing golden flowers, 535
Blown on the summit of the apparent fruit.
These have their sexes; and when summer shines,
The bee transports the fertilizing meal
From flower to flower, and even the breathing air
Wafts the rich prize to its appointed use. 540
Not so when winter scowls.　Assistant Art
Then acts in Nature's office, brings to pass
The glad espousals, and ensures the crop.

Grudge not, ye rich, (since Luxury must have
His dainties, and the World's more numerous half
Lives by contriving delicates for you)   546
Grudge not the cost.   Ye little know the cares,
The vigilance, the labour, and the skill,
That day and night are exercised, and hang
Upon the ticklish balance of suspense,   550
That ye may garnish your profuse regales
With summer fruits, brought forth by wintry suns.
Ten thousand dangers lie in wait to thwart
The process.   Heat and cold, and wind and steam,
Moisture and drought, mice, worms, and swarming
      flies   555
Minute as dust and numberless, oft work
Dire disappointment that admits no cure,
And which no care can obviate.   It were long,
Too long, to tell the expedients and the shifts
Which he that fights a season so severe   560
Devises, while he guards his tender trust,
And oft at last in vain.   The learned and wise,
Sarcastic, would exclaim, and judge the song
Cold as its theme, and like its theme the fruit
Of too much labour, worthless when produced.   565
   Who loves a garden loves a greenhouse too.
Unconscious of a less propitious clime,
There blooms exotic beauty, warm and snug,
While the winds whistle, and the snows descend.
The spiry myrtle with unwithering leaf   570
Shines there, and flourishes.   The golden boast
Of Portugal and Western India there,
The ruddier orange and the paler lime,
Peep through their polished foliage at the storm,
And seem to smile at what they need not fear.   575

The amomum there with intermingling flowers
And cherries hangs her twigs. Geranium boasts
Her crimson honours ; and the spangled beau,
Ficoides, glitters bright the winter long.*
All plants, of every leaf, that can endure   580
The winter's frown, if screened from his shrewd bite,
Live there, and prosper. Those Ausonia claims,
Levantine regions these, the Azores send
Their jessamine, her jessamine remote
Caffraria ;† foreigners from many lands,   585
They form one social shade, as if convened
By magic summons of the Orphean lyre.
Yet just arrangement, rarely brought to pass
But by a master's hand, disposing well
The gay diversities of leaf and flower,   590
Must lend its aid to illustrate all their charms,
And dress the regular yet various scene.
Plant behind plant aspiring, in the van
The dwarfish, in the rear retired, but still
Sublime above the rest, the statelier stand.   595
So once were ranged the sons of ancient Rome,
A noble show ! while Roscius trod the stage ;
And so, while Garrick, as renowned as he,
The sons of Albion ; fearing each to lose

* It is not easy to identify some of the plants mentioned
in this passage, Cowper's descriptions being poetical rather
than botanical. The *Myrtus Pimenta*, or Jamaica Pepper, may
have been the particular *Amomum* here alluded to ; whilst
the peculiar glittering points of the *Mesembryanthemum
crystallinum*, or Ice plant, will be recognized in "the spangled
beau, *Ficoides*." I have been kindly assisted on these botanical questions by W. C. Williamson, Esq., F. R. S., Professor
of Natural History in Owen's College, Manchester.

† "Caffraia ;" Eds. 1785, 1786, 1787, 1788, 1793, editions
down to 1821, except 1798, and Dale. " Caffraria ;" Eds.
1798, 1825, and subsequent editions, except that of Dale.

Some note of Nature's music from his lips,   600
And covetous of Shakespeare's beauty, seen
In every flash of his far-beaming eye.
Nor taste alone and well-contrived display
Suffice to give the marshalled ranks the grace
Of their complete effect.   Much yet remains   605
Unsung, and many cares are yet behind,
And more laborious; cares on which depends
Their vigour, injured soon, not soon restored.
The soil must be renewed, which often washed,
Loses its treasure of salubrious salts,   610
And disappoints the roots; the slender roots
Close interwoven, where they meet the vase,
Must smooth be shorn away; the sapless branch
Must fly before the knife; the withered leaf
Must be detached, and where it strews the floor, 615
Swept with a woman's neatness, breeding else
Contagion, and disseminating death.
Discharge but these kind offices, (and who
Would spare, that loves them, offices like these?)
Well they reward the toil.   The sight is pleased, 620
The scent regaled, each odoriferous leaf,
Each opening blossom, freely breathes abroad
Its gratitude, and thanks him with its sweets.
   So manifold, all pleasing in their kind,
All healthful, are the employs of rural life,   625
Reiterated as the wheel of time
Runs round; still ending, and beginning still.
Nor are these all.   To deck the shapely knoll,
That softly swelled and gaily dressed appears
A flowery island, from the dark green lawn   630
Emerging, must be deemed a labour due
To no mean hand, and asks the touch of taste.

Here also grateful mixture of well matched
And sorted hues (each giving each relief,
And by contrasted beauty shining more)   635
Is needful.   Strength may wield the ponderous
          spade,
May turn the clod, and wheel the compost home,
But elegance, chief grace the garden shows,
And most attractive, is the fair result
Of thought, the creature of a polished mind.   640
Without it, all is gothic as the scene
To which the insipid citizen resorts
Near yonder heath; where Industry mispent,
But proud of his uncouth ill-chosen task,   644
Has made a Heaven on earth; with suns and moons
Of close-rammed stones has charged the encum-
          bered soil,
And fairly laid the zodiac in the dust.
He, therefore, who would see his flowers disposed
Sightly, and in just order, ere he gives
The beds the trusted treasure of their seeds,   650
Forecasts the future whole; that when the scene
Shall break into its preconceived display,
Each for itself, and all as with one voice
Conspiring, may attest his bright design.
Nor even then, dismissing as performed   655
His pleasant work, may he suppose it done.
Few self-supported flowers endure the wind
Uninjured, but expect the upholding aid
Of the smooth-shaven prop, and neatly tied,
Are wedded thus, like beauty to old age,   660
For interest sake, the living to the dead.
Some clothe the soil that feeds them, far diffused
And lowly creeping, modest and yet fair,

Like virtue thriving most where little seen;
Some, more aspiring, catch the neighbour shrub 665
With clasping tendrils, and invest his branch,
Else unadorned, with many a gay festoon
And fragrant chaplet, recompensing well
The strength they borrow with the grace they lend.
All hate the rank society of weeds, 670
Noisome, and ever greedy to exhaust
The impoverished earth; an overbearing race,
That, like the multitude made faction-mad,
Disturb good order, and degrade true worth.
  Oh blest seclusion from a jarring world, 675
Which he, thus occupied, enjoys! Retreat
Cannot indeed to guilty man restore
Lost innocence, or cancel follies past,
But it has peace, and much secures the mind
From all assaults of evil, proving still 680
A faithful barrier, not o'erleaped with ease
By vicious Custom, raging uncontrolled
Abroad, and desolating public life.
When fierce Temptation, seconded within
By traitor Appetite, and armed with darts 685
Tempered in hell, invades the throbbing breast,
To combat may be glorious, and success
Perhaps may crown us, but to fly is safe.
Had I the choice of sublunary good,
What could I wish, that I possess not here? 690
Health, leisure, means to improve it, friendship,
        peace,
No loose or wanton, though a wandering Muse,
And constant occupation without care.
Thus blest, I draw a picture of that bliss;
Hopeless indeed that dissipated minds, 695

And profligate abusers of a world
Created fair so much in vain for them,
Should seek the guiltless joys that I describe,   '
Allured by my report: but sure no less,
That self-condemned they must neglect the prize,
And what they will not taste must yet approve. 701
    What we admire we praise, and when we praise,
Advance it into notice, that its worth
Acknowledged, others may admire it too.
I therefore recommend, though at the risk   705
Of popular disgust, yet boldly still,
The cause of piety, and sacred truth
And virtue, and those scenes which God ordained
Should best secure them, and promote them most;
Scenes that I love, and with regret perceive   710
Forsaken, or through folly not enjoyed.
Pure is the nymph, though liberal of her smiles,
And chaste, though unconfined, whom I extol.
Not as the prince in Shushan, when he called,
Vainglorious of her charms, his Vashti forth,   715
To grace the full pavilion.*   His design
Was but to boast his own peculiar good,
Which all might view with envy, none partake.
My charmer is not mine alone; my sweets,
And she that sweetens all my bitters too,   720
Nature, enchanting Nature, in whose form
And lineaments divine I trace a hand
That errs not, and find raptures still renewed,
Is free to all men—universal prize.
Strange that so fair a creature should yet want 725
Admirers, and be destined to divide
With meaner objects even the few she finds!

* Esther, i. 10, 11.

Stripped of her ornaments, her leaves, and flowers,
She loses all her influence.   Cities then
Attract us, and neglected Nature pines,   730
Abandoned as unworthy of our love.
But are not wholesome airs, though unperfumed
By roses, and clear suns though scarcely felt,
And groves, if unharmonious yet secure
From clamour, and whose very silence charms,   735
To be preferred to smoke, to the eclipse
That metropolitan volcanoes make,
Whose Stygian throats breathe darkness all day long;
And to the stir of Commerce, driving slow,
And thundering loud, with his ten thousand wheels?
They would be, were not madness in the head,   741
And folly in the heart; were England now
What England wás, plain, hospitable, kind,
And undebauched.   But we have bid farewell
To all the virtues of those better days,   745
And all their honest pleasures.   Mansions once
Knew their own masters, and laborious hinds,
Who * had survived the father, served the son.
Now the legitimate and rightful lord
Is but a transient guest, newly arrived   750
And soon to be supplanted.   He that saw
His patrimonial timber cast its leaf,
Sells the last scantling, and transfers the price
To some shrewd sharper, ere it buds again.
Estates are landscapes, gazed upon awhile,   755
Then advertised, and auctioneered away.

* " That;" Eds. 1785, 1786, Southey, Bell. " Who;" Ed.
1787, and subsequent editions, except those of Southey and
Bell. The same alteration, made at the same time in line 819,
has been followed by all subsequent editors, except Southey.

The country starves, and they that feed the o'er-
     charged
And surfeited lewd town with her fair dues,
By a just judgment strip and starve themselves.
The wings that waft our riches out of sight   760
Grow on the gamester's elbows, and the alert
And nimble motion of those restless joints
That never tire, soon fans them all away.
Improvement too, the idol of the age,
Is fed with many a victim.   Lo! he comes ;— 765
The omnipotent magician, Brown,* appears!
Down falls the venerable pile, the abode
Of our forefathers—a grave, whiskered race,
But tasteless.   Springs a palace in its stead,
But in a distant spot, where, more exposed,   770
It may enjoy the advantage of the north
And aguish east, till time shall have transformed
Those naked acres to a sheltering grove.
He speaks.   The lake in front becomes a lawn,
Woods vanish, hills subside, and valleys rise,   775
And streams, as if created for his use,
Pursue the track of his directing wand,
Sinuous or straight, now rapid and now slow,
Now murmuring soft, now roaring in cascades,
Even as he bids! The enraptured owner smiles. 780
'Tis finished, and yet, finished as it seems,
Still wants a grace, the loveliest it could show,
A mine to satisfy the enormous cost.
Drained to the last poor item of his wealth,
He sighs, departs, and leaves the accomplished plan,

* Lancelot, or, as he is more generally termed, " Capability
Brown," from his frequent use of that word in reference to
his professional operations as a landscape or ornamental
gardener.   He was born at Kirkharle in Northumberland in
1715, and died in 1773.

That he has touched, retouched, many a long day 786
Laboured, and many a night pursued in dreams,
Just when it meets his hopes, and proves the Heaven
He wanted, for a wealthier to enjoy !
And now perhaps the glorious hour is come,   790
When having no stake left, no pledge to endear
Her interests, or that gives her sacred cause
A moment's operation on his love,
He burns with most intense and flagrant zeal
To serve his country.   Ministerial grace   795
Deals him out money from the public chest;
Or if that mine be shut, some private purse
Supplies his need with a usurious loan,
To be refunded duly, when his vote
Well-managed shall have earned its worthy price.
Oh innocent, compared with arts like these,   801
Crape and cocked pistol, and the whistling ball
Sent through the traveller's temples ! He that finds
One drop of Heaven's sweet mercy in his cup,
Can dig, beg, rot, and perish, well content,   805
So he may wrap himself in honest rags
At his last gasp; but could not for a world
Fish up his dirty and dependent bread
From pools and ditches of the commonwealth,
Sordid and sickening at his own success.   810
    Ambition, Avarice, Penury incurred
By endless riot, Vanity, the Lust
Of pleasure and variety, dispatch,
As duly as the swallows disappear,
The world of wandering knights and squires to town.
London engulphs them all ! The shark is there, 816
And the shark's prey; the spendthrift, and the leech
That sucks him; there the sycophant, and he
Who, with bare-headed and obsequious bows,

Begs a warm office, doomed to a cold jail   820
And groat per diem, if his patron frown.
The levee swarms, as if in golden pomp
Were charactered on every statesman's door,
" Battered and bankrupt fortunes mended here."
These are the charms that sully and eclipse   825
The charms of Nature. 'Tis the cruel gripe
That lean hard-handed Poverty inflicts,
The hope of better things, the chance to win,
The wish to shine, the thirst to be amused,
That at the sound of Winter's hoary wing   830
Unpeople all our counties of such herds
Of fluttering, loitering, cringing, begging, loose
And wanton vagrants, as make London, vast
And boundless as it is, a crowded coop.
    Oh thou resort and mart of all the earth,   835
Chequered with all complexions of mankind,
And spotted with all crimes ; in whom I see
Much that I love, and more that I admire,
And all that I abhor ; thou freckled fair
That pleasest and yet shockest me,* I can laugh, 840
And I can weep, can hope, and can despond,
Feel wrath and pity, when I think on thee !
Ten righteous would have saved a city once,†
And thou hast many righteous.—Well for thee !
That salt preserves thee ; more corrupted else, 845
And therefore more obnoxious at this hour,
Than Sodom in her day had power to be,
For whom God heard his Abraham plead in vain.

* " That pleases and yet shocks me ;" Eds. 1785, 1786,
1787, 1788, Southey, Bell. " That pleasest and yet shock'st
me ;" Eds. 1793, 1794, 1798, 1799, 1800, 1808, 1810, 1812.
1817, 1821, 1825, Grimshawe, Dale. Eds. 1803, 1805,
1806(2) have the words as we have printed them.
  † Genesis, xviii. 32.

THE TASK.   BOOK IV.

THE WINTER EVENING.

ARGUMENT.

THE post comes in. The newspaper is read. The world contemplated at a distance. Address to Winter. The rural amusements of a winter evening compared with the fashionable ones. Address to Evening. A brown study. Fall of snow in the evening. The waggoner. A poor family piece. The rural thief. Public houses. The multitude of them censured. The farmer's daughter: what she was—what she is. The simplicity of country manners almost lost. Causes of the change. Desertion of the country by the rich. Neglect of magistrates. The militia principally in fault. The new recruit and his transformation. Reflection on bodies corporate. The love of rural objects natural to all, and never to be totally extinguished.

THE TASK.   BOOK IV.

THE WINTER EVENING.

ARK! 'tis the twanging horn!* O'er yonder bridge
That with its wearisome but needful length
Bestrides the wintry flood, in which the moon
Sees her unwrinkled face reflected bright,

---

* Different ways of punctuating this passage have produced two widely different readings. The first edition (1785) gave the passage thus:—

> Hark! 'tis the twanging horn! o'er yonder bridge
> That with its wearisome but needful length
> Bestrides the wintry flood, in which the moon
> Sees her unwrinkled face reflected bright,
> He comes, &c.

The second edition (1786) converted the comma after " bright" into a semicolon. The third edition (1787) added a comma after " bridge." Both these alterations were adopted in the fourth edition (1788). In 1793 the note of exclamation after " horn" was omitted, and a dash was added to the semicolon after " bright." By these successive alterations the passage was brought to stand as follows:—

> Hark! 'tis the twanging horn o'er yonder bridge,
> That with its wearisome but needful length

He comes, the herald of a noisy world,   5
With spattered boots, strapped waist, and frozen
     locks,
News from all nations lumbering at his back.
True to his charge, the close-packed load behind,
Yet careless what he brings, his one concern
Is to conduct it to the destined inn,   .   10
And, having dropped the expected bag, pass on.
He whistles as he goes, light-hearted wretch,
Cold and yet cheerful; messenger of grief
Perhaps to thousands, and of joy to some;
To him indifferent whether grief or joy.   15
Houses in ashes, and the fall of stocks,
Births, deaths, and marriages, epistles wet
With tears that trickled down the writer's cheeks
Fast as the periods from his fluent quill,

> Bestrides the wintry flood, in which the moon
> Sees her unwrinkled face reflected bright;—
> He comes, &c.

This was the text of the editions of 1794, and 1798, except
that in the latter edition the dash after "bright" was omitted.
The editions of 1799, 1800, 3, 5, 6 (2), 1810, 12, 17, and
1821, agreed with that of 1793, and the edition of 1825
with that of 1798.   Southey restored the reading of the
second edition; Grimshawe followed that of 1793, and Dale
that of the editions up to 1788 as to the insertion of a note
of exclamation after " horn," and the edition of 1793 as to a
semicolon and dash after " bright."   Bell followed the
editions up to 1788 in inserting a note of exclamation after
" horn," the third edition in giving a comma after " bridge,"
and the first edition in printing a comma, and not a semicolon, after " bright."   He also printed " o'er," in the first
line, with an initial capital letter.   On the whole we think
the reading of the first edition to be the one which best ex-
presses what may be inferred to have been the original
meaning.   We have therefore followed it, with the one alteration of the initial capital letter to " o'er" introduced by
Bell.

Or charged with amorous sighs of absent swains, 20
Or nymphs responsive, equally affect
His horse and him, unconscious of them all.
But oh the important budget! ushered in
With such heart-shaking music, who can say
What are its tidings? Have our troops awaked?
Or do they still, as if with opium drugged,   26
Snore to the murmurs of the Atlantic wave?
Is India free? And does she wear her plumed
And jewelled turban with a smile of peace?
Or do we grind her still? The grand debate,   30
The popular harangue, the tart reply,
The logic, and the wisdom, and the wit,
And the loud laugh—I long to know them all;
I burn to set the imprisoned wranglers free,   .
And give them voice and utterance once again. 35
    Now stir the fire, and close the shutters fast,
Let fall the curtains, wheel the sofa round,
And while the bubbling and loud-hissing urn
Throws up a steamy column, and the cups
That cheer but not inebriate, wait on each,   40
So let us welcome peaceful evening in.
Not such his evening, who with shining face
Sweats in the crowded theatre, and squeezed
And bored with elbow-points through both his sides,
Outscolds the ranting actor on the stage: 45
Nor his, who patient stands till his feet throb.
And his head thumps, to feed upon the breath
Of patriots bursting with heroic rage,
Or placemen all tranquillity and smiles.
This folio of four pages, happy work!   ˙   50
Which not even critics criticise; that holds
Inquisitive attention, while I read,

Fast bound in chains of silence, which the fair,
Though eloquent themselves, yet fear to break;
What is it, but a map of busy life,   55
Its fluctuations, and its vast concerns?
Here runs the mountainous and craggy ridge
That tempts Ambition. On the summit, see
The seals of office glitter in his eyes;
He climbs, he pants, he grasps them! At his heels,
Close at his heels, a demagogue ascends,   61
And with a dexterous jerk soon twists him down,
And wins them, but to lose them in his turn.
Here rills of oily eloquence in soft
Meanders lubricate the course they take;   65
The modest speaker is ashamed and grieved
To engross a moment's notice, and yet begs,
Begs a propitious ear for his poor thoughts,
However trivial all that he conceives.
Sweet bashfulness! it claims at least this praise; 70
The dearth of information and good sense
That it foretells us, always comes to pass.
Cataracts of declamation thunder here,
There forests of no meaning spread the page,
In which all comprehension wanders lost;   75
While fields of pleasantry amuse us there
With merry descants on a nation's woes.
The rest appears a wilderness of strange
But gay confusion; roses for the cheeks
And lilies for the brows of faded age,   80
Teeth for the toothless, ringlets for the bald,
Heaven, earth, and ocean, plundered of their sweets,
Nectareous essences, Olympian dews,
Sermons, and city feasts, and favourite airs,
Æthereal journeys, submarine exploits,   85

And Katterfelto,* with his hair on end
At his own wonders, wondering for his bread.
'Tis pleasant through the loopholes of retreat
To peep at such a world; to see the stir
Of the great Babel, and not feel the crowd;   90
To hear the roar she sends through all her gates
At a safe distance, where the dying sound
Falls a soft murmur on the uninjured ear.
Thus sitting, and surveying thus at ease
The globe and its concerns, I seem advanced   95
To some secure and more than mortal height,
That liberates and exempts me from them all.
It turns submitted to my view, turns round
With all its generations; I behold
The tumult, and am still. The sound of war   100
Has lost its terrors ere it reaches me;
Grieves, but alarms me not. I mourn the pride
And avarice that make† man a wolf to man;
Hear the faint echo of those brazen throats
By which he speaks the language of his heart,   105
And sigh, but never tremble at the sound.
He travels and expatiates, as the bee
From flower to flower, so he from land to land;
The manners, customs, policy of all
Pay contribution to the store he gleans;   110
He sucks intelligence in every clime,
And spreads the honey of his deep research
At his return, a rich repast for me.
He travels, and I too. I tread his deck,

* Dr. Katterfelto, an empiric of Cowper's time, who announced the performances of himself and his black Morocco cat in advertisements occasionally headed, " Wonders! Wonders! Wonders!" He died in 1799.
† The second edition alone (1786) has " makes."

Ascend his topmast, through his peering eyes   115
Discover countries, with a kindred heart
Suffer his woes and share in his escapes;
While fancy, like the finger of a clock,
Runs the great circuit, and is still at home.
    O Winter, ruler of the inverted year,   120
Thy scattered hair with sleet like ashes filled,
Thy breath congealed upon thy lips, thy cheeks
Fringed with a beard made white with other snows
Than those of age, thy forehead wrapped in clouds,
A leafless branch thy sceptre, and thy throne   125
A sliding car, indebted to no wheels,
But urged by storms along its slippery way;
I love thee, all unlovely as thou seemest,
And dreaded as thou art! Thou holdest the sun
A prisoner in the yet undawning east,   130
Shortening his journey between morn and noon,
And hurrying him, impatient of his stay,
Down to the rosy west; but kindly still
Compensating his loss with added hours
Of social converse and instructive ease,   135
And gathering, at short notice, in one group,
The family dispersed, and fixing thought,
Not less dispersed by daylight and its cares.
I crown thee king of intimate delights,
Fireside enjoyments, homeborn happiness,   140
And all the comforts that the lowly roof
Of undisturbed Retirement, and the hours
Of long uninterrupted evening know.
No rattling wheels stop short before these gates;
No powdered pert proficient in the art   145
Of sounding an alarm assaults these doors
Till the street rings; no stationary steeds

Cough their own knell, while, heedless of the sound,
The silent circle fan themselves, and quake;
But here the needle plies its busy task, 150
The pattern grows, the well-depicted flower,
Wrought patiently into the snowy lawn,
Unfolds its bosom; buds, and leaves, and sprigs,
And curling tendrils, gracefully disposed,
Follow the nimble finger of the fair; 155
A wreath that cannot fade, of flowers that blow
With most success when all besides decay.
The poet's or historian's page, by one
Made vocal for the amusement of the rest; 159
The sprightly lyre, whose treasure of sweet sounds
The touch from many a trembling chord shakes out;
And the clear voice, symphonious yet distinct,
And in the charming strife triumphant still,
Beguile the night, and set a keener edge
On female industry; the threaded steel 165
Flies swiftly, and unfelt the task proceeds.
The volume closed, the customary rites
Of the last meal commence. A Roman meal,
Such as the mistress of the world once found
Delicious, when her patriots of high note, 170
Perhaps by moonlight, at their humble doors,
And under an old oak's domestic shade,
Enjoyed, spare feast! a radish and an egg.
Discourse ensues, not trivial, yet not dull,
Nor such as with a frown forbids the play 175
Of fancy, or proscribes the sound of mirth:
Nor do we madly, like an impious world,
Who deem religion frenzy, and the God
That made them an intruder on their joys,
Start at his awful name, or deem his praise 180

A jarring note.   Themes of a graver tone,
Exciting oft our gratitude and love,
While we retrace with Memory's pointing wand,
That calls the past to our exact review,
The dangers we have 'scoped, the broken snare,   185
The disappointed foe, deliverance found
Unlooked for, life preserved, and peace restored,
Fruits of omnipotent, eternal love.
" O evenings worthy of the gods !" exclaimed
The Sabine bard.   O evenings, I reply,   190
More to be prized and coveted than yours,
As more illumined, and with nobler truths,
That I, and mine, and those we love, enjoy.
    Is winter hideous in a garb like this?
Needs he the tragic fur, the smoke of lamps,   195
The pent-up breath of an unsavoury throng,
To thaw him into feeling, or the smart
And snappish dialogue, that flippant wits
Call comedy, to prompt him with a smile?
The self-complacent actor, when he views   200
(Stealing a side-long glance at a full house)
The slope of faces from the floor to the roof,
(As if one master-spring controlled them all)
Relaxed into a universal grin,
Sees not a countenance there that speaks of joy 205
Half so refined or so sincere as ours.
Cards were superfluous here, with all the tricks
That idleness has ever yet contrived
To fill the void of an unfurnished brain,
To palliate dullness, and give time a shove.   210
Time as he passes us has a dove's wing,
Unsoiled and swift, and of a silken sound,
But the World's Time, is Time in masquerade.

Theirs, should I paint him, has his pinions fledged
With motley plumes, and, where the peacock shows
His azure eyes, is tinctured black and red,   216
With spots quadrangular of diamond form,
Ensanguined hearts, clubs typical of strife,
And spades the emblem of untimely graves.
What should be, and what was an hourglass once,
Becomes a dicebox, and a billiard-mast*   221
Well does the work of his destructive scythe.
Thus decked, he charms a world whom Fashion
    blinds -
To his true worth, most pleased when idle most;
Whose only happy are their wasted hours.   225
Even misses, at whose age their mothers wore
The backstring and the bib, assume the dress
Of womanhood, sit† pupils in the school
Of card-devoted Time, and night by night
Placed at some vacant corner of the board,   230
Learn every trick, and soon play all the game.
But truce with censure. Roving as I rove,
Where shall I find an end, or how proceed?
As he that travels far, oft turns aside
To view some rugged rock or mouldering tower, 235
Which seen delights him not; then coming home,
Describes and prints it, that the world may know
How far he went for what was nothing worth;
So I, with brush in hand and pallet spread,
With colours mixed for a far different use,   240

---

* All the editions down to 1806 have " billiard-mast."
In 1808 we find it altered to " mace," which has been followed
by subsequent editors, except Southey and Dale.
  † Ed. 1785, all the editions down to 1806, 1821, and 1825,
Southey and Dale, have " sit;" 1808, 1810, 1812, 1817,
Grimshawe and Bell, have " fit."

Paint cards and dolls, and every idle thing
That Fancy finds in her excursive flights.
   Come, Evening, once again, season of peace;
Return, sweet Evening, and continue long!
Methinks I see thee in the streaky west,   245
With matron step slow moving, while the Night
Treads on thy sweeping train; one hand employed
In letting fall the curtain of repose
On bird and beast, the other charged for man
With sweet oblivion of the cares of day: 250
Not sumptuously adorned, nor* needing aid,
Like homely-featured Night, of clustering gems;
A star or two, just twinkling on thy brow,
Suffices thee; save that the moon is thine
No less than hers, not worn indeed on high   255
With ostentatious pageantry, but set
With modest grandeur in thy purple zone,
Resplendent less, but of an ampler round.
Come then, and thou shalt find thy votary calm,
Or make me so. Composure is thy gift: 260
And whether I devote thy gentle hours
To books, to music, or the poet's toil;
To weaving nets for bird-alluring fruit;
Or twining silken threads round ivory reels,
When they command whom man was born to
        please;   265
I slight thee not, but make thee welcome still.
   Just when our drawing rooms begin to blaze
With lights, by clear reflection multiplied
From many a mirror, in which he of Gath,

* " Nor;" in Ed. 1785, in all the editions down to 1806,
and in 1821, 1825, Southey, Dale, and Bell. " Not;" in
1808, 1810, 1812, 1817, and Grimshawe.

Goliath,* might have seen his giant bulk   270
Whole without stooping, towering crest and all,
My pleasures too begin.   But me, perhaps,
The glowing hearth may satisfy awhile
With faint illumination, that uplifts
The shadow † to the ceiling, there by fits   275
Dancing uncouthly to the quivering flame.
Not undelightful is an hour to me
So spent in parlour twilight; such a gloom
Suits well the thoughtful, or unthinking mind,
The mind contemplative, with some new theme 280
Pregnant, or indisposed alike to all.
Laugh ye, who boast your more mercurial powers
That never felt a stupor, know no pause,
Nor need one; I am conscious and confess,
Fearless, a soul that does not always think.   285
Me oft has Fancy, ludicrous and wild,
Soothed with a waking dream of houses, towers,
Trees, churches, and strange visages, expressed
In the red cinders, while with poring eye
I gazed, myself creating what I saw.   290
Nor less amused, have I quiescent watched
The sooty films that play upon the bars,
Pendulous, and foreboding, in the view
Of superstition, prophesying still
Though still deceived, some stranger's near ap-
  proach.   295

 * It may be worth a passing remark that this word stood
" Goliah" in the first four editions, but was altered in 1793.
" Goliah" was restored in 1803, and again altered in 1810,
but has reappeared in the edition of Dale.
 † "Shadow;" in Ed. 1785, in all editions down to 1803,
and in Southey.   "Shadows;" Ed. 1805, and subsequent
editions, except Southey's.

'Tis thus the understanding takes repose
In indolent vacuity of thought,
And sleeps and is refreshed.   Meanwhile the face
Conceals the mood lethargic with a mask
Of deep deliberation, as the man   300
Were tasked to his full strength, absorbed and lost.
Thus oft, reclined at ease, I lose an hour
At evening, till at length the freezing blast,
That sweeps the bolted shutter, summons home
The recollected powers, and snapping short   305
The glassy threads with which the Fancy weaves
Her brittle toys,* restores me to myself.
How calm is my recess, and how the frost,
Raging abroad, and the rough wind, endear
The silence and the warmth enjoyed within.   310
I saw the woods and fields at close of day
A variegated show; the meadows green
Though faded; and the lands where lately waved
The golden harvest, of a mellow brown,
Upturned so lately by the forceful share.   315
I saw far off the weedy fallows smile
With verdure not unprofitable, grazed
By flocks, fast feeding and selecting each
His favourite herb; while all the leafless groves
That skirt the horizon, wore a sable hue,   320
Scarce noticed in the kindred dusk of eve.
To-morrow brings a change, a total change!
Which even now, though silently performed
And slowly, and by most unfelt, the face
Of universal nature undergoes.   325

---

* " Toys;" Ed. 1785, all editions down to 1800, and
Southey.   "Toils;" Ed. 1803, and subsequent editions, except that of Southey.

Fast falls a fleecy shower: the downy flakes
Descending, and with never-ceasing lapse
Softly alighting upon all below,
Assimilate all objects.   Earth receives
Gladly the thickening mantle, and the green   330
And tender blade, that feared the chilling blast,
Escapes unhurt beneath so warm a veil.
  In such a world, so thorny, and where none
Finds happiness unblighted, or if found,
Without some thistly sorrow at its side,   335
It seems the part of wisdom, and no sin
Against the law of love, to measure lots
With less distinguished than ourselves, that thus
We may with patience bear our moderate ills,
And sympathise with others suffering more.   340
Ill fares the traveller now, and he that stalks
In ponderous boots beside his recking team.
The wain goes heavily, impeded sore
By congregated loads adhering close
To the clogged wheels; and in its sluggish pace 345
Noiseless, appears a moving hill of snow.
The toiling steeds expand the nostril wide,
While every breath, by respiration strong
Forced downward, is consolidated soon
Upon their jutting chests.   He, formed to bear 350
The pelting brunt of the tempestuous night,
With half-shut eyes, and puckered cheeks, and teeth
Presented bare against the storm, plods on.
One hand secures his hat, save when with both
He brandishes his pliant length of whip,   355
Resounding oft, and never heard in vain.
O happy! and, in my account, denied
That sensibility of pain with which

Refinement is endued, thrice happy thou!
Thy frame, robust and hardy, feels indeed   360
The piercing cold, but feels it unimpaired.
The learned finger never need explore
Thy vigorous pulse, and the unhealthful East,
That breathes the spleen, and searches every bone
Of the infirm, is wholesome air to thee.   365
Thy days roll on exempt from household care;
Thy waggon is thy wife, and the poor beasts
That drag the dull companion to and fro,
Thine helpless charge, dependent on thy care.
Ah, treat him kindly! rude as thou appearest, 370
Yet show that thou hast mercy, which the great,
With needless hurry whirled from place to place,
Humane as they would seem, not always show.
  Poor, yet industrious, modest, quiet, neat,
Such claim compassion in a night like this,   375
And have a friend in every feeling heart.
Warmed, while it lasts, by labour, all day long
They brave the season, and yet find at eve,
Ill-clad and fed but sparely, time to cool.
The frugal housewife trembles when she lights 380
Her scanty stock of brushwood, blazing clear,
But dying soon, like all terrestrial joys.
The few small embers left she nurses well;
And while her infant race, with outspread hands
And crowded knees, sit cowering o'er the sparks,
Retires, content to quake, so they be warmed. 385
The man feels least, as more inured than she
To winter, and the current in his veins
More briskly moved by his severer toil;
Yet he too finds his own distress in theirs.   390
The taper soon extinguished, which I saw

Dangled along at the cold finger's end
Just when the day declined, and the brown loaf
Lodged on the shelf, half-eaten without sauce
Of savoury cheese, or butter costlier still,   395
Sleep seems their only refuge: for, alas!
Where penury is felt the thought is chained,
And sweet colloquial pleasures are but few.
With all this thrift they thrive not. All the care
Ingenious Parsimony takes, but just   400
Saves the small inventory, bed and stool,
Skillet and old carved chest, from public sale.
They live, and live without extorted alms
From grudging hands, but other boast have none
To soothe their honest pride, that scorns to beg;   405
Nor comfort else, but in their mutual love.
I praise you much, ye meek and patient pair,
For ye are worthy; choosing rather far
A dry but independent crust, hard earned
And eaten with a sigh, than to endure   410
The rugged frowns and insolent rebuffs
Of knaves in office, partial in the work
Of distribution; liberal of their aid
To clamorous importunity in rags,
But oft-times deaf to suppliants who would blush
To wear a tattered garb however coarse,   416
Whom famine cannot reconcile to filth;
These ask with painful shyness, and, refused
Because deserving, silently retire.
But be ye of good courage. Time itself   420
Shall much befriend you. Time shall give increase,
And all your numerous progeny, well trained
But helpless, in few years shall find their hands,
And labour too. Meanwhile ye shall not want

What, conscious of your virtues, we can spare, 425
Nor what a wealthier than ourselves may send.
I mean the man who, when the distant poor
Need help, denies them nothing but his name.*
  But poverty, with most who whimper forth
Their long complaints, is self-inflicted woe,   430
The effect of laziness or sottish waste.
Now goes the nightly thief prowling abroad
For plunder, much solicitous how best
He may compensate for a day of sloth,
By works of darkness and nocturnal wrong.   435
Woe to the gardener's pale, the farmer's hedge
Plashed neatly, and secured with driven stakes
Deep in the loamy bank.   Uptorn by strength,
Resistless in so bad a cause but lame
To better deeds, he bundles up the spoil,   440
An ass's burden, and when laden most
And heaviest, light of foot steals fast away.
Nor does the boarded hovel better guard
The well-stacked pile of riven logs and roots
From his pernicious force.   Nor will he leave 445
Unwrenched the door, however well secured,
Where chanticleer amidst his harem sleeps
In unsuspecting pomp.   Twitched from the perch,
He gives the princely bird, with all his wives,
To his voracious bag, struggling in vain,   450
And loudly wondering at the sudden change.
Nor this to feed his own !   'Twere some excuse,
Did pity of their sufferings warp aside

---

* Mr. Bell, in his edition of Cowper, drew attention to
Cowper's letter to Unwin, of 10th October, 1784, which proves
that this allusion was to Mr. Smith the banker, afterwards
created Lord Carrington.

His principle, and tempt him into sin
For their support, so destitute. But they   455
Neglected pine at home, themselves, as more
Exposed than others, with less scruple made
His victims, robbed of their defenceless all.
Cruel is all he does.   'Tis quenchless thirst
Of ruinous ebriety that prompts   460
His every action, and imbrutes the man.
Oh for a law to noose the villain's neck
Who starves his own, who persecutes the blood
He gave them in his children's veins, and hates
And wrongs the woman he has sworn to love ! 465
    Pass where we may, through city or through town,
Village or hamlet, of this merry land,
Though lean and beggared, every twentieth pace
Conducts the unguarded nose to such a whiff
Of stale debauch, forth-issuing from the styes   470
That law has licensed, as makes Temperance reel.
There sit, involved and lost in curling clouds
Of Indian fume, and guzzling deep, the boor,
The lackey, and the groom; the craftsman there
Takes a Lethean leave of all his toil;   475
Smith, cobbler, joiner, he that plies the shears,
And he that kneads the dough; all loud alike,
All learned, and all drunk.   The fiddle screams
Plaintive and piteous, as it wept and wailed
Its wasted tones, and harmony unheard: 480
Fierce the dispute whate'er the theme; while she,
Fell Discord, arbitress of such debate,
Perched on the signpost, holds with even hand
Her undecisive scales.   In this she lays
A weight of ignorance; in that, of pride; `   485
And smiles delighted with the eternal poise.

Dire is the frequent curse, and its twin sound
The cheek-distending oath, not to be praised
As ornamental, musical, polite,
Like those which modern senators employ, 490
Whose oath is rhetoric, and who swear for fame.
Behold the schools in which plebeian minds,
Once simple, are initiated in arts,
Which some may practise with politer grace,
But none with readier skill!—'Tis here they learn
The road that leads from competence and peace 495
To indigence and rapine; till at last
Society, grown weary of the load,
Shakes her encumbered lap, and casts them out.
But censure profits little: vain the attempt 500
To advertise in verse a public pest,
That like the filth with which the peasant feeds ·
His hungry acres, stinks and is of use.
The excise is fattened with the rich result
Of all this riot; and ten thousand casks, 505
For ever dribbling out their base contents,
Touched by the Midas finger of the state,
Bleed gold for ministers to sport away.
Drink and be mad then; 'tis your country bids!
Gloriously drunk, obey the important call! 510
Her cause demands the assistance of your throats;
Ye all can swallow, and she asks no more.
Would I had fallen upon those happier days
That poets celebrate; those golden times
And those Arcadian scenes that Maro sings, 515
And Sidney, warbler of poetic prose.
Nymphs were Dianas then, and swains had hearts
That felt their virtues; Innocence, it seems,
From courts dismissed, found shelter in the groves;

The footsteps of Simplicity, impressed   520
Upon the yielding herbage (so they sing),
Then were not all effaced; then speech profane,
And manners profligate, were rarely found,
Observed as prodigies, and soon reclaimed.
Vain wish! those days were never: airy dreams 525
Sat for the picture; and the poet's hand,
Imparting substance to an empty shade,
Imposed a gay delirium for a truth.
Grant it:—I still must envy them an age
That favoured such a dream, in days like these 530
Impossible, when Virtue is so scarce,
That to suppose a scene where she presides
Is tramontane, and stumbles all belief.
No: we are polished now! The rural lass,
Whom once her virgin modesty and grace,   535
Her artless manners, and her neat attire,
So dignified, that she was hardly less
Than the fair shepherdess of old romance,
Is seen no more. The character is lost!
Her head, adorned with lappets pinned aloft 540
And ribands streaming gay, superbly raised,
And magnified beyond all human size,
Indebted to some smart wig-weaver's hand
For more than half the tresses it sustains;
Her elbows ruffled, and her tottering form   545
Ill propped upon French heels; she might be
    deemed
(But that the basket dangling on her arm
Interprets her more truly) of a rank
Too proud for dairy work, or sale of eggs.
Expect her soon with footboy at her heels,   550
No longer blushing for her awkward load,

Her train and her umbrella all her care.

The town has tinged the country; and the stain
Appears a spot upon a vestal's robe,
The worse for what it soils. The fashion runs 555
Down into scenes still rural; but, alas,
Scenes rarely graced with rural manners now!
Time was when in the pastoral retreat
The unguarded door was safe; men did not watch
To invade another's right, or guard their own. 560
Then sleep was undisturbed by Fear, unscared
By drunken howlings; and the chilling tale
Of midnight murder was a wonder heard
With doubtful credit, told to frighten babes.
But farewell now to unsuspicious nights, 565
And slumbers unalarmed! Now, ere you sleep,
See that your polished arms be primed with care,
And drop the night-bolt;—ruffians are abroad;
And the first larum of the cock's shrill throat
May prove a trumpet, summoning your ear 570
To horrid sounds of hostile feet within.
Even daylight has its dangers; and the walk
Through pathless wastes and woods, unconscious
        once
Of other tenants than melodious birds
Or harmless flocks, is hazardous and bold. 575
Lamented change! to which full many a cause
Inveterate, hopeless of a cure, conspires.
The course of human things from good to ill,
From ill to worse, is fatal, never fails.
Increase of power begets increase of wealth; 580
Wealth luxury, and luxury excess;
Excess, the scrofulous and itchy plague
That seizes first the opulent, descends

To the next rank contagious, and in time
Taints downward all the graduated scale   585
Of order, from the chariot to the plough.
The rich, and they that have an arm to check
The licence of the lowest in degree,
Desert their office; and themselves intent
On pleasure, haunt the capital, and thus,   590
To all the violence of lawless hands
Resign the scenes their presence might protect.
Authority herself not seldom sleeps,
Though resident, and witness of the wrong.
The plump convivial parson often bears   595
The magisterial sword in vain, and lays
His reverence and his worship both to rest
On the same cushion of habitual sloth.
Perhaps timidity restrains his arm;
When he should strike, he trembles and sets free,
Himself enslaved by terror of the band,   601
The audacious convict, whom he dares not bind.
Perhaps, though by profession ghostly pure,
He too may have his vice, and sometimes prove
Less dainty than becomes his grave outside,   605
In lucrative concerns.   Examine well
His milkwhite hand; the palm is hardly clean—
But here and there an ugly smutch appears.
Foh! 'twas a bribe that left it: he has touched
Corruption! Whoso seeks an audit here   610
Propitious, pays his tribute, game or fish,
Wildfowl or venison, and his errand speeds.
    But faster far, and more than all the rest,
A noble cause, which none who bears a spark
Of public virtue ever wished removed,   615
Works the deplored and mischievous effect.

'Tis universal soldiership has stabbed
The heart of merit in the meaner class.
Arms, through the vanity and brainless rage
Of those that bear them, in whatever cause,   620
Seem most at variance with all moral good,
And incompatible with serious thought.
The clown, the child of nature, without guile,
Blest with an infant's ignorance of all
But his own simple pleasures, now and then   625
A wrestling match, a footrace, or a fair,
Is balloted, and trembles at the news:
Sheepish he doffs his hat, and mumbling swears
A Bible-oath to be whate'er they please,
To do he knows not what. The task performed,
That instant he becomes the serjeant's care,   631
His pupil, and his torment, and his jest.
His awkward gait, his introverted toes,
Bent knees, round shoulders, and dejected looks,
Procure him many a curse. By slow degrees,   635
Unapt to learn, and formed of stubborn stuff,
He yet by slow degrees puts off himself,
Grows conscious of a change, and likes it well:
He stands erect; his slouch becomes a walk;
He steps right onward, martial in his air,   640
His form, and movement; is as smart above
As meal and larded locks can make him; wears
His hat, or his plumed helmet, with a grace;
And his three years of heroship expired,
Returns indignant to the slighted plough.   645
He hates the field in which no fife or drum
Attends him, drives his cattle to a march,
And sighs for the smart comrades he has left.
'Twere well if his exterior change were all—

But with his clumsy port the wretch has lost 650
His ignorance and harmless manners too.
To swear, to game, to drink; to show at home
By lewdness, idleness, and sabbath-breach,
The great proficiency he made abroad;
To astonish and to grieve his gazing friends; 655
To break some maiden's and his mother's heart;
To be a pest where he was useful once;
Are his sole aim, and all his glory now.
 Man in society is like a flower
Blown in its native bed; 'tis there alone 660
His faculties, expanded in full bloom,
Shine out; there only reach their proper use.
But man associated and leagued with man
By regal warrant, or self-joined by bond
For interest sake, or swarming into clans 665
Beneath one head for purposes of war,
Like flowers selected from the rest, and bound
And bundled close to fill some crowded vase,
Fades rapidly, and by compression marred,
Contracts defilement not to be endured. 670
Hence chartered boroughs are such public plagues;
And burghers, men immaculate perhaps
In all their private functions, once combined,
Become a loathsome body, only fit
For dissolution, hurtful to the main. 675
Hence merchants, unimpeachable of sin
Against the charities of domestic life,
Incorporated, seem at once to lose
Their nature, and disclaiming all regard
For mercy and the common rights of man, 680
Build factories with blood, conducting trade
At the sword's point, and dyeing the white robe

Of innocent commercial Justice red.
Hence, too, the field of glory, as the world
Misdeems it, dazzled by its bright array,   685
With all its majesty of thundering pomp,
Enchanting music, and immortal wreaths,
Is but a school where thoughtlessness is taught
On principle, where foppery atones
For folly, gallantry for every vice.   690
    But slighted as it is, and by the great
Abandoned, and which still I more regret,
Infected with the manners and the modes
It knew not once, the country wins me still.
I never framed a wish, or formed a plan,   695
That flattered me with hopes of earthly bliss,
But there I laid the scene.   There early strayed
My Fancy, ere yet liberty of choice
Had found me, or the hope of being free.
My very dreams were rural; rural too   700
The firstborn efforts of my youthful Muse,
Sportive, and jingling her poetic bells,
Ere yet her ear was mistress of their powers.
No bard could please me but whose lyre was tuned
To Nature's praises.   Heroes and their feats   705
Fatigued me, never weary of the pipe
Of Tityrus, assembling, as he sang,
The rustic throng beneath his favourite beech.
Then MILTON had indeed a poet's charms:
New to my taste his Paradise surpassed   710
The struggling efforts of my boyish tongue
To speak its excellence; I danced for joy;
I marvelled much that, at so ripe an age
As twice seven years, his beauties had then first
Engaged my wonder, and admiring still,   715

And still admiring, with regret supposed
The joy half lost, because not sooner found.
Thee* too enamoured of the life I loved,
Pathetic in its praise, in its pursuit
Determined, and possessing it at last   720
With transports such as favoured lovers feel,
I studied, prized, and wished that I had known,
Ingenious COWLEY! and though now reclaimed
By modern lights from an erroneous taste,
I cannot but lament thy splendid wit   725
Entangled in the cobwebs of the schools,
I still revere thee, courtly though retired;
Though stretched at ease in Chertsey's silent bowers,
Not unemployed, and finding rich amends
For a lost world in solitude and verse.   730
'Tis born with all: the love of Nature's works
Is an ingredient in the compound, man,
Infused at the creation of the kind.
And though the Almighty Maker has throughout
Discriminated each from each, by strokes   735
And touches of his hand, with so much art
Diversified, that two were never found
Twins at all points—yet this obtains in all,
That all discern a beauty in his works,
And all can taste them: minds that have been
    formed   740
And tutored with a relish more exact,
But none without some relish, none unmoved.
It is a flame that dies not even there
Where nothing feeds it. Neither business, crowds,

* "Thee;" Eds. 1785, 1786, 1787, 1788, Southey, Bell,
and Dale. "There;" Ed. 1793, and subsequent editions, except as before mentioned.

Nor habits of luxurious city-life,   745
Whatever else they smother of true worth
In human bosoms, quench it or abate.
The villas with which London stands begirt,
Like a swarth Indian with his belt of beads,
Prove it.   A breath of unadulterate air,   750
The glimpse of a green pasture, how they cheer
The citizen, and brace his languid frame !
Even in the stifling bosom of the town,
A garden in which nothing thrives, has charms
That soothe the rich possessor ; much consoled 755
That here and there some sprigs of mournful mint,
Of nightshade, or valerian, grace the well*
He cultivates.   These serve him with a hint
That Nature lives ; that sight-refreshing green
Is still the livery she delights to wear,   760
Though sickly samples of the exuberant whole.
What are the casements lined with creeping herbs,
The prouder sashes fronted with a range
Of orange, myrtle, or the fragrant weed
The Frenchman's darling?†   Are they not all
        proofs   765
That man immured in cities, still retains
His inborn inextinguishable thirst
Of rural scenes, compensating his loss
By supplemental shifts, the best he may ?
The most unfurnished with the means of life,   770
And they that never pass their brick-wall bounds
To range the fields and treat their lungs with air,
Yet feel the burning instinct : over-head

---

* Ed. 1786 has " wall;" but the mistake was corrected
in Ed. 1787, and has never reappeared.
    † Mignonette.—C.

Suspend their crazy boxes, planted thick,
And watered duly.   There the pitcher stands   775
A fragment, and the spoutless teapot there;
Sad witnesses how close-pent man regrets
The country, with what ardour he contrives
A peep at Nature, when he can no more.
˙ Hail, therefore, patroness of health and ease   780
And contemplation, heart-consoling joys
And harmless pleasures, in the thronged abode
Of multitudes unknown! Hail, rural life!
Address himself who will to the pursuit
Of honours, or emolument, or fame,   785
I shall not add myself to such a chase,
Thwart his attempts, or envy his success.
Some must be great.   Great offices will have
Great talents: and God gives to every man
The virtue, temper, understanding, taste,   790
That lifts him into life, and lets him fall
Just in the niche he was ordained to fill.
To the deliverer of an injured land
He gives a tongue to enlarge upon, a heart
To feel, and courage to redress her wrongs;   795
To monarchs dignity; to judges sense;
To artists ingenuity and skill;
To me an unambitious mind, content
In the low vale of life, that early felt
A wish for ease and leisure, and ere long   800
Found here that leisure and that ease I wished.

THE TASK.   BOOK V.

THE WINTER MORNING WALK.

ARGUMENT.

A FROSTY morning. The foddering of cattle. The woodman
and his dog. The poultry. Whimsical effects of frost at a
waterfall. The Empress of Russia's palace of ice. Amusements of monarchs. War, one of them. Wars, whence.
And whence monarchy. The evils of it. English and French
loyalty contrasted. The Bastille, and a prisoner there. Liberty
the chief recommendation of this country. Modern patriotism
questionable, and why. The perishable nature of the best
human institutions. Spiritual liberty not perishable. The
slavish state of man by nature. Deliver him, Deist, if you
can. Grace must do it. The respective merits of patriots
and martyrs stated. Their different treatment. Happy
freedom of the man whom grace makes free. His relish of
the works of God. Address to the Creator.

THE TASK.   BOOK V.

THE WINTER MORNING WALK.

IS morning; and the sun, with ruddy orb
Ascending, fires the horizon; while the
   clouds
That crowd away before the driving
   wind,
More ardent as the disk emerges more,
Resemble most some city in a blaze,   5
Seen through the leafless wood.   His slanting ray
Slides ineffectual down the snowy vale,
And, tinging all with his own rosy hue,
From every herb and every spiry blade
Stretches a length of shadow o'er the field.   10
Mine, spindling into longitude immense,
In spite of gravity, and sage remark
That I myself am but a fleeting shade,
Provokes me to a smile.   With eye askance
I view the muscular proportioned limb   15
Transformed to a lean shank.   The shapeless pair,
As they designed to mock me, at my side
Take step for step; and as I near approach
The cottage, walk along the plastered wall,
Preposterous sight! the legs without the man. 20

The verdure of the plain lies buried deep
Beneath the dazzling deluge; and the bents
And coarser grass, upspearing o'er the rest,
Of late unsightly and unseen, now shine
Conspicuous, and in bright apparel clad,   25
And fledged with icy feathers, nod superb.
The cattle mourn in corners where the fence
Screens them, and seem half petrified to sleep
In unrecumbent sadness.   There they wait
Their wonted fodder, not like hungering man,   30
Fretful if unsupplied, but silent, meek,
And patient of the slow-paced swain's delay.
He from the stack carves out the accustomed load,
Deep-plunging and again deep-plunging oft,
His broad keen knife into the solid mass: 35
Smooth as a wall the upright remnant stands,
With such undeviating and even force
He severs it away: no needless care,
Lest storms should overset the leaning pile
Deciduous, or its own unbalanced weight.   40
    Forth goes the woodman, leaving unconcerned
The cheerful haunts of man, to wield the axe
And drive the wedge in yonder forest drear,
From morn to eve his solitary task.
Shaggy, and lean, and shrewd, with pointed ears 45
And tail cropped short, half lurcher and half cur,
His dog attends him.   Close behind his heel
Now creeps he slow; and now, with many a frisk
Wide scampering, snatches up the drifted snow
With ivory teeth, or ploughs it with his snout; 50
Then shakes his powdered coat, and barks for joy.
Heedless of all his pranks, the sturdy churl
Moves right toward the mark; nor stops for aught,

But, now and then, with pressure of his thumb
To adjust the fragrant charge of a short tube,   55
That fumes beneath his nose: the trailing cloud
Streams far behind him, scenting all the air.
Now from the roost, or from the neighbouring pale,
Where diligent to catch the first faint gleam
Of smiling day, they gossipped side by side,   60
Come trooping at the housewife's well-known call
The feathered tribes domestic.   Half on wing
And half on foot, they brush the fleecy flood,
Conscious, and fearful of too deep a plunge.
The sparrows peep, and quit the sheltering eaves,
To seize the fair occasion.   Well they eye   66
The scattered grain, and thievishly resolved
To escape the impending famine, often scared
As oft return, a pert voracious kind.
Clean riddance quickly made, one only care   70
Remains to each, the search of sunny nook,
Or shed impervious to the blast.   Resigned
To sad necessity, the cock foregoes
His wonted strut, and wading at their head
With well considered steps, seems to resent   75
His altered gait and stateliness retrenched.
How find the myriads that in summer cheer
The hills and valleys with their ceaseless songs,
Due sustenance, or where subsist they now?
Earth yields them naught: the imprisoned worm
        is safe   80
Beneath the frozen clod; all seeds of herbs
Lie covered close; and berry-bearing thorns
That feed the thrush (whatever some suppose)
Afford the smaller minstrels no supply.
The long protracted rigour of the year   85

Thins all their numerous flocks.   In chinks and
    holes
Ten thousand seek an unmolested end,
As instinct prompts; self-buried ere they die.
The very rooks and daws forsake the fields,
Where neither grub, nor root, nor earth-nut, now
Repays their labour more; and perched aloft   91
By the wayside, or stalking in the path,
Lean pensioners upon the traveller's track,
Pick up their nauseous dole, though sweet to them,
Of voided pulse or half-digested grain.   95
The streams are lost amid the splendid blank,
O'erwhelming all distinction.   On the flood,
Indurated and fixed, the snowy weight
Lies undissolved; while silently beneath,
And unperceived, the current steals away.   100
Not so, where, scornful of a check, it leaps
The mill-dam, dashes on the restless wheel,
And wantons in the pebbly gulf below:
No frost can bind it there; its utmost force
Can but arrest the light and smoky mist   105
That in its fall the liquid sheet throws wide.
And see where it has hung the embroidered banks
With forms so various, that no powers of art,
The pencil, or the pen, may trace the scene!
Here glittering turrets rise, upbearing high   110
(Fantastic misarrangement!) on the roof
Large growth of what may seem the sparkling trees
And shrubs of fairy land.   The crystal drops
That trickle down the branches, fast congealed,
Shoot into pillars of pellucid length,   115
And prop the pile they but adorned before.
Here grotto within grotto safe defies

The sunbeam; there embossed and fretted wild,
The growing wonder takes a thousand shapes
Capricious, in which Fancy seeks in vain   120
The likeness of some object seen before.
Thus Nature works as if to mock at Art,
And in defiance of her rival powers;
By these fortuitous and random strokes
Performing such inimitable feats,   125
As she with all her rules can never reach.
Less worthy of applause, though more admired,
Because a novelty, the work of man,
Imperial mistress of the fur-clad Russ!
Thy most magnificent and mighty freak,   130
The wonder of the North.*   No forest fell
When thou wouldst build, no quarry sent its stores
To enrich thy walls, but thou didst hew the floods,
And make thy marble of the glassy wave.
In such a palace Aristæus found   135
Cyrene, when he bore the plaintive tale
Of his lost bees to her maternal ear.†

* This "mighty freak" of the Empress Anna, constructed
on the bank of the Neva in 1740, is minutely described in
Tooke's Life of Catherine II., vol. I., p. 13.   According to
Levesque (Histoire de Russie, v. 216), the purpose for which
it was primarily designed, was the degradation of Prince
Golitsin.   Having abandoned the Greek Church for that of
Rome, the Empress subjected him to various kinds of ridicule.
On the death of his wife, she compelled him to marry a girl
of low station in life, and after the public performance of the
nuptial ceremony, the newly married couple were conducted
to the ice-palace, and were compelled to pass the night in a
chamber furnished with seeming propriety, but in which, as
throughout the building, every article was of ice.

† Aristæus, it will be remembered, was punished by the
loss of his bees for having been accessory to the death of
Eurydice.   His appeal to his mother " *ad extremi sacrum caput
amnis,*" is described by Virgil, Georg. iv. 317.

In such a palace Poetry might place
The armoury of Winter; where his troops,
The gloomy clouds, find weapons, arrowy sleet, 140
Skin-piercing volley, blossom-bruising hail,
And snow that often blinds the traveller's course,
And wraps him in an unexpected tomb.
Silently as a dream the fabric rose;
No sound of hammer or of saw was there. 145
Ice upon ice, the well-adjusted parts
Were soon conjoined; nor other cement asked
Than water interfused to make them one.
Lamps gracefully disposed, and of all hues,
Illumined every side: a watery light 150
Gleamed through the clear transparency, that
      seemed
Another moon new risen, or meteor fallen
From Heaven to Earth, of lambent flame serene.
So stood the brittle prodigy; though smooth
And slippery the materials, yet frostbound 155
Firm as a rock. Nor wanted aught within,
That royal residence might well befit,
For grandeur or for use. Long wavy wreaths
Of flowers that feared no enemy but warmth,
Blushed on the panels. Mirror needed none 160
Where all was vitreous; but in order due
Convivial table and commodious seat
(What seemed at least commodious seat) were there,
Sofa, and couch, and high built throne august.
The same lubricity was found in all, 165
And all was moist to the warm touch; a scene
Of evanescent glory, once a stream,
And soon to slide into a stream again.
Alas! 'twas but a mortifying stroke

Of undesigned severity, that glanced   170
(Made by a monarch) on her own estate,
On human grandeur and the courts of kings.
'Twas transient in its nature, as in show
'Twas durable; as worthless as it seemed
Intrinsically precious; to the foot   175
Treacherous and false; it smiled, and it was cold.
   Great princes have great playthings. Some have
     played
At hewing mountains into men, and some
At building human wonders mountain high.
Some have amused the dull sad years of life,   180
Life spent in indolence, and therefore sad,
With schemes of monumental fame; and sought
By pyramids and mausolean pomp,
Shortlived themselves, to immortalize their bones.
Some seek diversion in the tented field,   185
And make the sorrows of mankind their sport.
But war's a game, which were their subjects wise,
Kings would * not play at. Nations would do well
To extort their truncheons from the puny hands
Of heroes, whose infirm and baby minds   190
Are gratified with mischief, and who spoil,
Because men suffer it, their toy the World.
   When Babel was confounded, and the great
Confederacy of projectors wild and vain
Was split into diversity of tongues,   195
Then, as a shepherd separates his flock,
These to the upland, to the valley those,
God drave asunder, and assigned their lot
To all the nations. Ample was the boon

* "Should;" Eds. 1785, 1786, and Southey; "Would;"
Ed. 1787, and subsequent Eds., except Southey's.

He gave them, in its distribution fair 200
And equal, and he bade them dwell in peace.
Peace was awhile their care : they ploughed and
    sowed,
And reaped their plenty without grudge or strife.
But Violence can never longer sleep
Than human passions please.   In every heart 205
Are sown the sparks that kindle fiery war ;
Occasion needs but fan them, and they blaze.
Cain had already shed a brother's blood ;
The Deluge washed it out ; but left unquenched
The seeds of murder in the breast of man. 210
Soon, by a righteous judgment, in the line
Of his descending progeny was found
The first artificer of death ; the shrewd
Contriver who first sweated at the forge,
And forced the blunt and yet unbloodied steel 215
To a keen edge, and made it bright for war.
Him, Tubal* named, the Vulcan of old times,
The sword and falchion their inventor claim,
And the first smith was the first murderer's son.
His art survived the waters ; and ere long, 220
When man was multiplied and spread abroad
In tribes and clans, and had begun to call
These meadows and that range of hills his own,
The tasted sweets of property begat
Desire of more ; and industry in some 225
To improve and cultivate their just demesne,
Made others covet what they saw so fair.
Thus war began on earth : these fought for spoil,
And those in self-defence.   Savage at first
The onset, and irregular.   At length 230

      * Genesis, iv. 22.

One eminent above the rest for strength,
For stratagem, or courage, or for all,
Was chosen leader; him they served in war,
And him in peace, for sake of warlike deeds
Reverenced no less. Who could with him compare?
Or who so worthy to control themselves,   236
As he whose prowess had subdued their foes?
Thus war affording field for the display
Of virtue, made one chief, whom times of peace,
Which have their exigencies too, and call   240
For skill in government, at length made king.
King was a name too proud for man to wear
With modesty and meekness,* and the crown,
So dazzling in their eyes who set it on,
Was sure to intoxicate the brows it bound.   215
It is the abject property of most,
That being parcel of the common mass,
And destitute of means to raise themselves,
They sink and settle lower than they need.
They know not what it is to feel within   250
A comprehensive faculty that grasps,
Great purposes with ease, that turns and wields,
Almost without an effort, plans too vast
For their conception, which they cannot move.
Conscious of impotence they soon grow drunk   255
With gazing, when they see an able man
Step forth to notice; and, besotted thus,
Build him a pedestal, and say, " Stand there,
And be our admiration and our praise."
They roll themselves before him in the dust,   260
Then most deserving in their own account,
When most extravagant in his applause,

* " Weakness," Southey.

As if exalting him they raised themselves.
Thus by degrees self-cheated of their sound
And sober judgment that he is but man,   265
They demi-deify and fume him so,
That in due season he forgets it too.
Inflated and astrut with self-conceit,
He gulphs the windy diet, and ere long,
Adopting their mistake, profoundly thinks   270
The world was made in vain, if not for him.
Thenceforth they are his cattle: drudges born
To bear his burdens, drawing in his gears,
And sweating in his service; his caprice
Becomes the soul that animates them all.   275
He deems a thousand or ten thousand lives,
Spent in the purchase of renown for him,
An easy reckoning, and they think the same.
Thus kings were first invented, and thus kings
Were burnished into heroes, and became   280
The arbiters of this terraqueous swamp,
Storks among frogs, that have but croaked and
        died.
Strange that such folly as lifts bloated man
To eminence fit only for a God,   ＼
Should ever drivel out of human lips,   285
Even in the cradled weakness of the world!
Still stranger much that when at length mankind
Had reached the sinewy firmness of their youth,
And could discriminate and argue well
On subjects more mysterious, they were yet   290
Babes in the cause of freedom, and should fear
And quake before the Gods themselves had made.
But above measure strange, that neither proof
Of sad experience, nor examples set

By some whose patriot virtue has prevailed,   295
Can even now, when they are grown mature
In wisdom, and with philosophic deeps*
Familiar, serve to emancipate the rest!
Such dupes are men to custom, and so prone
To reverence what is ancient, and can plead   300
A course of long observance for its use,
That even servitude, the worst of ills,
Because delivered down from sire to son,
Is kept and guarded as a sacred thing.
But is it fit, or can it bear the shock   305
Of rational discussion, that a man,
Compounded and made up like other men
Of elements tumultuous, in whom lust
And folly in as ample measure meet
As in the bosoms of the slaves he rules,   310
Should be a despot absolute, and boast
Himself the only freeman of his land?
Should, when he pleases, and on whom he will,
Wage war, with any or with no pretence
Of provocation given or wrong sustained,   315
And force the beggarly last doit, by means
That his own humour dictates, from the clutch
Of Poverty, that thus he may procure
His thousands, weary of penurious life,
A splendid opportunity to die?   320
Say ye, who (with less prudence than of old
Jotham † ascribed to his assembled trees

---

* " Deeps;" Eds. 1785, 1786, 1787, 1788, 1793, 1794,
1798, 1800, Southey, Bell.   " Deeds;" Eds. 1799, 1805,
1806 (2), 1808, 1810, 1812, 1817, 1821, 1825, Grimshawe,
Dale.
    † Judges, ix. 8-15.

In politic convention) put your trust
In the shadow of a bramble, and reclined
In fancied peace beneath his dangerous branch, 325
Rejoice in him, and celebrate his sway,
Where find ye passive fortitude? Whence springs
Your self-denying zeal, that holds it good
To stroke the prickly grievance, and to hang
His thorns with streamers of continual praise? 330
We too are friends to loyalty. We love
The king who loves the law, respects his bounds,
And reigns content within them : him we serve
Freely and with delight, who leaves us free:
But recollecting still that he is man, 335
We trust him not too far. King though he be,
And king in England too, he may be weak
And vain enough to be ambitious still,
May exercise amiss his proper powers,
Or covet more than freemen choose to grant: 340
Beyond that mark is treason. He is ours,
To administer, to guard, to adorn the state,
But not to warp or change it. We are his,
To serve him nobly in the common cause,
True to the death, but not to be his slaves. 345
Mark now the difference, ye that boast your love
Of kings, between your loyalty and ours.
We love the man ; the paltry pageant you:
We the chief patron of the commonwealth ;
You the regardless author of its woes: 350
We, for the sake of liberty, a king ;
You chains and bondage for a tyrant's sake.
Our love is principle, and has its root
In reason, is judicious, manly, free ;
Yours, a blind instinct, crouches to the rod, 355

And licks the foot that treads it in the dust.
Were kingship as true treasure as it seems,
Sterling, and worthy of a wise man's wish,
I would not be a king to be beloved
Causeless, and daubed with undiscerning praise,
Where love is mere attachment to the throne,   361
Not to the man who fills it as he ought.

Whose freedom is by sufferance, and at will
Of a superior, he is never free.
Who lives, and is not weary of a life   365
Exposed to manacles, deserves them well.
The State that strives for liberty, though foiled,
And forced to abandon what she bravely sought,
Deserves at least applause for her attempt,
And pity for her loss.   But that's a cause   370
Not often unsuccessful: power usurped
Is weakness when opposed; conscious of wrong,
'Tis pusillanimous and prone to flight.
But slaves that once conceive the glowing thought
Of freedom, in that hope itself possess   375
All that the contest calls for; spirit, strength,
The scorn of danger, and united hearts,
The surest presage of the good they seek.*

Then shame to manhood, and opprobrious more
To France than all her losses and defeats,   380
Old or of later date, by sea or land,
Her house of bondage, worse than that of old
Which God avenged on Pharaoh—the Bastille.

---

* The author hopes that he shall not be censured for un-
necessary warmth upon so interesting a subject. He is aware
that it is become almost fashionable to stigmatize such sentiments as no better than empty declamation; but it is an
ill symptom, and peculiar to modern times.—(C.)

Ye horrid towers, the abode of broken hearts,
Ye dungeons and ye cages of despair,   385
That monarchs have supplied, from age to age,
With music such as suits their sovereign ears,
The sighs and groans of miserable men!
There's not an English heart that would not leap
To hear that ye were fallen at last; to know   390
That even our enemies, so oft employed
In forging chains for us, themselves were free.
For he who* values Liberty confines
His zeal for her predominance within
No narrow bounds; her cause engages him   395
Wherever pleaded.   'Tis the cause of man.
There dwell the most forlorn of human kind,
Immured though unaccused, condemned untried,
Cruelly spared, and hopeless of escape!
There, like the visionary emblem seen   400
By him of Babylon,† life stands a stump,
And filleted about with hoops of brass,
Still lives, though all its‡ pleasant boughs are gone.
To count the hour-bell, and expect no change;
And ever, as the sullen sound is heard,   405
Still to reflect, that though a joyless note
To him whose moments all have one dull pace,
Ten thousand rovers in the world at large
Account it music; that it summons some
To theatre, or jocund feast, or ball;   410

  * Originally written " that," but altered to "who" in Ed.
1787, which has been followed in subsequent editions, except that of Southey.
  † Daniel, ii. 31.
  ‡ Eds. up to 1803 had " its;" in 1803 the word was
altered to " his," which has been followed by subsequent
editors except Southey.

The wearied hireling finds it a release
From labour; and the lover, who has chid
Its long delay, feels every welcome stroke
Upon his heart-strings, trembling with delight—
To fly for refuge from distracting thought   415
To such amusements as ingenious woe
Contrives, hard shifting, and without her tools—
To read, engraven on the mouldy walls
In staggering types, his predecessor's tale,
A sad memorial, and subjoin his own—   420
To turn purveyor to an overgorged
And bloated spider, till the pampered pest
Is made familiar, watches his approach,
Comes at his call, and serves him for a friend—
To wear out time in numbering to and fro   425
The studs that thick emboss his iron door,
Then downward and then upward, then aslant
And then alternate, with a sickly hope
By dint of change to give his tasteless task
Some relish, till the sum, exactly found   430
In all directions, he begins again—
Oh comfortless existence! hemmed around
With woes, which who that suffers would not kneel
And beg for exile, or the pangs of death?
That man should thus encroach on fellow man, 435
Abridge him of his just and native rights,
Eradicate him, tear him from his hold
Upon the endearments of domestic life
And social, nip his fruitfulness and use,
And doom him for perhaps a heedless word   440
To barrenness, and solitude, and tears,
Moves indignation, makes the name of king,
(Of king whom such prerogative can please)

As dreadful as the Manichean God,
Adored through fear, strong only to destroy.   445
    'Tis Liberty alone that gives the flower
Of fleeting life its lustre and perfume,
And we are weeds without it.   All constraint,
Except what wisdom lays on evil men,
Is evil; hurts the faculties, impedes   450
Their progress in the road of science; blinds
The eyesight of Discovery; and begets,
In those that suffer it, a sordid mind
Bestial, a meagre intellect, unfit
To be the tenant of man's noble form.   455
Thee therefore still, blame-worthy as thou art,
With all thy loss of empire, and though squeezed
By public exigence, till annual food
Fails for the craving hunger of the state,
Thee I account still happy, and the chief   460
Among the nations, seeing thou art free,
My native nook of earth! Thy clime is rude,
Replete with vapours, and disposes much
All hearts to sadness, and none more than mine;
Thine unadulterate manners are less soft   465
And plausible than social life requires,
And thou hast need of discipline and art
To give thee what politer France receives
From Nature's bounty—that humane address
And sweetness, without which no pleasure is   470
In converse, either starved by cold reserve,
Or flushed with fierce dispute, a senseless brawl;
Yet being free, I love thee: for the sake
Of that one feature can be well content,
Disgraced as thou hast been, poor as thou art,   475
To seek no sublunary rest beside.

But once enslaved, farewell! I could endure
Chains nowhere patiently, and chains at home,
Where I am free by birthright, not at all.
Then what were left of roughness in the grain 480
Of British natures, wanting its excuse
That it belongs to freemen, would disgust
And shock me. I should then with double pain
Feel all the rigour of thy fickle clime;
And if I must bewail the blessing lost,   485
For which our Hampdens and our Sidneys bled,
I would at least bewail it under skies
Milder, among a people less austere,   .
In scenes which, having never known me free,
Would not reproach me with the loss I felt.   490
Do I forebode impossible events,
And tremble at vain dreams? Heaven grant I may!
But the age of virtuous politics is past,
And we are deep in that of cold pretence.
Patriots are grown too shrewd to be sincere,   495
And we too wise to trust them. He that takes
Deep in his soft credulity the stamp
Designed by loud declaimers on the part
Of Liberty, themselves the slaves of lust,
Incurs derision for his easy faith   500
And lack of knowledge, and with cause enough:
For when was public virtue to be found
Where private was not? Can he love the whole
Who loves no part? He be a nation's friend
Who is, in truth, the friend of no man there? 505
Can he be strenuous in his country's cause,
Who slights the charities for whose dear sake
That country, if at all, must be beloved?
    'Tis therefore sober and good men are sad

For England's glory, seeing it wax pale   510
And sickly, while her champions wear their hearts
So loose to private duty, that no brain,
Healthful and undisturbed by factious fumes,
Can dream them trusty to the general weal.
Such were not they of old, whose tempered blades
Dispersed the shackles of usurped control,   516
And hewed them link from link. Then Albion's sons
Were sons indeed; they felt a filial heart
Beat high within them at a mother's wrongs,
And shining each in his domestic sphere,   520
Shone brighter still, once called to public view.
'Tis therefore, many whose sequestered lot
Forbids their interference, looking on,
Anticipate perforce some dire event;
And seeing the old castle of the state,   525
That promised once more firmness, so assailed
That all its tempest-beaten turrets shake,
Stand motionless expectants of its fall.
All has its date below; the fatal hour
Was registered in Heaven ere time began.   530
We turn to dust, and all our mightiest works
Die too: the deep foundations that we lay,
Time ploughs them up, and not a trace remains.
We build with what we deem eternal rock;
A distant age asks where the fabric stood,   535
And in the dust, sifted and searched in vain,
The undiscoverable secret sleeps.
     But there is yet a Liberty unsung
By poets, and by senators unpraised,
Which monarchs cannot grant, nor all the powers *
Of Earth and Hell confederate take away: 541

* " Power," Southey.

A Liberty which persecution, fraud,
Oppression, prisons, have no power to bind,
Which whoso tastes can be enslaved no more.
'Tis Liberty of Heart, derived from Heaven,   545
Bought with His blood who gave it to mankind,
And sealed with the same token.   It is held
By charter, and that charter sanctioned sure
By the unimpeachable and awful oath
And promise of a God.   His other gifts   550
All bear the royal stamp that speaks them his,
And are august, but this transcends them all.
His other works, the visible display
Of all-creating energy and might,
Are grand, no doubt, and worthy of the Word 555
That finding an interminable space
Unoccupied, has filled the void so well,
And made so sparkling what was dark before.
But these are not his glory.   Man, 'tis true,
Smit with the beauty of so fair a scene,   560
Might well suppose the artificer divine
Meant it eternal, had he not himself
Pronounced it transient, glorious as it is,
And still designing a more glorious far,
Doomed it, as insufficient for his praise.   565
These, therefore, are occasional, and pass;
Formed for the confutation of the fool
Whose lying heart disputes against a God;
That office served, they must be swept away.
Not so the labours of his love: they shine   570
In other heavens than these that we behold,
And fade not.   There is Paradise that fears
No forfeiture, and of its fruits he sends
Large prelibation oft to saints below.

Of these the first in order, and the pledge   575
And confident assurance of the rest,
Is Liberty: a flight into his arms,
Ere yet mortality's fine threads give way;
A clear escape from tyrannizing lust,
And full immunity from penal woe.   580
   Chains are the portion of revolted man,
Stripes, and a dungeon; and his body serves
The triple purpose. In that sickly, foul,
Opprobrious residence, he finds them all.
Propense his heart to idols, he is held   585
In silly dotage on created things,
Careless of their Creator. And that low
And sordid gravitation of his powers
To a vile clod, so draws him, with such force
Resistless from the centre he should seek,   590
That he at last forgets it. All his hopes
Tend downward; his ambition is to sink,
To reach a depth profounder still, and still
Profounder, in the fathomless abyss
Of folly, plunging in pursuit of death.   595
But ere he gain the comfortless repose
He seeks, and* acquiescence of his soul
In heaven-renouncing exile, he endures—
What does he not, from lusts opposed in vain,
And self-reproaching conscience? He foresees 600
The fatal issue to his health, fame, peace,
Fortune, and dignity; the loss of all
That can ennoble man, and make frail life,
Short as it is, supportable. Still worse,
Far worse than all the plagues with which his sins

---

* "An;" Eds. 1785, 1786, Southey. "And;" Eds.
1787, and subsequent Eds., except Southey's.

Infect his happiest moments, he forebodes   606
Ages of hopeless misery.   Future death,
And death still future.   Not a hasty stroke,
Like that which sends him to the dusty grave,
But unrepealable enduring death.   610
Scripture is still a trumpet to his fears:
What none can prove a forgery, may be true;
What none but bad men wish exploded, must.
That scruple checks him.   Riot is not loud
Nor drunk enough to drown it.   In the midst 615
Of laughter his compunctions are sincere,
And he abhors the jest by which he shines.
Remorse begets reform.   His master-lust
Falls first before his resolute rebuke,
And seems dethroned and vanquished.   Peace
        ensues,   620
But spurious and short-lived; the puny child
Of self-congratulating Pride, begot
On fancied Innocence.   Again he falls,
And fights again; but finds his best essay
A presage ominous, portending still   625
Its own dishonour by a worse relapse.
Till Nature, unavailing Nature, foiled
So oft, and wearied in the vain attempt,
Scoffs at her own performance.   Reason now
Takes part with Appetite, and pleads the cause 630
Perversely, which of late she so condemned;
With shallow shifts and old devices, worn
And tattered in the service of debauch,
Covering his shame from his offended sight.
    " Hath God indeed given appetites to man, 635
" And stored the earth so plenteously with means
" To gratify the hunger of his wish,

" And doth he reprobate and will he damn
" The use of his own bounty?—making first
" So frail a kind, and then enacting laws   640
" So strict, that less than perfect must despair?
" Falsehood! which whoso but suspects of truth
" Dishonours God, and makes a slave of man.
" Do they themselves, who undertake for hire
" The teacher's office, and dispense at large   645
" Their weekly dole of edifying strains,
" Attend to their own music?   Have they faith
" In what, with such solemnity of tone
" And gesture, they propound to our belief?
" Nay—conduct hath the loudest tongue. The voice
" Is but an instrument on which the priest   651
" May play what tune he pleases.   In the deed,
" The unequivocal, authentic deed,
" We find sound argument, we read the heart."
    Such reasonings (if that name must needs be-
        long   655
To excuses in which reason has no part)
Serve to compose a spirit well inclined
To live on terms of amity with vice,
And sin without disturbance.   Often urged,
(As often as libidinous discourse   660
Exhausted, he resorts to solemn themes
Of theological and grave import)
They gain at last his unreserved assent;
Till hardened his heart's temper in the forge
Of lust, and on the anvil of despair,   665
He slights the strokes of conscience.   Nothing
        moves,
Or nothing much, his constancy in ill,
Vain tampering has but fostered his disease,

'Tis desperate, and he sleeps the sleep of death.
Haste now, philosopher, and set him free.   670
Charm the deaf serpent wisely.   Make him hear
Of rectitude and fitness, moral truth
How lovely, and the moral sense how sure,
Consulted and obeyed, to guide his steps
Directly to the FIRST AND ONLY FAIR.   675
Spare not in such a cause.   Spend all the powers
Of rant and rhapsody in virtue's praise :
Be most sublimely good, verbosely grand,
And with poetic trappings grace thy prose,
Till it out-mantle all the pride of verse.—   680
Ah, tinkling cymbal and high-sounding brass,
Smitten in vain ! such music cannot charm
The eclipse that intercepts truth's heavenly beam,
And chills and darkens a wide-wandering soul.
The still small voice is wanted.   He must speak,
Whose word leaps forth at once to its effect,   686
Who calls for things that are not, and they come.
    Grace makes the slave a freeman.   'Tis a change
That turns to ridicule the turgid speech
And stately tone of moralists, who boast,   690
As if, like him of fabulous renown,
They had indeed ability to smooth
The shag of savage nature, and were each
An Orpheus, and omnipotent in song.
But transformation of apostate man   695
From fool to wise, from earthly to divine,
Is work for him that made him.   He alone,
And He by means in philosophic eyes
Trivial and worthy of disdain, achieves
The wonder ; humanizing what is brute   700
In the lost kind, extracting from the lips

Of asps their venom, overpowering strength
By weakness, and hostility by love.

    Patriots have toiled, and in their country's cause
Bled nobly, and their deeds, as they deserve,   705
Receive proud recompense. We give in charge
Their names to the sweet lyre. The Historic Muse,
Proud of the treasure, marches with it down
To latest times; and Sculpture, in her turn,
Gives bond in stone and ever-during brass   710
To guard them, and to immortalize her trust.
But fairer wreaths are due, though never paid,
To those who, posted at the shrine of Truth,
Have fallen in her defence. A Patriot's blood,
Well spent in such a strife, may earn indeed,   715
And for a time ensure, to his loved land
The sweets of Liberty and equal laws;
But Martyrs struggle for a brighter prize,
And win it with more pain. Their blood is shed
In confirmation of the noblest claim,   720
Our claim to feed upon immortal truth,
To walk with God, to be divinely free,
To soar, and to anticipate the skies.
Yet few remember them. They lived unknown
Till Persecution dragged them into fame,   725
And chased them up to Heaven. Their ashes flew—
No marble tells us whither. With their names
No bard embalms and sanctifies his song;
And History, so warm on meaner themes,
Is cold on this. She execrates indeed   730
The tyranny that doomed them to the fire,
But gives the glorious sufferers little praise.*

    He is the freeman whom the Truth makes free,

* See Hume [cap. xxxvii].—(C).

And all are slaves beside.   There's not a chain
That hellish foes, confederate for his harm,   735
Can wind around him, but he casts it off
With as much ease as Samson his green withes.*
He looks abroad into the varied field
Of Nature, and though poor perhaps compared
With those whose mansions glitter in his sight, 740
Calls the delightful scenery all his own.
His are the mountains, and the valleys his,
And the resplendent rivers.   His to enjoy
With a propriety that none can feel,
But who, with filial confidence inspired,   745
Can lift to Heaven an unpresumptuous eye,
And smiling say—" My Father made them all."
Are they not his by a peculiar right,
And by an emphasis of interest his,
Whose eye they fill with tears of holy joy,   750
Whose heart with praise, and whose exalted mind
With worthy thoughts of that unwearied Love
That planned, and built, and still upholds a world
So clothed with beauty, for rebellious man ?
Yes—ye may fill your garners, ye that reap   755
The loaded soil, and ye may waste much good
In senseless riot ; but ye will not find
In feast or in the chase, in song or dance,
A liberty like his, who unimpeached
Of usurpation, and to no man's wrong,   760
Appropriates nature as his Father's work,
And has a richer use of yours than you.†
He is indeed a freeman.   Free by birth
Of no mean city, planned or ere the hills
Were built, the fountains opened, or the sea   765

* Judges xvi. 7, 8, 9.   † " Ye," Southey.

With all his roaring multitude of waves.
His freedom is the same in every state,
And no condition of this changeful life,
So manifold in cares, whose every day
Brings its own evil with it, makes it less ;   770
For he has wings that neither sickness, pain,
Nor penury, can cripple or confine.
No nook so narrow but he spreads them there
With ease, and is at large.   The oppressor holds
His body bound, but knows not what a range   775
His spirit takes, unconscious of a chain ;
And that to bind him is a vain attempt,
Whom God delights in, and in whom He dwells.
    Acquaint thyself with God, if thou wouldst taste
His works.   Admitted once to his embrace,   780
Thou shalt perceive that thou wast blind before :
Thine eye shall be instructed, and thine heart
Made pure, shall relish with divine delight
'Till then unfelt, what hands divine have wrought.
Brutes graze the mountain-top, with faces prone,
And eyes intent upon the scanty herb   786
It yields them, or recumbent on its brow,
Ruminate heedless of the scene outspread
Beneath, beyond, and stretching far away
From inland regions to the distant main.   790
Man views it and admires, but rests content
With what he views.   The landscape has his praise,
But not its Author.   Unconcerned who formed
The Paradise he sees, he finds it such,
And such well pleased to find it, asks no more. 795
Not so the mind that has been touched from Heaven,
And in the school of sacred wisdom taught
To read his wonders, in whose thought the world,

Fair as it is, existed ere it was.
Not for its own sake merely, but for his   800
Much more who fashioned it, he gives it praise ;
Praise that from earth resulting, as it ought,
To earth's acknowledged Sovereign, finds at once
Its only just proprietor in him.
The soul that sees him, or receives sublimed   805
New faculties, or learns at least to employ
More worthily the powers she owned before,
Discerns in all things what, with stupid gaze
Of ignorance, till then she overlooked,
A ray of heavenly light gilding all forms   810
Terrestrial, in the vast and the minute
The unambiguous footsteps of the God
Who gives its lustre to an insect's wing,
And wheels his throne upon the rolling worlds.
Much conversant with Heaven, she often holds 815
With those fair ministers of light to man,
That fill the skies nightly with silent pomp,
Sweet conference ; inquires what strains were they
With which Heaven rang, when every star, in haste
To gratulate the new-created earth,   820
Sent forth a voice, and all the sons of God
Shouted for joy.—" Tell me, ye shining hosts
" That navigate a sea that knows no storms,
" Beneath a vault unsullied with a cloud,
" If from your elevation, whence ye view   825
" Distinctly scenes invisible to man,
" And systems of whose birth no tidings yet
" Have reached this nether world, ye spy a race
" Favoured as ours, transgressors from the womb,
" And hasting to a grave, yet doomed to rise,   830
" And to possess a brighter Heaven than yours ?

" As one who long detained on foreign shores
" Pants to return, and when he sees afar
" His country's weather-bleached and battered
      rocks
" From the green wave emerging, darts an eye 835
" Radiant with joy towards the happy land,
" So I with animated hopes behold,
" And many an aching wish, your beamy fires,
" That show like beacons in the blue abyss,
" Ordained to guide the embodied spirit home 840
" From toilsome life to never ending rest.
" Love kindles as I gaze.   I feel desires
" That give assurance of their own success,
" And that, infused from Heaven, must thither
      tend."
  So reads he Nature, whom the lamp of truth 845
Illuminates.   Thy lamp, mysterious Word!
Which whoso sees no longer wanders lost,
With intellects bemazed in endless doubt,
But runs the road of wisdom.   Thou hast built
With means that were not till by thee employed, 850
Worlds that had never been hadst Thou in strength
Been less, or less benevolent than strong.   ·
They are thy witnesses, who speak thy power
And goodness infinite, but speak in ears
That hear not, or receive not their report.   855
In vain thy creatures testify of thee,
Till Thou proclaim thyself.   Theirs is indeed
A teaching voice; but 'tis the praise of thine
That whom it teaches it makes prompt to learn,
And with the boon gives talents for its use.   860
Till Thou art heard, imaginations vain
Possess the heart, and fables false as hell

Yet deemed oracular, lure down to death
The uninformed and heedless souls of men.
We give to Chance, blind Chance, ourselves as
    blind,   865
The glory of thy work, which yet appears
Perfect and unimpeachable of blame,
Challenging human scrutiny, and proved
Then skilful most when most severely judged.
But Chance is not; or is not where Thou reignest:
Thy Providence forbids that fickle power   871
(If power she be that works but to confound)
To mix her wild vagaries with thy laws.
Yet thus we dote, refusing while we can
Instruction, and inventing to ourselves   875
Gods such as guilt makes welcome; gods that
    sleep,
Or disregard our follies, or that sit
Amused spectators of this bustling stage.
Thee we reject, unable to abide
Thy purity, till pure as Thou art pure,   880
Made such by thee, we love thee for that cause
For which we shunned and hated thee before.
Then we are free. Then Liberty like day
Breaks on the soul, and by a flash from Heaven
Fires all the faculties with glorious joy.   885
A voice is heard that mortal ears hear not
Till Thou hast touched them; 'tis the voice of song,
A loud Hosanna sent from all thy works,
Which he that hears it with a shout repeats,
And adds his rapture to the general praise.   890
In that blest moment, Nature throwing wide
Her veil opaque, discloses with a smile
The Author of her beauties, who, retired

Behind his own creation, works unseen
By the impure, and hears his power denied.   895
Thou art the source and centre of all minds,
Their only point of rest, Eternal Word!
From thee departing, they are lost, and rove
At random, without honour, hope, or peace.
From thee is all that soothes the life of man,   900
His high endeavour, and his glad success,
His strength to suffer, and his will to serve.
But, O Thou bounteous giver of all good!
Thou art of all thy gifts thyself the crown;
Give what Thou canst, without thee we are poor,
And with thee rich, take what Thou wilt away. 906

THE TASK.   BOOK VI.

THE WINTER WALK AT NOON.

ARGUMENT.

Bells at a distance. Their effect. A fine noon in winter.
A sheltered walk. Meditation better than books. Our fa-
miliarity with the course of nature makes it appear less
wonderful than it is. The transformation that Spring effects
in a shrubbery described. A mistake concerning the course
of nature corrected. God maintains it by an unremitted act.
The amusements fashionable at this hour of the day reproved.
Animals happy, a delightful sight. Origin of cruelty to
animals. That it is a great crime proved from scripture.
That proof illustrated by a tale. A line drawn between the
lawful and unlawful destruction of them. Their good and
useful properties insisted on. Apology for the encomiums
bestowed by the author on animals. Instances of man's
extravagant praise of man. The groans of the creation shall
have an end. A view taken of the restoration of all things.
An invocation and an invitation of him who shall bring it
to pass. The retired man vindicated from the charge of
uselessness. Conclusion.

THE TASK.   BOOK VI.

THE WINTER WALK AT NOON.

HERE is in souls a sympathy with
    sounds,
And as the mind is pitched the ear is
    pleased
With melting airs or martial, brisk or grave :
Some chord in unison with what we hear
Is touched within us, and the heart replies.   5
How soft the music of those village bells,
Falling at intervals upon the ear
In cadence sweet, now dying all away,
Now pealing loud again, and louder still,
Clear and sonorous, as the gale comes on !   10
With easy force it opens all the cells
Where Memory slept.   Wherever I have heard
A kindred melody, the scene recurs,
And with it all its pleasures and its pains.
Such comprehensive views the spirit takes,   15
That in a few short moments I retrace
(As in a map the voyager his course)
The windings of my way through many years.
Short as in retrospect the journey seems,

It seemed not always short; the rugged path,   20
And prospect oft so dreary and forlorn,
Moved many a sigh at its disheartening length.
Yet feeling present evils, while the past
Faintly impress the mind, or not at all,
How readily we wish time spent revoked,   25
That we might try the ground again, where once
(Through inexperience, as we now perceive,)
We missed that happiness we might have found!
Some friend is gone, perhaps his son's best friend,
A father, whose authority, in show   30
When most severe, and mustering all its force,
Was but the graver countenance of love;
Whose favour, like the clouds of spring, might
          lower,
And utter now and then an awful voice,
But had a blessing in its darkest frown,   35
Threatening at once and nourishing the plant.
We loved, but not enough, the gentle hand
That reared us.   At a thoughtless age, allured
By every gilded folly, we renounced
His sheltering side, and wilfully forewent   40
That converse which we now in vain regret.
How gladly would the man recall to life
The boy's neglected sire! a mother too,
That softer friend, perhaps more gladly still,
Might he demand them at the gates of death.   45
Sorrow has, since they went, subdued and tamed
The playful humour; he could now endure
(Himself grown sober in the vale of tears)
And feel a parent's presence no restraint.
But not to understand a treasure's worth   50
Till time has stolen away the slighted good,

Is cause of half the poverty we feel,
And makes the world the wilderness it is.
The few that pray at all pray oft amiss,
And seeking grace to improve the prize they hold,
Would urge a wiser suit than asking more.   56
     The night was winter in his roughest mood;
The morning sharp and clear. But now at noon
Upon the southern side of the slant hills,
And where the woods fence off the northern blast,
The season smiles, resigning all its rage,   61
And has the warmth of May. The vault is blue
Without a cloud, and white without a speck
The dazzling splendour of the scene below.
Again the harmony comes o'er the vale,   65
And through the trees I view the embattled tower
Whence all the music. I again perceive
The soothing influence of the wafted strains,
And settle in soft musings as I tread
The walk, still verdant, under oaks and elms,   70
Whose outspread branches overarch the glade.
The roof, though moveable through all its length
As the wind sways it, has yet well sufficed,
And intercepting in their silent fall
The frequent flakes, has kept a path for me.   75
No noise is here, or none that hinders thought.
The redbreast warbles still, but is content
With slender notes, and more than half suppressed:
Pleased with his solitude, and flitting light
From spray to spray, where'er he rests he shakes
From many a twig the pendent drops of ice,   81
That tinkle in the withered leaves below.
Stillness, accompanied with sounds so soft,
Charms more than silence. Meditation here

May think down hours to moments. Here the heart
May give a* useful lesson to the head,   86
And Learning wiser grow without his books.
Knowledge and Wisdom, far from being one,
Have ofttimes no connexion. Knowledge dwells
In heads replete with thoughts of other men,   90
Wisdom in minds attentive to their own.
Knowledge, a rude unprofitable mass,
The mere materials with which Wisdom builds,
Till smoothed and squared and fitted to its place,
Does but encumber whom it seems to enrich.   95
Knowledge is proud that he has learned so much,
Wisdom is humble that he knows no more.
Books are not seldom talismans and spells,
By which the magic art of shrewder wits
Holds an unthinking multitude enthralled.   100
Some to the fascination of a name
Surrender judgment hoodwinked. Some the style
Infatuates, and through labyrinths and wilds
Of error, leads them by a tune entranced.
While sloth seduces more, too weak to bear   105
The insupportable fatigue of thought,
And swallowing therefore without pause or choice
The total grist unsifted, husks and all.
But trees, and rivulets whose rapid course
Defies the check of winter, haunts of deer,   110
And sheepwalks populous with bleating lambs,
And lanes in which the primrose ere her time
Peeps through the moss that clothes the hawthorn
            root,

---

* "An;" Eds. 1785, 1786, 1787, 1788, 1793, and all
editions down to 1806, with the addition of Southey's.
"A;" Ed. 1808, and subsequent editions, except Southey's.

Deceive no student.   Wisdom there, and Truth,
Not shy as in the world, and to be won   115
By slow solicitation, seize at once
The roving thought, and fix it on themselves.
   What prodigies can power divine perform
More grand than it produces year by year,
And all in sight of inattentive man ?   120
Familiar with the effect we slight the cause,
And in the constancy of Nature's course,
The regular return of genial months,
And renovation of a faded world,
See naught to wonder at.   Should God again,   125
As once in Gibeon,* interrupt the race
Of the undeviating and punctual sun,
How would the world admire !   But speaks it less
An agency divine, to make him know
His moment when to sink and when to rise,   130
Age after age, than to arrest his course ?
All we behold is miracle, but seen
So duly, all is miracle in vain.
Where now the vital energy that moved,
While summer was, the pure and subtle lymph 135
Through the imperceptible meandering veins
Of leaf and flower ?   It sleeps; and the icy touch
Of unprolific winter has impressed
A cold stagnation on the intestine tide.
But let the months go round, a few short months,
And all shall be restored.   These naked shoots, 141
Barren as lances, among which the wind
Makes wintry music, sighing as it goes,
Shall put their graceful foliage on again,
And more aspiring, and with ampler spread,   145

* Joshua, x. 12, 13.

Shall boast new charms, and more than they have
    lost.
Then each in its peculiar honours clad,
Shall publish, even to the distant eye,
Its family and tribe.   Laburnum, rich
In streaming gold; Syringa, ivory pure;   150
The scentless and the scented Rose, this red,
And of an humbler growth, the other* tall,
And throwing up into the darkest gloom
Of neighbouring Cypress, or more sable Yew,
Her silver globes, light as the foamy surf,   155
That the wind severs from the broken wave;
The Lilac, various in array, now white,
Now sanguine, and her beauteous head now set
With purple spikes pyramidal, as if ·
Studious of ornament, yet unresolved   160
Which hue she most approved, she chose them all;
Copious of flowers the Woodbine, pale and wan,
But well compensating her sickly looks
With never cloying odours, early and late;
Hypericum all bloom, so thick a swarm   165
Of flowers, like flies clothing her slender rods,
That scarce a leaf appears;† Mezereon too,
Though leafless, well attired, and thick beset
With blushing wreaths, investing every spray;
Althæa with the purple eye;‡ the Broom,   170
Yellow and bright, as bullion unalloyed,
Her blossoms; and luxuriant above all
The Jasmine, throwing wide her elegant sweets,
The deep dark green of whose unvarnished leaf

* The Guelder rose.—(C.)
† *Hypericum perforatum*, the common St. John's wort.
‡ The mallow.

Makes more conspicuous, and illumines more   175
The bright profusion of her scattered stars.—
These have been, and these shall be in their day;
And all this uniform uncoloured scene
Shall be dismantled of its fleecy load,
And flush into variety again.   180
From dearth * to plenty, and from death to life,
Is Nature's progress, when she lectures man
In heavenly truth; evincing as she makes
The grand transition, that there lives and works
A soul in all things, and that soul is God.   185
The beauties of the wilderness are his,
That make so gay the solitary place,
Where no eye sees them. And the fairer forms
That cultivation glories in, are his.
He sets the bright procession on its way,   190
And marshals all the order of the year;
He marks the bounds which Winter may not pass,
And blunts his pointed fury; in its case,
Russet and rude, folds up the tender germ
Uninjured, with inimitable art;   195
And ere one flowery season fades and dies,
Designs the blooming wonders of the next.
    Some say that in the origin of things,
When all creation started into birth,
The infant elements received a law   200
From which they swerve not since. That under
    force
Of that controlling ordinance they move,
And need not his immediate hand, who first
Prescribed their course, to regulate it now.
Thus dream they, and contrive to save a God   205

* " Death;" Ed. 1798.

The incumbrance of his own concerns, and spare
The Great Artificer of all that moves
The stress of a continual act, the pain
Of unremitted vigilance and care,
As too laborious and severe a task.   210
So man, the moth, is not afraid, it seems,
To span Omnipotence, and measure might
That knows no measure, by the scanty rule
And standard of his own, that is to-day,
And is not ere to-morrow's sun go down.   215
But how should matter occupy a charge,
Dull as it is, and satisfy a law
So vast in its demands, unless impelled
To ceaseless service by a ceaseless force,
And under pressure of some conscious cause?   220
The Lord of all, himself through all diffused,
Sustains and is the life of all that lives.
Nature is but a name for an effect,
Whose cause is God. He feeds the secret fire
By which the mighty process is maintained,   225
Who sleeps not, is not weary; in whose sight
Slow-circling ages are as transient days;
Whose work is without labour; whose designs
No flaw deforms, no difficulty thwarts;
And whose beneficence no charge exhausts.   230
Him blind antiquity profaned, not served,
With self-taught rites, and under various names,
Female and male, Pomona, Pales, Pan,
And Flora, and Vertumnus; peopling earth
With tutelary goddesses and gods   235
That were not; and commending as they would
To each some province, garden, field, or grove.
But all are under One. One Spirit—His

Who wore * the platted thorns with bleeding brows,
Rules universal nature. Not a flower   240
But shows some touch, in freckle, streak, or stain,
Of his unrivalled pencil.   He inspires
Their balmy odours, and imparts their hues,
And bathes their eyes with nectar, and includes
In grains as countless as the seaside sands,   245
The forms with which he sprinkles all the earth.
Happy who walks with him ! whom what he finds
Of flavour or of scent in fruit or flower,
Or what he views of beautiful or grand
In nature, from the broad majestic oak   250
To the green blade that twinkles in the sun,
Prompts with remembrance of a present God.
His presence, who made all so fair, perceived,
Makes all still fairer. ' As with him no scene
Is dreary, so with him all seasons please.   255
Though winter had been none, had man been
         true,
And earth be punished for its tenant's sake,
Yet not in vengeance ; as this smiling sky,
So soon succeeding such an angry night,   .
And these dissolving snows, and this clear stream
Recovering fast its liquid music, prove.   261
    Who then that has a mind well strung and tuned
To contemplation, and within his reach
A scene so friendly to his favourite task,
Would waste attention at the chequered board,   265
His host of wooden warriors to and fro

---

* " Wore" was the original reading (1785). " Bore"
crept into the second edition (1786), but " wore" was restored
in the third (1787), and " bore" did not reappear until
Southey's time. He, Dale, and Bell read " bore."

Marching and countermarching, with an eye
As fixed as marble, with a forehead ridged
And furrowed into storms, and with a hand
Trembling, as if eternity were hung   270
In balance on his conduct of a pin?
Nor envies he aught more their idle sport,
Who pant with application misapplied
To trivial toys, and pushing ivory balls
Across a velvet level, feel a joy   275
Akin to rapture, when the bauble finds
Its destined goal of difficult access.
Nor deems he wiser him who gives his noon
To miss, the mercer's plague, from shop to shop
Wandering, and littering with unfolded silks 280
The polished counter, and approving none,
Or promising with smiles to call again.
Nor him who, by his vanity seduced,
And soothed into a dream that he discerns
The difference of a Guido from a daub,   285
Frequents the crowded auction.   Stationed there
As duly as the Langford* of the show,
With glass at eye, and catalogue in hand,
And tongue accomplished in the fulsome cant
And pedantry that coxcombs learn with ease,   290
Oft as the price-deciding hammer falls,
He notes it in his book, then raps his box,
Swears 'tis a bargain, rails at his hard fate
That he has let it pass—but never bids.
     Here unmolested, through whatever sign   295
The sun proceeds, I wander.   Neither mist,

---

* A celebrated auctioneer of books and pictures; a predecessor of George Robins in the well-known rooms in Covent
Garden.

Nor freezing sky nor sultry, checking me,
Nor stranger intermeddling with my joy.
Even in the spring and play-time of the year,
That calls the unwonted villager abroad   300
With all her little ones, a sportive train,
To gather king-cups in the yellow mead,
And prink their hair with daisies, or to pick
A cheap but wholesome salad from the brook,
These shades are all my own.   The timorous hare,
Grown so familiar with her frequent guest,   306
Scarce shuns me ; and the stockdove unalarmed
Sits cooing in the pine-tree, nor suspends
His long love-ditty for my near approach.
Drawn from his refuge in some lonely elm,   310
That age or injury has hollowed deep,
Where on his bed of wool and matted leaves
He has outslept the winter, ventures forth
To frisk awhile, and bask in the warm sun,
The squirrel, flippant, pert, and full of play.   315
He sees me, and at once, swift as a bird,
Ascends the neighbouring beech ; there whisks his
          brush,
And perks his ears, and stamps, and scolds* aloud,
With all the prettiness of feigned alarm,
And anger insignificantly fierce.   320
    The heart is hard in nature, and unfit
For human fellowship, as being void
Of sympathy, and therefore dead alike
To love and friendship both, that is not pleased
With sight of animals enjoying life,   325

---

* " Scolds ;" Eds. 1785, 1786, 1787, 1788, 1793, Southey,
Bell. " Cries ;" Ed. 1794, and subsequent editions, except
those of Southey and Bell.

Nor feels their happiness augment his own.
The bounding fawn that darts across the glade
When none pursues, through mere delight of heart,
And spirits buoyant with excess of glee;
The horse, as wanton and almost as fleet, 330
That skims the spacious meadow at full speed,
Then stops and snorts, and throwing high his heels,
Starts to the voluntary race again;
The very kine that gambol at high noon,
The total herd receiving first from one 335
That leads the dance a summons to be gay,
Though wild their strange vagaries, and uncouth
Their efforts, yet resolved with one consent
To give such act and utterance as they may
To ecstasy too big to be suppressed— 340
These, and a thousand images of bliss,
With which kind Nature graces every scene
Where cruel man defeats not her design,
Impart to the benevolent, who wish
All that are capable of pleasure, pleased, 345
A far superior happiness to theirs,
The comfort of a reasonable joy.
Man scarce had risen, obedient to his call
Who formed him from the dust, his future grave,
When he was crowned as never king was since. 350
God set the diadem upon his head,
And angel choirs attended. Wondering stood
The new-made monarch, while before him passed,
All happy and all perfect in their kind,
The creatures, summoned from their various haunts
To see their sovereign, and confess his sway. 356
Vast was his empire, absolute his power,
Or bounded only by a law whose force

'Twas his sublimest privilege to feel
And own, the law of universal love.   360
He ruled with meekness, they obeyed with joy ;
No cruel purpose lurked within his heart,
And no distrust of his intent in theirs.
So Eden was a scene of harmless sport,
Where kindness on his part who ruled the whole, 365
Begat a tranquil confidence in all,
And fear as yet was not, nor cause for fear.
But sin marred all ; and the revolt of man,
That source of evils not exhausted yet,
Was punished with revolt of his from him.   370
Garden of God, how terrible the change
Thy groves and lawns then witnessed!   Every
        heart,
Each animal of every name, conceived
A jealousy and an instinctive fear,
And conscious of some danger, either fled   375
Precipitate the loathed abode of man,
Or growled defiance in such angry sort,
As taught him too to tremble in his turn.
Thus harmony and family accord
Were driven from Paradise ; and in that hour 380
The seeds of cruelty, that since have swelled
To such gigantic and enormous growth,
Were sown in human nature's fruitful soil.
Hence date the persecution and the pain
That man inflicts on all inferior kinds,   385
Regardless of their plaints.   To make him sport,
To gratify the frenzy of his wrath,
Or his base gluttony, are causes good
And just in his account, why bird and beast
Should suffer torture, and the streams be dyed 390

With blood of their inhabitants impaled.
Earth groans beneath the burden of a war
Waged with defenceless innocence, while he,
Not satisfied to prey on all around,
Adds tenfold bitterness to death by pangs 395
Needless, and first torments ere he devours.
Now happiest they that occupy the scenes
The most remote from his abhorred resort,
Whom once, as delegate of God on earth,
They feared, and as his perfect image loved. 400
The wilderness is theirs, with all its caves,
Its hollow glens, its thickets, and its plains
Unvisited by man. There they are free,
And howl and roar as likes them, uncontrolled,
Nor ask his leave to slumber or to play. 405
Woe to the tyrant, if he dare intrude
Within the confines of their wild domain:
The lion tells him—"I am monarch here!"
And if he spare* him, spares him on the terms
Of royal mercy, and through generous scorn 410
To rend a victim trembling at his foot.
In measure, as by force of instinct drawn,
Or by necessity constrained, they live
Dependent upon man; those in his fields,
These at his crib, and some beneath his roof. 415
They prove too often at how dear a rate
He sells protection. Witness, at his foot
The spaniel dying for some venial fault,
Under dissection of the knotted scourge;
Witness the patient ox, with stripes and yells 420
Driven to the slaughter, goaded, as he runs,

* "Spare;" Ed. 1785, and subsequent editions, except those of 1786 and Southey, which have "spares."

To madness, while the savage at his heels
Laughs at the frantic sufferer's fury, spent
Upon the guiltless passenger o'erthrown.
He too is witness, noblest of the train   425
That wait on man. the flight-performing horse:
With unsuspecting readiness he takes
His murderer on his back, and pushed all day,
With bleeding sides and flanks that heave for life,
To the far-distant goal, arrives and dies.   430
So little mercy shows who needs so much!
Does law, so jealous in the cause of man,
Denounce no doom on the delinquent?   None.
He lives, and o'er his brimming beaker boasts
(As if barbarity were high desert)   435
The inglorious feat, and clamorous in praise
Of the poor brute, seems wisely to suppose
The honours of his matchless horse his own.
But many a crime deemed innocent on earth
Is registered in Heaven; and these no doubt   440
Have each their record, with a curse annexed.
Man may dismiss compassion from his heart,
But God will never.   When He charged the Jew
To assist his foe's down-fallen beast to rise;*
And when the bush-exploring boy that seized   445
The young, to let the parent bird go free;†
Proved He not plainly that his meaner works
Are yet his care, and have an interest all,
All, in the universal Father's love?
On Noah, and in him on all mankind,   450
The charter was conferred, by which we hold
The flesh of animals in fee, and claim
O'er all we feed on, power of life and death.

* Exodus, xxiii. 5.   † Deuteron. xxii. 6, 7.

But read the instrument, and mark it well : *
The oppression of a tyrannous control   455
Can find no warrant there.   Feed then, and yield
Thanks for thy food.   Carnivorous through sin,
Feed on the slain, but spare the living brute.
   The Governor of all, himself to all
So bountiful, in whose attentive ear   460
The unfledged raven and the lion's whelp
Plead not in vain for pity on the pangs
Of hunger unassuaged, has interposed,
Not seldom, his avenging arm, to smite
The injurious trampler upon Nature's law,   465
That claims forbearance even for a brute.
He hates the hardness of a Balaam's heart ;
And prophet as he was, he might not strike
The blameless animal, without rebuke,
On which he rode.   Her opportune offence   470
Saved him, or the unrelenting seer had died.
He sees that human equity is slack
To interfere, though in so just a cause,
And makes the task his own.   Inspiring dumb
And helpless victims with a sense so keen   475
Of injury, with such knowledge of their strength,
And such sagacity to take revenge,
That oft the beast has seemed to judge the man.
An ancient, not a legendary tale,
By one of sound intelligence rehearsed   480
(If such who plead for Providence may seem
In modern eyes), shall make the doctrine clear.
   Where England, stretched towards the setting
       sun,   .
Narrow and long, o'erlooks the western wave,

* Genesis, ix. 2, 3.

Dwelt young Misagathus ; a scorner he   485
Of God and goodness, atheist in ostent,
Vicious in act, in temper savage-fierce.
He journeyed ; and his chance was as he went
To join a traveller, of far different note,
Evander, famed for piety, for years   490
Deserving honour, but for wisdom more.
Fame had not left the venerable man
A stranger to the manners of the youth,
Whose face too was familiar to his view.
Their way was on the margin of the land,   495
O'er the green summit of the rocks, whose base
Beats back the roaring surge, scarce heard so high.
The charity that warmed his heart was moved
At sight of the man-monster.   With a smile
Gentle, and affable, and full of grace,   500
As fearful of offending whom he wished
Much to persuade, he plied his ear with truths
Not harshly thundered forth, or rudely pressed,
But like his purpose, gracious, kind, and sweet.
" And dost thou dream," the impenetrable man 505
Exclaimed, " that me, the lullabies of age,
And fantasies of dotards, such as thou,
Can cheat, or move a moment's fear in me ?
Mark now the proof I give thee, that the brave
Need no such aids as Superstition lends,   510
To steel their hearts against the dread of Death."
He spoke, and to the precipice at hand
Pushed with a madman's fury.   Fancy shrinks,
And the blood thrills and curdles at the thought
Of such a gulf as he designed his grave.   515
But though the felon on his back could dare
The dreadful leap, more rational his steed

Declined the death, and wheeling swiftly round,
Or e'er * his hoof had pressed the crumbling verge,
Baffled his rider, saved against his will.   520
The frenzy of the brain may be redressed
By medicine well applied; but without grace
The heart's insanity admits no cure.
Enraged the more by what might have reformed
His horrible intent, again he sought   525
Destruction, with a zeal to be destroyed,
With sounding whip, and rowels dyed in blood.
But still in vain.   The Providence that meant
A longer date to the far nobler beast,
Spared yet again the ignobler for his sake.   530
And now, his prowess proved, and his sincere
Incurable obduracy evinced,
His rage grew cool; and pleased perhaps to have
          earned
So cheaply the renown of that attempt,
With looks of some complacence he resumed   535
His road, deriding much the blank amaze
Of good Evander, still where he was left
Fixed motionless, and petrified with dread.
So on they fared.   Discourse on other themes
Ensuing seemed to obliterate the past,   540
And tamer far for so much fury shown,
(As is the course of rash and fiery men)
The rude companion smiled, as if transformed.
But 'twas a transient calm.   A storm was near,
An unsuspected storm.   His hour was come.   545
The impious challenger of power divine

* "Or ere;" Eds. 1785, 1786, Southey, Bell. " Or e'er;"
Eds. 1787, 1788, 1793, 1794, and subsequent editions, except
those of Southey and Bell.

Was now to learn that Heaven, though slow to
    wrath,
Is never with impunity defied.
His horse, as he had caught his master's mood,
Snorting, and starting into sudden rage,   550
Unbidden, and not now to be controlled,
Rushed to the cliff, and having reached it, stood.
At once the shock unseated him : he flew
Sheer o'er the craggy barrier, and immersed
Deep in the flood, found, when he sought it not, 555
The death he had deserved, and died alone.
So God wrought double justice ; made the fool
The victim of his own tremendous choice,
And taught a brute the way to safe revenge.

    I would not enter on my list of friends   560
(Though graced with polished manners and fine
    sense,
Yet wanting sensibility) the man
Who needlessly sets foot upon a worm.
An inadvertent step may crush the snail
That crawls at evening in the public path ;   565
But he that has humanity, forewarned,
Will tread aside, and let the reptile live.
The creeping vermin, loathsome to the sight,
And charged perhaps with venom, that intrudes,
A visitor unwelcome, into scenes   570
Sacred to neatness and repose, the alcove,
The chamber, or refectory, may die :
A necessary act incurs no blame.
Not so, when, held within their proper bounds
And guiltless of offence, they range the air,   575
Or take their pastime in the spacious field :
There they are privileged ; and he that hunts

Or harms them there, is guilty of a wrong,
Disturbs the economy of Nature's realm,
Who, when she formed, designed them an abode. 580
The sum is this.   If man's convenience, health,
Or safety interfere, his rights and claims
Are paramount, and must extinguish theirs.
Else they are all—the meanest things that are,
As free to live, and to enjoy that life,   585
As God was free to form them at the first,
Who in his sovereign wisdom made them all.
Ye, therefore, who love mercy, teach your sons
To love it too.   The spring-time of our years
Is soon dishonoured and defiled in most   590
By budding ills, that ask a prudent hand
To check them.   But, alas! none sooner shoots,
If unrestrained, into luxuriant growth,
Than cruelty, most devilish of them all.
Mercy to him that shows it, is the rule   595
And righteous limitation of its act,
By which Heaven moves in pardoning guilty man ;
And he that shows none, being ripe in years,
And conscious of the outrage he commits,
Shall seek it, and not find it, in his turn.   600
     Distinguished much by reason, and still more
By our capacity of grace divine,
From creatures that exist but for our sake,
Which having served us, perish, we are held
Accountable, and God, some future day,   605
Will reckon with us roundly for the abuse
Of what he deems no mean or trivial trust.
Superior as we are, they yet depend
Not more on human help, than we on theirs.
Their strength, or speed, or vigilance, were given

In aid of our defects. In some are found   611
Such teachable and apprehensive parts,
That man's attainments in his own concerns,
Matched with the expertness of the brutes in theirs,
Are oft-times vanquished and thrown far behind.
Some show that nice sagacity of smell,   616
And read with such discernment, in the port
And figure of the man, his secret aim,
That oft we owe our safety to a skill
We could not teach, and must despair to learn. 620
But learn we might, if not too proud to stoop
To quadruped instructors, many a good
And useful quality, and virtue too,
Rarely exemplified among ourselves.
Attachment never to be weaned or changed   625
By any change of fortune; proof alike
Against unkindness, absence, and neglect;
Fidelity that neither bribe nor threat
Can move or warp; and gratitude for small
And trivial favours, lasting as the life,   630
And glistening even in the dying eye.
    Man praises man. Desert in arts or arms
Wins public honour; and ten thousand sit
Patiently present at a sacred song,
Commemoration-mad; content to hear   635
(O wonderful effect of music's power!)
Messiah's eulogy, for Handel's sake.
But less, methinks, than sacrilege might serve—
(For was it less? What heathen would have dared
To strip Jove's statue of his oaken wreath,   640
And hang it up in honour of a man?)
Much less might serve, when all that we design
Is but to gratify an itching ear,

And give the day to a musician's praise.
Remember Handel! Who that was not born   645
Deaf as the dead to harmony, forgets,
Or can, the more than Homer of his age?
Yes—we remember him ; and while we praise
A talent so divine, remember too
That his most holy book, from whom it came,   650
Was never meant, was never used before,
To buckram out the memory of a man.
But hush !—the Muse perhaps is too severe,
And with a gravity beyond the size
And measure of the offence, rebukes a deed   655
Less impious than absurd, and owing more
To want of judgment than to wrong design.
So in the chapel of old Ely House,
When wandering Charles, who meant to be the
          third,
Had fled from William,* and the news was fresh,
The simple clerk, but loyal, did announce   661
And eke did rear right merrily, two staves,
Sung to the praise and glory of king George !
    Man praises man ; and Garrick's memory next,
When time hath somewhat mellowed it, and made
The idol of our worship while he lived   666
The god of our idolatry once more,
Shall have its altar ; and the world shall go
In pilgrimage to bow before his shrine.
The theatre, too small, shall suffocate   670
Its squeezed contents, and more than it admits

---

* William Duke of Cumberland, the victor at Culloden,
fought on the 16th April, 1746. Old Ely House was of course
the ancient episcopal residence in Holborn. The chapel still
remains.

Shall sigh at their exclusion, and return
Ungratified.   For there some noble lord
Shall stuff his shoulders with king Richard's bunch,
Or wrap himself in Hamlet's inky cloak,   675
And strut, and storm, and straddle, stamp, and stare,
To show the world how Garrick did not act.
For Garrick was a worshipper himself;
He drew the liturgy, and framed the rites
And solemn ceremonial of the day,   680
And called the world to worship on the banks
Of Avon, famed in song.*   Ah, pleasant proof
That piety has still in human hearts
Some place, a spark or two not yet extinct!
The mulberry-tree was hung with blooming
        wreaths;   685
The mulberry-tree stood centre of the dance;
The mulberry-tree was hymned with dulcet airs;
And from his touchwood trunk the mulberry-tree
Supplied such relics as devotion holds
Still sacred, and preserves with pious care.   690
So 'twas a hallowed time: decorum reigned,
And mirth without offence.   No few returned,
Doubtless, much edified, and all refreshed.
  Man praises man.   The rabble all alive,
From tippling benches, cellars, stalls, and styes, 695
Swarm in the streets.   The statesman of the day,
A pompous and slow-moving pageant, comes.
Some shout him, and some hang upon his car,
To gaze in his eyes, and bless him.   Maidens wave
Their kerchiefs, and old women weep for joy;   700
While others, not so satisfied, unhorse

* Garrick's Shakespeare Commemoration, held at Stratford-
on-Avon in September, 1769.

The gilded equipage, and turning loose
His steeds, usurp a place they well deserve.
Why? What has charmed them? Hath he saved
  the state?
No. Doth he purpose its salvation? No. 705
Enchanting novelty, that moon at full
That finds out every crevice of the head
That is not sound and perfect, hath in theirs
Wrought this disturbance. But the wane is near,
And his own cattle must suffice him soon. 710
Thus idly do we waste the breath of praise,
And dedicate a tribute, in its use
And just direction sacred, to a thing
Doomed to the dust, or lodged already there.
Encomium in old time was poet's work; 715
But poets having lavishly long since
Exhausted all materials of the art,
The task now falls into the public hand;
And I, contented with an humble theme,
Have poured my stream of panegyric down 720
The vale of Nature, where it creeps and winds
Among her lovely works, with a secure
And unambitious course, reflecting clear,
If not the virtues, yet the worth of brutes.
And I am recompensed, and deem the toils 725
Of poetry not lost, if verse of mine
May stand between an animal and woe,
And teach one tyrant pity for his drudge.
  The groans of Nature in this nether world,
Which Heaven has heard for ages, have an end. 730
Foretold by prophets, and by poets sung,
Whose fire was kindled at the prophets' lamp,
The time of rest, the promised Sabbath, comes.

Six thousand years of sorrow have well nigh
Fulfilled their tardy and disastrous course   735
Over a sinful world; and what remains
Of this tempestuous state of human things,
Is merely as the working of a sea
Before a calm, that rocks itself to rest:
For He, whose car the winds are, and the clouds 740
The dust that waits upon his sultry march,
When sin hath moved him, and his wrath is hot,
Shall visit earth in mercy; shall descend   ˙
Propitious in his chariot paved with love;
And what his storms have blasted and defaced 745
For man's revolt, shall with a smile repair.

Sweet is the harp of prophecy; too sweet
Not to be wronged by a mere mortal touch:
Nor can the wonders it records be sung
To meaner music, and not suffer loss.   750
But when a poet, or when one like me,
Happy to rove among poetic flowers
Though poor in skill to rear them, lights at last
On some fair theme, some theme divinely fair,
Such is the impulse and the spur he feels   755
To give it praise proportioned to its worth,
That not to attempt it, arduous as he deems
The labour, were a task more arduous still.

O scenes surpassing fable, and yet true,
Scenes of accomplished bliss! which who can see,
Though but in distant prospect, and not feel   761
His soul refreshed with foretaste of the joy?
Rivers of gladness water all the earth,
And clothe all climes with beauty. The reproach
Of barrenness is passed. The fruitful field   765
Laughs with abundance, and the land, once lean,

Or fertile only in its own disgrace,
Exults to see its thistly curse repealed.
The various seasons woven into one,
And that one season an eternal spring,   770
The garden fears no blight, and needs no fence,
For there is none to covet, all are full.
The lion, and the libbard,* and the bear
Graze with the fearless flocks; all bask at noon
Together, or all gambol in the shade   775
Of the same grove, and drink one common stream.
Antipathies are none.   No foe to man
Lurks in the serpent now: the mother sees,
And smiles to see, her infant's playful hand
Stretched forth to dally with the crested worm,   780
To stroke his azure neck, or to receive
The lambent homage of his arrowy tongue.
All creatures worship man, and all mankind,
One Lord, one Father.   Error has no place;
That creeping pestilence is driven away;   785
The breath of Heaven has chased it.   In the heart
No passion touches a discordant string,
But all is harmony and love.   Disease
Is not.   The pure and uncontaminate blood
Holds its due course, nor fears the frost of age.   790
One song employs all nations, and all cry,
" Worthy the Lamb, for he was slain for us!"
The dwellers in the vales and on the rocks
Shout to each other, and the mountain tops
From distant mountains catch the flying joy,   795
Till nation after nation taught the strain,
Earth rolls the rapturous Hosanna round.

* The leopard; the word is found in Spenser and Shakespeare.

Behold the measure of the promise filled;
See Salem built, the labour of a God!
Bright as a sun the sacred city shines;   800
All kingdoms and all princes of the earth
Flock to that light; the glory of all lands
Flows into her; unbounded is her joy,
And endless her increase.   Thy rams are there,
Nebaioth, and the flocks of Kedar there; *   805
The looms of Ormus, and the mines of Ind,
And Saba's spicy groves pay tribute there.
Praise is in all her gates: upon her walls,
And in her streets, and in her spacious courts,
Is heard salvation.   Eastern Java there   810
Kneels with the native of the farthest west;
And Æthiopia spreads abroad the hand,
And worships.   Her report has travelled forth
Into all lands.   From every clime they come
To see thy beauty, and to share thy joy,   815
O Sion! an assembly such as earth
Saw never, such as Heaven stoops down to see.
   Thus Heavenward all things tend.   For all were
      once
Perfect, and all must be at length restored.
So God has greatly purposed; who would else   820
In his dishonoured works himself endure
Dishonour, and be wronged without redress.
Haste, then, and wheel away a shattered world,
Ye slow-revolving seasons!   We would see
(A sight to which our eyes are strangers yet)   825

* Nebaioth and Kedar, the sons of Ishmael, and progeni-
tors of the Arabs, in the prophetic scripture here alluded to,
may be reasonably considered as representatives of the Gen-
tiles at large.—(C.)

A world that does not dread and hate his laws,
And suffer for its crime; would learn how fair
The creature is that God pronounces good,
How pleasant in itself what pleases him.
Here every drop of honey hides a sting, 830
Worms wind themselves into our sweetest flowers,
And even the joy that haply some poor heart
Derives from Heaven, pure as the fountain is,
Is sullied in the stream, taking a taint
From touch of human lips, at best impure. 835
Oh for a world in principle as chaste
As this is gross and selfish! over which
Custom and Prejudice shall bear no sway,
That govern all things here, shouldering aside
The meek and modest Truth, and forcing her 8:0
To seek a refuge from the tongue of Strife
In nooks obscure, far from the ways of men:
Where Violence shall never lift the sword,
Nor Cunning justify the proud man's wrong,
Leaving the poor no remedy but tears: 845
Where he that fills an office, shall esteem
The occasion it presents of doing good
More than the perquisite: where Law shall speak
Seldom, and never but as Wisdom prompts
And Equity; not jealous more to guard 850
A worthless form, than to decide aright:
Where Fashion shall not sanctify abuse,
Nor smooth Good-breeding (supplemental grace)
With lean performance ape the work of Love.
  Come then, and added to thy many crowns, 855
Receive yet one, the crown of all the Earth,
Thou who alone art worthy! It was thine
By ancient covenant ere Nature's birth,

And thou hast made it thine by purchase since,
And overpaid its value with thy blood.   860
Thy saints proclaim thee king; and in their hearts
Thy title is engraven with a pen
Dipped in the fountain of eternal love.
Thy saints proclaim thee king; and thy delay
Gives courage to their foes, who, could they see 865
The dawn of thy last advent, long-desired,
Would creep into the bowels of the hills,
And flee for safety to the falling rocks.
The very spirit of the world is tired
Of its own taunting question, asked so long,   870
" Where is the promise of your Lord's approach?"*
The infidel has shot his bolts away,
Till his exhausted quiver yielding none,
He gleans the blunted shafts that have recoiled,
And aims them at the shield of Truth again.   875
The veil is rent, rent too by priestly hands,
That hides divinity from mortal eyes;
And all the mysteries to faith proposed,
Insulted and traduced, are cast aside
As useless, to the moles and to the bats.   880
They now are deemed the faithful, and are praised,
Who, constant only in rejecting thee,
Deny thy Godhead with a martyr's zeal,
And quit their office for their error's sake.†
Blind and in love with darkness! yet even these
Worthy, compared with sycophants, who knee 885
Thy name, adoring, and then preach thee man.
So fares thy church.   But how thy church may fare

---

* 2 Peter iii. 4.
† Lindsey and other Unitarian seceders from the Church
of England are here alluded to.

The world takes little thought. Who will may
  preach,
And what they will. All pastors are alike   890
To wandering sheep, resolved to follow none.
Two gods divide them all—Pleasure and Gain.
For these they live, they sacrifice to these,
And in their service wage perpetual war
With Conscience and with thee. Lust in their
  hearts,   895
And mischief in their hands, they roam the earth
To prey upon each other: stubborn, fierce,
High-minded, foaming out their own disgrace.
Thy prophets speak of such; and, noting down
The features of the last degenerate times,   900
Exhibit every lineament of these.
Come then, and added to thy many crowns,
Receive yet one, as radiant as the rest,
Due to thy last and most effectual work,
Thy word fulfilled, the conquest of a world!   905
    He is the happy man, whose life even now
Shows somewhat of that happier life to come;
Who doomed to an obscure but tranquil state,
Is pleased with it, and were he free to choose,
Would make his fate his choice; whom Peace, the
  fruit   910
Of virtue, and whom Virtue, fruit of faith,
Prepare for happiness; bespeak him one
Content indeed to sojourn while he must
Below the skies, but having there his home.
The World o'erlooks him in her busy search   915
Of objects more illustrious in her view;
And occupied as earnestly as she,
Though more sublimely, he o'erlooks the World.

She scorns his pleasures, for she knows them not;
He seeks not hers, for he has proved them vain. 920
He cannot skim the ground like summer birds
Pursuing gilded flies, and such he deems
Her honours, her emoluments, her joys.
Therefore in Contemplation is his bliss,
Whose power is such, that whom she lifts from earth
She makes familiar with a Heaven unseen,   926
And shows him glories yet to be revealed.
Not slothful he, though seeming unemployed,
And censured oft as useless.   Stillest streams
Oft water fairest meadows, and the bird   930
That flutters least is longest on the wing.
Ask him, indeed, what trophies he has raised,
Or what achievements of immortal fame
He purposes, and he shall answer—None.
His warfare is within.   There unfatigued   935
His fervent spirit labours.   There he fights,
And there obtains fresh triumphs o'er himself,
And never-withering wreaths, compared with which
The laurels that a Cæsar reaps are weeds.
Perhaps the self-approving haughty World,   940
That as she sweeps him with her whistling silks
Scarce deigns to notice him, or if she see,
Deems him a cipher in the works of God,
Receives advantage from his noiseless hours,
Of which she little dreams.   Perhaps she owes 945
Her sunshine and her rain, her blooming spring
And plenteous harvest, to the prayer he makes,
When, Isaac like, the solitary saint
Walks forth to meditate at eventide,*
And think on her, who thinks not for herself. 950

* Genesis xxiv. 63.

Forgive him, then, thou bustler in concerns
Of little worth, and* idler in the best,
If author of no mischief and some good,
He seek his proper happiness by means
That may advance, but cannot hinder, thine.   955
Nor though he tread the secret path of life,
Engage no notice, and enjoy much ease,
Account him an encumbrance on the state,
Receiving benefits, and rendering none.
His sphere though humble, if that humble sphere
Shine with his fair example, and though small   961
His influence, if that influence all be spent
In soothing sorrow and in quenching strife,
In aiding helpless indigence, in works
From which at least a grateful few derive   965
Some taste of comfort in a world of woe;
Then let the supercilious great confess
He serves his country, recompenses well
The state, beneath the shadow of whose vine
He sits secure, and in the scale of life   970
Holds no ignoble, though a slighted, place.
The man whose virtues are more felt than seen,
Must drop indeed the hope of public praise;
But he may boast what few that win it can,
That if his country stand not by his skill,   975
At least his follies have not wrought her fall.
Polite Refinement offers him in vain
Her golden tube, through which a sensual World
Draws gross impurity, and likes it well,
The neat conveyance hiding all the offence.   980
Not that he peevishly rejects a mode

* "And;" Eds. 1785, 1786, 1787, 1788, and Southey.
"An;" Ed. 1793, and subsequent editions, except Southey's.

Because that World adopts it. If it bear
The stamp and clear impression of good sense,
And be not costly more than of true worth,
He puts it on, and for decorum sake,   985
Can wear it even as gracefully as she.
She judges of refinement by the eye,
He by the test of conscience, and a heart
Not soon deceived; aware that what is base
No polish can make sterling, and that Vice,   990
Though well perfumed and elegantly dressed,
Like an unburied carcass tricked with flowers,
Is but a garnished nuisance, fitter far
For cleanly riddance than for fair attire.
So life glides smoothly and by stealth away,   995
More golden than that Age of fabled Gold
Renowned in ancient song; not vexed with care
Or stained with guilt, beneficent, approved
Of God and man, and peaceful in its end.
So glide my life away! and so at last,   1000
My share of duties decently fulfilled,
May some disease, not tardy to perform
Its destined office, yet with gentle stroke,
Dismiss me weary to a safe retreat,
Beneath the turf that I have often trod.   1005
It shall not grieve me, then, that once, when called
To dress a Sofa with the flowers of verse,
I played awhile, obedient to the fair,
With that light task; but soon, to please her more,
Whom flowers alone I knew would little please,   1010
Let fall the unfinished wreath, and roved for fruit;
Roved far, and gathered much: some harsh, 'tis
        true,
Picked from the thorns and briers of reproof,

But wholesome, well-digested ; grateful some
To palates that can taste immortal truth,   1015
Insipid else, and sure to be despised.
But all is in his hand whose praise I seek.
In vain the Poet sings, and the World hears,
If He regard not, though divine the theme.
'Tis not in artful measures, in the chime   1020
And idle tinkling of a minstrel's lyre,
To charm his ear, whose eye is on the heart,
Whose frown can disappoint the proudest strain,
Whose approbation prosper—even mine.

AN EPISTLE TO JOSEPH HILL, ESQ.*

EAR Joseph—five and twenty years
  ago—
Alas, how time escapes!—'tis even so—
With frequent intercourse, and always
  sweet,
And always friendly, we were wont to cheat
A tedious hour—and now we never meet!   5
As some grave gentleman in Terence says,
('Twas therefore much the same in ancient days)
Good lack, we know not what to-morrow brings—
Strange fluctuation of all human things!
True. Changes will befall, and friends may part,
But distance only cannot change the heart: 11
And were I called to prove the assertion true,
One proof should serve—a reference to you.

Whence comes it then, that in the wane of life,
Though nothing have occurred to kindle strife,   15
We find the friends we fancied we had won,
Though numerous once, reduced to few or none?
Can gold grow worthless that has stood the touch?
No; gold they seemed, but they were never such.

Horatio's servant once, with bow and cringe,   20
Swinging the parlour door upon its hinge,

* Poems, Ed. 1785, I. 285.

Dreading a negative, and overawed
Lest he should trespass, begged to go abroad.
" Go, fellow!—whither?"—turning short about—
" Nay—stay at home—you're always going out."
" 'Tis but a step, sir, just at the street's end."— 26
" For what?"—" An please you, sir, to see a
    friend."—
" A friend!" Horatio cried, and seemed to start—
" Yea marry shalt thou, and with all my heart.
" And fetch my cloak; for, though the night be raw,
" I'll see him too—the first I ever saw." 31
    I knew the man, and knew his nature mild,
And was his plaything often when a child;
But somewhat at that moment pinched him close,
Else he was seldom bitter or morose. 35
Perhaps his confidence just then betrayed,
His grief might prompt him with the speech he
    made;
Perhaps 'twas mere good humour gave it birth,
The harmless play of pleasantry and mirth.
Howe'er it was, his language, in my mind, 40
Bespoke at least a man that knew mankind.
    But not to moralize too much, and strain
To prove an evil of which all complain,
(I hate long arguments verbosely spun);
One story more, dear Hill, and I have done. 45
Once on a time an Emperor, a wise man,
No matter where, in China or Japan,
Decreed that whosoever should offend
Against the well-known duties of a friend,
Convicted once, should ever after wear 50
But half a coat, and show his bosom bare.
The punishment importing this, no doubt,

That all was naught within, and all found out.
   Oh, happy Britain ! we have not to fear
Such hard and arbitrary measure here ;   55
Else, could a law like that which I relate,
Once have the sanction of our triple state,
Some few that I have known in days of old,
Would run most dreadful risk of catching cold ;
While you, my friend, whatever wind should blow,
Might traverse England safely to and fro,   61
An honest man, close-buttoned to the chin,   ·
Broad-cloth without, and a warm heart within.

TIROCINIUM;

OR, A REVIEW OF SCHOOLS.

Κεφαλαιον δη παιδειας ορθη τροφη.—PLATO.
Αρχη πολιτειας απασης, νεων τροφα.—DIOG. LAERT.

TO THE

REV. WILLIAM CAWTHORNE UNWIN,

RECTOR OF STOCK IN ESSEX,

THE TUTOR OF HIS TWO SONS,

THE FOLLOWING POEM,

RECOMMENDING PRIVATE TUITION IN PREFERENCE

TO AN EDUCATION AT SCHOOL,

IS INSCRIBED,

BY HIS AFFECTIONATE FRIEND,

WILLIAM COWPER.

Olney, Nov. 6, 1784.

TIROCINIUM.*

T is not from his form, in which we trace
    Strength joined with beauty, dignity
        with grace,
    That man, the master of this globe,
        derives
His right of empire over all that lives.
That form, indeed, the associate of a mind   5
Vast in its powers, ethereal in its kind,—
That form, the labour of Almighty skill,
Framed for the service of a free-born will,
Asserts precedence, and bespeaks control,
But borrows all its grandeur from the soul.   10
Hers is the state, the splendour, and the throne,
An intellectual kingdom, all her own.
For her, the Memory fills her ample page
With truths poured down from every distant age ;
For her, amasses an unbounded store,   15
The wisdom of great nations, now no more ;
Though laden, not encumbered with her spoil,
Laborious, yet unconscious of her toil,

* First published in the same volume with " The Task,"
1785. The date of the dedication, which is printed on the
preceding page, indicates the period of its completion. Its
composition was begun in 1782.

When copiously supplied, then most enlarged,
Still to be fed, and not to be surcharged.   20
For her the Fancy, roving unconfined,
The present Muse of every pensive mind,
Works magic wonders, adds a brighter hue
To Nature's scenes, than Nature ever knew.
At her command winds rise and waters roar,   25
Again she lays them slumbering on the shore ;
With flower and fruit the wilderness supplies,
Or bids the rocks in ruder pomp arise.
For her the Judgment, umpire in the strife
That Grace and Nature have to wage through life,
Quick-sighted arbiter of good and ill,   31
Appointed sage preceptor to the Will,
Condemns, approves, and with a faithful voice
Guides the decision of a doubtful choice.

Why did the fiat of a God give birth   35
To yon fair Sun and his attendant Earth ?
And when descending he resigns the skies,
Why takes the gentler Moon her turn to rise,
Whom Ocean feels through all his countless waves,
And owns her power on every shore he laves ?   40
Why do the seasons still enrich the year,
Fruitful and young as in their first career ?
Spring hangs her infant blossoms on the trees,
Rocked in the cradle of the western breeze ;
Summer in haste the thriving charge receives,   45
Beneath the shade of her expanded leaves,
Till Autumn's fiercer heats and plenteous dews
Dye them at last in all their glowing hues.—
'Twere wild profusion all, and bootless waste,
Power misemployed, munificence misplaced,   50
Had not its author dignified the plan,

And crowned it with the majesty of man.
Thus formed, thus placed, intelligent, and taught,
Look where he will, the wonders God has wrought,
The wildest scorner of his Maker's laws   55
Finds in a sober moment time to pause,
To press the important question on his heart,
" Why formed at all, and wherefore as thou art?"
If man be what he seems, this hour a slave,
The next mere dust and ashes in the grave ;   60
Endued with reason only to descry
His crimes and follies with an aching eye ;
With passions, just that he may prove, with pain,
The force he spends against their fury vain ;
And if, soon after having burned, by turns,   65
With every lust with which frail Nature burns,
His being end where death dissolves the bond,
The tomb take all, and all be blank beyond ;
Then he, of all that Nature has brought forth,
Stands self-impeached the creature of least worth,
And useless while he lives, and when he dies,   71
Brings into doubt the wisdom of the skies.
    Truths that the learned pursue with eager thought
Are not important always as dear-bought,
Proving at last, though told in pompous strains, 75
A childish waste of philosophic pains ;
But truths on which depends our main concern,
That 'tis our shame and misery not to learn,
Shine by the side of every path we tread,
With such a lustre he that runs may read.   80
'Tis true that, if to trifle life away
Down to the sunset of their latest day,
Then perish on futurity's wide shore
Like fleeting exhalations, found no more,

Were all that Heaven required of human kind, 85
And all the plan their destiny designed,
What none could reverence all might justly blame,
And man would breathe but for his Maker's shame.
But Reason heard, and Nature well perused,
At once the dreaming mind is disabused. 90
If all we find possessing earth, sea, air,
Reflect his attributes who placed them there,
Fulfil the purpose, and appear designed
Proofs of the wisdom of the all-seeing mind,
'Tis plain the creature whom He chose to invest 95
With kingship and dominion o'er the rest,
Received his nobler nature, and was made
Fit for the power in which he stands arrayed,
That first or last, hereafter if not here,
He too might make his author's wisdom clear, 100
Praise him on earth, or obstinately dumb,
Suffer his justice in a world to come.
This once believed, 'twere logic misapplied
To prove a consequence by none denied,
That we are bound to cast the minds of youth 105
Betimes into the mould of heavenly truth,
That taught of God they may indeed be wise,
Nor ignorantly wandering miss the skies.
    In early days the Conscience has in most
A quickness, which in later life is lost: 110
Preserved from guilt by salutary fears,
Or, guilty, soon relenting into tears.
Too careless often, as our years proceed,
What friends we sort with, or what books we read,
Our parents yet exert a prudent care 115
To feed our infant minds with proper fare,
And wisely store the nursery by degrees

With wholesome learning, yet acquired with ease.
Neatly secured from being soiled or torn
Beneath a pane of thin translucent horn,   120
A book (to please us at a tender age
'Tis called a book, though but a single page)
Presents the prayer the Saviour deigned to teach,
Which children use, and parsons—when they
    preach.
Lisping our syllables, we scramble next   125
Through moral narrative, or sacred text,
And learn with wonder how this world began,
Who made, who marred, and who has ransomed
    man;
Points, which, unless the Scripture made them plain,
The wisest heads might agitate in vain.   130
Oh thou,* whom, borne on Fancy's eager wing
Back to the season of life's happy spring,
I pleased remember, and, while memory yet
Holds fast her office here, can ne'er forget;
Ingenious dreamer, in whose well-told tale   135
Sweet fiction and sweet truth alike prevail;
Whose humorous vein, strong sense, and simple
    style,
May teach the gayest, make the gravest smile,
Witty, and well-employed, and, like thy Lord,
Speaking in parables his slighted word,   140
I name thee not, lest so despised a name
Should move a sneer at thy deserved fame,
Yet even in transitory life's late day,
That mingles all my brown with sober gray,
Revere the man whose PILGRIM marks the road,   145
And guides the PROGRESS of the soul to God.

        * John Bunyan.

'Twere well with most, if books that could engage
Their childhood, pleased them at a riper age;
The man approving what had charmed the boy,
Would die at last in comfort, peace, and joy,   150
And not with curses on his art who stole
The gem of truth from his unguarded soul.
The stamp of artless piety impressed
By kind tuition on his yielding breast,
The youth now bearded, and yet pert and raw,   155
Regards with scorn, though once received with awe,
And warped into the labyrinth of lies,
That babblers, called philosophers, devise,
Blasphemes his creed, as founded on a plan
Replete with dreams, unworthy of a man.   160
Touch but his nature in its ailing part,
Assert the native evil of his heart,
His pride resents the charge, although the proof*
· Rise in his forehead, and seem rank enough:
Point to the cure, describe a Saviour's cross   165
As God's expedient to retrieve his loss,
The young apostate sickens at the view,
And hates it with the malice of a Jew.
How weak the barrier of mere Nature proves,
Opposed against the pleasures Nature loves !   170
While self-betrayed, and wilfully undone,
She longs to yield, no sooner wooed than won.
Try now the merits of this blest exchange
Of modest truth for wit's eccentric range.
Time was he closed as he began the day,   175
With decent duty, not ashamed to pray;
The practice was a bond upon his heart,
A pledge he gave for a consistent part;

* See 2 Chron. xxvi. 19.

Nor could he dare presumptuously displease
A power, confessed so lately on his knees.   180
But now, farewell all legendary tales,
The shadows fly, philosophy prevails,
Prayer to the winds, and caution to the waves,
Religion makes the free by nature slaves,
Priests have invented, and the world admired,   185
What knavish priests promulgate as inspired,
Till Reason, now no longer overawed,
Resumes her powers, and spurns the clumsy fraud;
And common sense diffusing real day,
The meteor of the Gospel dies away.   190
Such rhapsodies our shrewd discerning youth
Learn from expert inquirers after truth;
Whose only care, might truth presume to speak,
Is not to find what they profess to seek.
And thus, well tutored only while we share   195
A mother's lecture and a nurse's care,
And taught at schools much mythologic stuff,*
But sound religion sparingly enough,
Our early notices of truth, disgraced,
Soon lose their credit, and are all effaced.   200
    Would you your son should be a sot or dunce,
Lascivious, headstrong, or all these at once;
That in good time, the stripling's finished taste
For loose expense and fashionable waste,
Should prove your ruin, and his own at last,   205

---

* The author begs leave to explain.—Sensible that, without such knowledge, neither the ancient poets nor historians
can be tasted, or indeed understood, he does not mean to
censure the pains that are taken to instruct a schoolboy in
the religion of the heathen, but merely that neglect of Christian culture which leaves him shamefully ignorant of his
own.—(C.)

Train him in public with a mob of boys,
Childish in mischief only and in noise,
Else of a mannish growth, and five in ten
In infidelity and lewdness, men.
There shall he learn, ere sixteen winters old,   210
That authors are most useful, pawned or sold;
That pedantry is all that schools impart,
But taverns teach the knowledge of the heart;
There waiter Dick, with Bacchanalian lays,
Shall win his heart, and have his drunken praise,
His counsellor and bosom-friend shall prove,   216
And some street-pacing harlot his first love.
Schools, unless discipline were doubly strong,
Detain their adolescent charge too long;
The management of tyros of eighteen   220
Is difficult, their punishment obscene.
The stout tall captain, whose superior size
The minor heroes view with envious eyes,
Becomes their pattern, upon whom they fix
Their whole attention, and ape all his tricks.   225
His pride, that scorns to obey or to submit,
With them is courage; his effrontery wit;
His wild excursions, window-breaking feats,
Robbery of gardens, quarrels in the streets,   229
His hairbreadth 'scapes, and all his daring schemes
Transport them, and are made their favourite
          themes;
In little bosoms such achievements strike
A kindred spark, they burn to do the like.
Thus, half accomplished ere he yet begin
To show the peeping down upon his chin,   235
And as maturity of years comes on,
Made just the adept that you designed your son,

To ensure the perseverance of his course,
And give your monstrous project all its force,
Send him to college.   If he there be tamed,   240
Or in one article of vice reclaimed,
Where no regard of ord'nances is shown,
Or looked for now, the fault must be his own.
Some sneaking virtue lurks in him, no doubt,
Where neither strumpets' charms, nor drinking bout,
Nor gambling practices, can find it out.   246
Such youths of spirit, and that spirit too,
Ye nurseries of our boys, we owe to you :
Though from ourselves the mischief more proceeds,
For public schools 'tis public folly feeds.   250
The slaves of custom and established mode,
With packhorse constancy we keep the road,
Crooked or straight, through quags or thorny dells,
True to the jingling of our leader's bells.
To follow foolish precedents, and wink   255
With both our eyes, is easier than to think,
And such an age as ours balks no expense,
Except of caution and of common sense ;
Else sure, notorious fact and proof so plain,
Would turn our steps into a wiser train.   260
I blame not those who, with what care they can,
O'erwatch the numerous and unruly clan,
Or if I blame, 'tis only that they dare
Promise a work of which they must despair.
Have ye, ye sage intendants of the whole,   265
An ubiquarian presence and control,
Elisha's eye, that when Gehazi strayed,
Went with him, and saw all the game he played ?
Yes—ye are conscious ; and on all the shelves
Your pupils strike upon, have struck yourselves. 270

Or if by nature sober, ye had then,
Boys as ye were, the gravity of men,
Ye knew at least, by constant proofs addressed
To ears and eyes, the vices of the rest.
But ye connive at what ye cannot cure,   275
And evils not to be endured, endure,
Lest power exerted, but* without success,
Should make the little ye retain still less.
Ye once were justly famed for bringing forth
Undoubted scholarship and genuine worth,   280
And in the firmament of fame still shines
A glory bright as that of all the signs,
Of poets raised by you, and statesmen, and divines.
Peace to them all ! those brilliant times are fled,
And no such lights are kindling in their stead. 285
Our striplings shine indeed, but with such rays
As set the midnight riot in a blaze,
And seem, if judged by their expressive looks,
Deeper in none than in their surgeons' books.
    Say, Muse, (for education made the song,   290
No Muse can hesitate or linger long)
What causes move us, knowing, as we must,
That these menageries all fail their trust,
To send our sons to scout and scamper there,
While colts and puppies cost us so much care ? 295
    Be it a weakness, it deserves some praise,
We love the play-place of our early days.
The scene is touching, and the heart is stone
That feels not at that sight, and feels at none.
The wall on which we tried our graving skill, 300

___

* An imperfect "b" in this word in the edition of 1785
was followed by "out" in Ed. 1786, but the mistake was
corrected in Ed. 1787, and has not been reproduced.

The very name we carved subsisting still,
The bench on which we sat while deep employed,
Though mangled, hacked, and hewed, not yet de-
   stroyed;
The little ones, unbuttoned, glowing hot,
Playing our games, and on the very spot,   305
As happy as we once, to kneel and draw
The chalky ring, and knuckle down at taw;
To pitch the ball into the grounded hat,
Or drive it devious with a dexterous pat;
The pleasing spectacle at once excites   310
Such recollection of our own delights,
That viewing it, we seem almost to obtain
Our innocent sweet simple years again.
This fond attachment to the well-known place,
Whence first we started into life's long race,   315
Maintains its hold with such unfailing sway,
We feel it even in age, and at our latest day.
Hark! how the sire of chits, whose future share
Of classic food begins to be his care,
With his own likeness placed on either knee,   320
Indulges all a father's heart-felt glee,
And tells them, as he strokes their silver locks,
That they must soon learn Latin, and to box;
Then turning, he regales his listening wife
With all the adventures of his early life,   325
His skill in coachmanship, or driving chaise,
In bilking tavern bills, and spouting plays;
What shifts he used, detected in a scrape,
How he was flogged, or had the luck to escape,
What sums he lost at play, and how he sold   330
Watch, seals, and all—till all his pranks are told.
Retracing thus his *frolics* ('tis a name

That palliates deeds of folly and of shame)
He gives the local bias all its sway,
Resolves that where he played his sons shall play,
And destines their bright genius to be shown   336
Just in the scene where he displayed his own.
The meek and bashful boy will soon be taught
To be as bold and forward as he ought,
The rude will scuffle through with ease enough,   340
Great schools suit best the sturdy and the rough.
Ah happy designation, prudent choice,
Tho event is sure, expect it, and rejoice !
Soon see your wish fulfilled in either child,
The pert made perter, and the tame made wild.   345
    The great, indeed, by titles, riches, birth,
Excused the incumbrance of more solid worth,
Are best disposed of where with most success
They may acquire that confident address,
Those habits of profuse and lewd expense,   350
That scorn of all delights but those of sense,
Which though in plain plebeians we condemn,
With so much reason all expect from them.
But families of less illustrious fame,
Whose chief distinction is their spotless name,   355
Whose heirs, their honours none, their income small,
Must shine by true desert, or not at all,
What dream they of, that, with so little care
They risk their hopes, their dearest treasure, there?
They dream of little Charles or William graced   360
With wig prolix, down-flowing to his waist,
They see the attentive crowds his talents draw,
They hear him speak—the oracle of law.
The father who designs his babe a priest,
Dreams him episcopally such at least,   365

And while the playful jockey scours the room
Briskly, astride upon the parlour broom,
In fancy sees him more superbly ride
In coach with purple lined, and mitres on its side.
Events improbable and strange as these,   370
Which only a parental eye foresees,
A public school shall bring to pass with ease.
But how? resides such virtue in that air,
As must create an appetite for prayer?
And will it breathe into him all the zeal   375
That candidates for such a prize should feel,
To take the lead and be the foremost still
In all true worth and literary skill?
" Ah blind to bright futurity, untaught
" The knowledge of the world, and dull of thought!
" Church-ladders are not always mounted best 381
" By learned clerks, and Latinists professed.
" The exalted prize demands an upward look,
" Not to be found by poring on a book.
" Small skill in Latin, and still less in Greek, 385
" Is more than adequate to all I seek.
" Let erudition grace him or not grace,
" I give the bauble but the second place,
" His wealth, fame, honours, all that I intend,
" Subsist and centre in one point—a friend.   390
" A friend, whate'er he studies or neglects,
" Shall give him consequence, heal all defects.
" His intercourse with peers, and sons of peers—
" There dawns the splendour of his future years,
" In that bright quarter his propitious skies 395
" Shall blush betimes, and there his glory rise.
" ' Your Lordship!' and ' Your Grace!' what school
      can teach

" A rhetoric equal to those parts of speech ?
" What need of Homer's verse, or Tully's prose,
" Sweet interjections ! if he learn but those ?   400
" Let reverend churls his ignorance rebuke,
" Who starve upon a dog's-ear'd Pentateuch,
" The parson knows enough who knows a Duke."
Egregious purpose ! worthily begun
In barbarous prostitution of your son ;   405
Pressed on his part by means that would disgrace
A scrivener's clerk, or footman out of place,
And ending, if at last its end be gained,
In sacrilege, in God's own house profaned.
It may succeed ; and if his sins should call   410
For more than common punishment, it shall.
The wretch shall rise, and be the thing on earth
Least qualified in honour, learning, worth,
To occupy a sacred, awful post,
In which the best and worthiest tremble most.   415
The royal letters are a thing of course,
A king, that would, might recommend his horse,
And Deans, no doubt, and Chapters, with one
       voice,
As bound in duty, would confirm the choice.
Behold your Bishop ! well he plays his part,   420
Christian in name, and infidel in heart,
Ghostly in office, earthly in his plan,
A slave at court, elsewhere a lady's man,
Dumb as a senator, and as a priest
A piece of mere church-furniture at best ;   425
To live estranged from God his total scope,
And his end sure, without one glimpse of hope.
But fair although and feasible it seem,
Depend not much upon your golden dream ;

For Providence, that seems concerned to exempt 430
The hallowed bench from absolute contempt,
In spite of all the wrigglers into place,
Still keeps a seat or two for worth and grace;
And therefore 'tis, that, though the sight be rare,
We sometimes see a Lowth or Bagot* there. 435
Besides, school-friendships are not always found,
Though fair in promise, permanent and sound;
The most disinterested and virtuous minds,
In early years connected, time unbinds;
New situations give a different cast 440
Of habit, inclination, temper, taste;
And he that seemed our counterpart at first,
Soon shows the strong similitude reversed.
Young heads are giddy, and young hearts are warm,
And make mistakes for manhood to reform. 445
Boys are, at best, but pretty buds unblown,
Whose scent and hues are rather guessed than
    known;
Each dreams that each is just what he appears,
But learns his error in maturer years,
When disposition, like a sail unfurled, 450
Shows all its rents and patches to the world.
If, therefore, even when honest in design,

* Bishop Lowth does not need a note. His biography of
William of Wykeham, and his work on the Sacred Poetry
of the Hebrews, have given him a prominent station in
literature, and will long keep his name in remembrance.
Bishop Bagot, besides being a Westminster man, a younger
brother of Cowper's friend, the Rev. Walter Bagot, and a
poet, all strong claims upon the affection of Cowper, adorned
the episcopal bench by his preaching and by great kindness
and amiability of temper and disposition. He was successively Bishop of Bristol, Norwich, and St. Asaph, and died in
1802. See Cowper's letter to Bagot, 15th Jan. 1786.

A boyish friendship may so soon decline,
'Twere wiser sure to inspire a little heart
With just abhorrence of so mean a part,   455
Than set your son to work at a vile trade
For wages so unlikely to be paid.
  Our public hives of puerile resort,
That are of chief and most approved report,
To such base hopes, in many a sordid soul,   460
Owe their repute in part, but not the whole.
A principle, whose proud pretensions pass
Unquestioned, though the jewel be but glass,
That with a world, not often over-nice,
Ranks as a virtue, and is yet a vice,   465
Or rather a gross compound, justly tried,
Of envy, hatred, jealousy, and pride,
Contributes most perhaps to enhance their fame,
And Emulation is its specious name.
Boys, once on fire with that contentious zeal,   470
Feel all the rage that female rivals feel,
The prize of beauty in a woman's eyes
Not brighter than in theirs the scholar's prize.
The spirit of that competition burns
With all varieties of ill by turns,   475
Each vainly magnifies his own success,
Resents his fellow's, wishes it were less,
Exults in his miscarriage if he fail,
Deems his reward too great if he prevail.
And labours to surpass him day and night,   480
Less for improvement than to tickle spite.
The spur is powerful, and I grant its force,
It pricks the genius forward in its course,
Allows short time for play, and none for sloth,
And felt alike by each, advances both,   485

But judge, where so much evil intervenes,
The end, though plausible, not worth the means.
Weigh, for a moment, classical desert
Against a heart depraved and temper hurt,
Hurt too perhaps for life, for early wrong   490
Done to the nobler part affects it long;
And you are staunch indeed in learning's cause
If you can crown a discipline that draws
Such mischiefs after it, with much applause.
    Connexion formed for interest, and endeared 495
By selfish views, thus censured and cashiered;
And Emulation, as engendering hate,
Doomed to a no less ignominious fate:
The props of such proud seminaries fall,
The Jachin and the Boaz* of them all.   500
Great schools rejected then, as those that swell
Beyond a size that can be managed well,
Shall royal institutions miss the bays,
And small academies win all the praise?
Force not my drift beyond its just intent,   505
I praise a school as Pope a government;
So take my judgment in his language dressed,
" Whate'er is best administered, is best."
Few boys are born with talents that excel,
But all are capable of living well;   510
Then ask not, whether limited or large?
But, watch they strictly, or neglect their charge?
If anxious only that their boys may learn,
While morals languish, a despised concern,
The great and small deserve one common blame, 515
Different in size, but in effect the same.
Much zeal in virtue's cause all teachers boast,

* 1 Kings, vii. 21.

Though motives of mere lucre sway the most;
Therefore in towns and cities they abound,
For there the game they seek is easiest found,   520
Though there, in spite of all that care can do,
Traps to catch youth are most abundant too.
If shrewd, and of a well-constructed brain,
Keen in pursuit, and vigorous to retain,
Your son come forth a prodigy of skill;   525
As wheresoever taught, so formed, he will,
The pedagogue, with self-complacent air,
Claims more than half the praise as his due share;
But if, with all his genius, he betray,
Not more intelligent than loose and gay,   530
Such vicious habits as disgrace his name,
Threaten his health, his fortune, and his fame,
Though want of due restraint alone have bred
The symptoms that you see with so much dread,
Unenvied there, he may sustain alone   535
The whole reproach, the fault was all his own.
    Oh! 'tis a sight to be with joy perused,
By all whom sentiment has not abused,
New-fangled sentiment, the boasted grace
Of those who never feel in the right place,   540
A sight surpassed by none that we can show,
Though Vestris on one leg still shine below,
A father blest with an ingenuous son,
Father, and friend, and tutor, all in one.
How!—turn again to tales long since forgot,   545
Æsop, and Phædrus, and the rest?—Why not?
He will not blush, that has a father's heart,
To take in childish plays a childish part,
But bends his sturdy back to any toy
That youth takes pleasure in, to please his boy;   550

Then why resign into a stranger's hand
A task as much within your own command,
That God and Nature, and your interest too,
Seem with one voice to delegate to you?
Why hire a lodging in a house unknown   555
For one whose tenderest thoughts all hover round
      your own?
This second weaning, needless as it is,
How does it lacerate both your heart and his!
The indented stick, that loses day by day
Notch after notch till all are smoothed away,   560
Bears witness, long ere his dismission come,
With what intense desire he wants his home.
But though the joys he hopes beneath your roof
Bid fair enough to answer in the proof,
Harmless, and safe, and natural, as they are,   565
A disappointment waits him even there:
Arrived, he feels an unexpected change,
He blushes, hangs his head, is shy, and strange,
No longer takes, as once, with fearless ease,
His favourite stand between his father's knees,   570
But seeks the corner of some distant seat,
And eyes the door, and watches a retreat,
And least familiar where he should be most,
Feels all his happiest privileges lost.
Alas, poor boy!—the natural effect   575
Of love by absence chilled into respect.
Say, what accomplishments, at school acquired,
Brings he to sweeten fruits so undesired?
Thou well deservest an alienated son,
Unless thy conscious heart acknowledge—none;   580
None that, in thy domestic snug recess,
He had not made his own with more address,

Though some, perhaps, that shock thy feeling mind,
And better never learned, or left behind.
Add too, that thus estranged, thou canst obtain 585
By no kind arts his confidence again ;
That here begins with most that long complaint
Of filial frankness lost, and love grown faint,
Which, oft neglected, in life's waning years
A parent pours into regardless ears. 590
    Like caterpillars dangling under trees
By slender threads, and swinging in the breeze,
Which filthily bewray and sore disgrace
The boughs in which are bred the unseemly race,
While every worm industriously weaves 595
And winds his web about the rivelled leaves ;
So numerous are the follies that annoy
The mind and heart of every sprightly boy ;
Imaginations noxious and perverse,
Which admonition can alone disperse. 600
The encroaching nuisance asks a faithful hand,
Patient, affectionate, of high command,
To check the procreation of a breed
Sure to exhaust the plant on which they feed.
'Tis not enough that Greek or Roman page, 605
At stated hours, his freakish thoughts engage ;
Even in his pastimes he requires a friend
To warn, and teach him safely to unbend,
O'er all his pleasures gently to preside,
Watch his emotions and control their tide, 610
And levying thus, and with an easy sway,
A tax of profit from his very play,
To impress a value, not to be erased,
On moments squandered else, and running all to
    waste.

And seems it nothing in a father's eye 615
That unimproved those many moments fly?
And is he well content his son should find
No nourishment to feed his growing mind,
But conjugated verbs, and nouns declined?
For such is all the mental food purveyed 620
By public hackneys in the schooling trade;
Who feed a pupil's intellect with store
Of syntax, truly, but with little more,
Dismiss their cares when they dismiss their flock,
Machines themselves, and governed by a clock. 625
Perhaps a father, blessed with any brains,
Would deem it no abuse, or waste of pains,
To improve this diet, at no great expense,
With savoury truth and wholesome common sense;
To lead his son, for prospects of delight, 630
To some not steep, though philosophic, height,
Thence to exhibit to his wondering eyes
Yon circling worlds, their distance, and their size,
The moon of Jove, and Saturn's belted ball,
And the harmonious order of them all; 635
To show him in an insect, or a flower,
Such microscopic proof* of skill and power,
As, hid from ages passed, God now displays
To combat atheists with in modern days;
To spread the earth before him and commend, 640
With designation of the finger's end,
Its various parts to his attentive note,
Thus bringing home to him the most remote;
To teach his heart to glow with generous flame,
Caught from the deeds of men of ancient fame; 645

*" Proofs;" Eds. 1785, 1786, 1787, and Southey. " Proof;"
Ed. 1788, and subsequent editions, except Southey's.

And, more than all, with commendation due,
To set some living worthy in his view,
Whose fair example may at once inspire
A wish to copy what he must admire.
Such knowledge, gained betimes, and which ap-
    pears,   650
Though solid, not too weighty for his years,
Sweet in itself, and not forbidding sport,
When health demands it, of athletic sort,
Would make him what some lovely boys have been,
And more than one perhaps that I have seen,   655
An evidence and reprehension both
Of the mere schoolboy's lean and tardy growth.
    Art thou a man professionally tied,
With all thy faculties elsewhere applied,
Too busy to intend a meaner care   660
Than how to enrich thyself, and next, thine heir;
Or art thou (as, though rich, perhaps thou art)
But poor in knowledge, having none to impart:—
Behold that figure, neat, though plainly clad,
His sprightly mingled with a shade of sad;   665
Not of a nimble tongue, though now and then
Heard to articulate like other men,
No jester, and yet lively in discourse,
His phrase well-chosen, clear, and full of force,
And his address, if not quite French in ease, 670
Not English stiff, but frank, and formed to please,
Low in the world, because he scorns its arts,
A man of letters, manners, morals, parts,
Unpatronized, and therefore little known,
Wise for himself and his few friends alone—   675
In him thy well-appointed proxy see,
Armed for a work too difficult for thee;

Prepared by taste, by learning, and true worth,
To form thy son, to strike his genius forth,
Beneath thy roof, beneath thine eye, to prove   680
The force of discipline when backed by love,
To double all thy pleasure in thy child,
His mind informed, his morals undefiled.
Safe under such a wing, the boy shall show
No spots contracted among grooms below,   685
Nor taint his speech with meannesses, designed
By footman Tom for witty and refined.
There, in his commerce with the liveried herd,
Lurks the contagion chiefly to be feared;
For since (so fashion dictates) all, who claim   690
A higher than a mere plebeian fame,
Find it expedient, come what mischief may,
To entertain a thief or two in pay,
And they that can afford the expense of more,
Some half a dozen, and some half a score,   695
Great cause occurs to save him from a band
So sure to spoil him, and so near at hand,
A point secured, if once he be supplied
With some such Mentor always at his side.
Are such men rare? perhaps they would abound
Were occupation easier to be found,   701
Were education, else so sure to fail,
Conducted on a manageable scale,
And schools, that have outlived all just esteem,
Exchanged for the secure domestic scheme.—   705
But having found him, be thou Duke or Earl,
Show thou hast sense enough to prize the pearl,
And as thou wouldst the advancement of thine heir
In all good faculties beneath his care,
Respect, as is but rational and just,   710

A man deemed worthy of so dear a trust.
Despised by thee, what more can he expect
From youthful folly, than the same neglect?
A flat and fatal negative obtains
That instant, upon all his future pains;　　715
His lessons tire, his mild rebukes offend,
And all the instructions of thy son's best friend
Are a stream choked, or trickling to no end.
Doom him not then to solitary meals,
But recollect that he has sense, and feels,　　720
And that, possessor of a soul refined,
An upright heart, and cultivated mind,
His post not mean, his talents not unknown,
He deems it hard to vegetate alone.
And if admitted at thy board he sit,　　725
Account him no just mark for idle wit,
Offend not him, whom modesty restrains
From repartee, with jokes that he disdains,
Much less transfix his feelings with an oath,
Nor frown, unless he vanish with the cloth.—　730
And trust me, his utility may reach
To more than he is hired or bound to teach,
Much trash unuttered, and some ills undone,
Through reverence of the censor of thy son.
　　But, if thy table be indeed unclean,　　735
Foul with excess, and with discourse obscene,
And thou a wretch, whom, following her old plan,
The world accounts an honourable man,
Because forsooth thy courage has been tried
And stood the test, perhaps on the wrong side;　740
Though thou hadst never grace enough to prove
That any thing but vice could win thy love;—
Or hast thou a polite, card-playing wife,

Chained to the routs that she frequents for life;
Who, just when industry begins to snore, 745
Flies, winged with joy, to some coach-crowded door;
And thrice in every winter throngs thine own
With half the chariots and sedans in town,
Thyself meanwhile e'en shifting as thou mayst,
Not very sober though, nor very chaste;— 750
Or is thine house, though less superb thy rank,
If not a scene of pleasure, a mere blank,
And thou at best, and in thy soberest mood,
A trifler vain, and empty of all good?
Though mercy for thyself thou canst have none,
Hear Nature plead, show mercy to thy son, 756
Saved from his home, where every day brings forth
Some mischief fatal to his future worth,
Find him a better in a distant spot,
Within some pious pastor's humble cot, 760
Where vile example (yours I chiefly mean,
The most seducing, and the oftenest seen)
May never more be stamped upon his breast,
Not yet perhaps incurably impressed.
Where early rest makes early rising sure, 765
Disease or comes not, or finds easy cure,
Prevented much by diet neat and plain;
Or if it enter, soon starved out again:
Where all the attention of his faithful host,
Discreetly limited to two at most, 770
May raise such fruits as shall reward his care,
And not at last evaporate in air:
Where, stillness aiding study, and his mind
Serene, and to his duties much inclined,
Not occupied in day-dreams, as at home, 775
Of pleasures past, or follies yet to come,

His virtuous toil may terminate at last
In settled habit and decided taste.—
But whom do I advise? the fashion-led,
The incorrigibly wrong, the deaf, the dead!   780
Whom care and cool deliberation suit
Not better much than spectacles a brute;
Who if their sons some slight tuition share,
Deem it of no great moment whose, or where;
Too proud to adopt the thoughts of one unknown,
And much too gay to have any of their own.   786
But courage, man! methought the Muse replied,
Mankind are various, and the world is wide:
The ostrich, silliest of the feathered kind,
And formed of God without a parent's mind,   790
Commits her eggs, incautious, to the dust,
Forgetful that the foot may crush the trust;
And while on public nurseries they rely,
Not knowing, and too oft not caring, why,
Irrational in what they thus prefer,   795
No few, that would seem wise, resemble her.
But all are not alike.   Thy warning voice
May here and there prevent erroneous choice;
And some perhaps, who, busy as they are,
Yet make their progeny their dearest care   800
(Whose hearts will ache, once told what ills may
        reach
Their offspring, left upon so wild a beach),
Will need no stress of argument to enforce
The expedience of a less adventurous course:
The rest will slight thy counsel, or condemn;   805
But *they* have human feelings—turn to *them*.
    To you, then, tenants of life's middle state,
Securely placed between the small and great,

Whose character, yet undebauched, retains
Two thirds of all the virtue that remains,　　810
Who wise yourselves, desire your sons should learn
Your wisdom and your ways—to you I turn.
Look round you on a world perversely blind;
See what contempt is fallen on humankind;
See wealth abused, and dignities misplaced,　　815
Great titles, offices, and trusts disgraced,
Long lines of ancestry, renowned of old,
Their noble qualities all quenched and cold;
See Bedlam's closeted and handcuffed charge
Surpassed in frenzy by the mad at large;　　820
See great commanders making war a trade,
Great lawyers, lawyers without study made:
Churchmen, in whose esteem their best employ
Is odious, and their wages all their joy,
Who far enough from furnishing their shelves　825
With Gospel lore, turn infidels themselves;
See womanhood despised, and manhood shamed
With infamy too nauseous to be named,
Fops at all corners, ladylike in mien,
Civeted fellows, smelt ere they are seen,　　830
Else coarse and rude in manners, and their tongue
On fire with curses, and with nonsense hung,
Now flushed with drunkenness, now with whore-
　　　　dom pale,
Their breath a sample of last night's regale;
See volunteers in all the vilest arts,　　835
Men well endowed, of honourable parts,
Designed by Nature wise, but self-made fools;
All these, and more like these, were bred at schools.
And if it chance, as sometimes chance it will,
That though school-bred the boy be virtuous still,

Such rare exceptions, shining in the dark,   841
Prove, rather than impeach, the just remark,
As here and there a twinkling star descried
Serves but to show how black is all beside.
Now look on him, whose very voice in tone   845
Just echoes thine, whose features are thine own,
And stroke his polished cheek of purest red,
And lay thine hand upon his flaxen head,
And say,—" My boy, the unwelcome hour is come,
" When thou, transplanted from thy genial home,
" Must find a colder soil and bleaker air,   851
" And trust for safety to a stranger's care.
" What character, what turn, thou wilt assume
" From constant converse with I know not whom ;
" Who there will court thy friendship, with what
            views,   855
" And, artless as thou art, whom thou wilt choose ;
" Though much depends on what thy choice shall be,
" Is all chance-medley, and unknown to me."—
Canst thou, the tear just trembling on thy lids,
And while the dreadful risk foreseen forbids ;   860
Free, too, and under no constraining force,
Unless the sway of custom warp thy course ;
Lay such a stake upon the losing side,
Merely to gratify so blind a guide ?
Thou canst not ! Nature, pulling at thine heart, 865
Condemns the unfatherly, the imprudent part.
Thou wouldst not, deaf to Nature's tenderest plea,
Turn him adrift upon a rolling sea,
Nor say,—" Go thither ;"—conscious that there lay
A brood of asps, or quicksands, in his way ;   870
Then, only governed by the self-same rule
Of natural pity, send him not to school.

No!—guard him better.   Is he not thine own,
Thyself in miniature, thy flesh, thy bone?
And hopest thou not ('tis every father's hope)   875
That since thy strength must with thy years elope,
And thou wilt need some comfort to assuage
Health's last farewell, a staff of thine old age,
That then, in recompense of all thy cares,
Thy child shall show respect to thy gray hairs,   880
Befriend thee, of all other friends bereft,
And give thy life its only cordial left?
Aware then how much danger intervenes,
To compass that good end, forecast the means.
His heart, now passive, yields to thy command;   885
Secure it thine, its key is in thine hand.
If thou desert thy charge, and throw it wide,
Nor heed what guests there enter and abide,
Complain not if attachments lewd and base
Supplant thee in it, and usurp thy place.   890
But if thou guard its sacred chambers sure
From vicious inmates and delights impure,
Either his gratitude shall hold him fast,
And keep him warm and filial to the last;
Or if he prove unkind (as who can say,   895
But being man, and therefore frail, he may)
One comfort yet shall cheer thine aged heart;—
Howe'er he slight thee, thou hast done thy part.
" Oh, barbarous! wouldst thou with a Gothic hand
Pull down the schools—what!—all the schools
        i' th' land;   900
Or throw them up to livery-nags and grooms,
Or turn them into shops and auction rooms?"
A captious question, sir, and yours is one,
Deserves an answer similar, or none.

Wouldst thou, possessor of a flock, employ   905
(Apprised that he is such) a careless boy,
And feed him well, and give him handsome pay,
Merely to sleep, and let them run astray?
Survey our schools and colleges, and see
A sight not much unlike my simile.   910
From education, as the leading cause,
The public character its colour draws;
Thence the prevailing manners take their cast,
Extravagant or sober, loose or chaste.
And, though I would not advertise them yet,   915
Nor write on each—" This building to be let,"
Unless the world were all prepared to embrace
A plan well worthy to supply their place;
Yet, backward as they are, and long have been,
To cultivate and keep the MORALS clean   920
(Forgive the crime), I wish them, I confess,
Or better managed, or encouraged less.

TO THE REVEREND MR. NEWTON.

AN INVITATION INTO THE COUNTRY.*

THE swallows in their torpid state
    Compose their useless wing,
And bees in hives as idly wait
    The call of early Spring.

The keenest frost that binds the stream,   5
    The wildest wind that blows,
Are neither felt nor feared by them,
    Secure of their repose.

But man, all feeling and awake,
    The gloomy scene surveys,   10
With present ills his heart must ache,
    And pant for brighter days.

Old Winter, halting o'er the mead,
    Bids me and Mary mourn;
But lovely Spring peeps o'er his head,   15
    And whispers your return.

Then April, with her sister May,
    Shall chase him from the bowers,

* Poems, Ed. 1782, p. 351.

And weave fresh garlands every day,
To crown the smiling hours. 20

And if a tear, that speaks regret
Of happier times, appear,
A glimpse of joy, that we have met,
Shall shine and dry the tear.

CATHARINA.

ADDRESSED TO MISS STAPLETON.*

HE came—she is gone—we have met—
And meet perhaps never again ;
The sun of that moment is set,
And seems to have risen in vain.
Catharina has fled like a dream— 5
(So vanishes Pleasure, alas !)
But has left a regret and esteem
That will not so suddenly pass.

The last evening-ramble we made,
Catharina, Maria, and I, 10
Our progress was often delayed
By the nightingale warbling nigh.

* Written probably in 1790; see Letter to Mrs. King,
dated 31st. Dec. in that year. The lines were printed in
the Poems, Ed. 1794, vol. II. p. 352. The "Catharina"
alluded to was the lady mentioned in our Memoir of the
Poet, vol. I. p. clii. "Now Mrs. Courtenay" was added to
the title in Ed. 1803. A poem written by Cowper on her
marriage, will be found in our third volume.

We paused under many a tree,
　　And much she was charmed with a tone,
Less sweet to Maria and me,　　　　　　　　15
　　Who so lately had witnessed her own.*

My numbers that day she had sung,
　　And gave them a grace so divine,
As only her musical tongue
　　Could infuse into numbers of mine.　　20
The longer I heard, I esteemed
　　The work of my Fancy the more,
And e'en to myself never seemed
　　So tuneful a poet before.

Though the pleasures of London exceed　25
　　In number the days of the year,
Catharina, did nothing impede,
　　Would feel herself happier here ;
For the close-woven arches of limes
　　On the banks of our river, I know,　　30
Are sweeter to her many times
　　Than aught† that the city can show.

So it is, when the mind is endued
　　With a well-judging taste from above,
Then, whether embellished or rude,　　　35
　　'Tis Nature alone that we love.

---

* This stands in Eds. 1794, 1798, 1799, 1800, 1803, 1805,
1806(2), "Who had witness'd so lately her own."　The
transposition now adopted is found in Eds. 1808, 1810, 1812,
1817, and all subsequent editions.

† " All ;" in the Eds. enumerated in the last note from
1794 to 1806. " Aught " was introduced in 1808, and has
been followed from that time.

The achievements of Art may amuse,
　　May even our wonder excite,
But groves, hills, and valleys diffuse
　　A lasting, a sacred delight.　　　　　40

Since then in the rural recess
　　Catharina alone can rejoice,
May it still be her lot to possess
　　The scene of her sensible choice!
To inhabit a mansion remote　　　　　45
　　From the clatter of street-pacing steeds,
And by Philomel's annual note
　　To measure the life that she leads.

With her book, and her voice, and her lyre,
　　To wing all her moments at home ;　　50
And with scenes that new rapture inspire,
　　As oft as it suits her to roam;
She will have just the life she prefers,
　　With little to hope or to fear,
And ours would be pleasant as hers,　　55
　　Might we view her enjoying it here.

THE MORALIZER CORRECTED.*

A TALE.

HERMIT (or if 'chance you hold
That title now too trite and old),
A man once young, who lived retired
As hermit could have well desired,
His hours of study closed at last,   5
And finished his concise repast,
Stoppled his cruise, replaced his book
Within its customary nook,
And, staff in hand, set forth to share
The sober cordial of sweet air,   10
Like Isaac,† with a mind applied
To serious thought at evening-tide.
Autumnal rains had made it chill,
And from the trees that fringed his hill,
Shades slanting at the close of day   15
Chilled more his else delightful way.
Distant a little mile he spied
A western bank's still sunny side,
And right toward the favoured place
Proceeding with his nimblest pace,   20
In hope to bask a little yet,
Just reached it when the sun was set.
   Your hermit, young and jovial sirs!
Learns something from whate'er occurs—

* Poems, Ed. 1794, vol. II. p. 355.
† Gen. xxiv. 63.

And " Hence," he said, " my mind computes 25
The real worth of man's pursuits.
His object chosen, wealth or fame,
Or other sublunary game,
Imagination to his view
Presents it decked with every hue 30
That can seduce him not to spare
His powers of best exertion there,
But youth, health, vigour to expend
On so desirable an end.
Ere long approach life's evening shades, 35
The glow that Fancy gave it fades;
And, earned too late, it wants the grace
That first engaged him in the chase."
    " True," answered an angelic guide,
Attendant at the senior's side— 40
" But whether all the time it cost,
To urge the fruitless chase be lost,
Must be decided by the worth
Of that which called his ardour forth.
Trifles pursued, whate'er the event, 45
Must cause him shame or discontent;
A vicious object still is worse,
Successful there, he wins a curse;
But he, whom e'en in life's last stage
Endeavours laudable engage, 50
Is paid at least in peace of mind,
And sense of having well designed;
And if, ere he attain his end,
His sun precipitate descend,
A brighter prize than that he meant 55
Shall recompense his mere intent.
No virtuous wish can bear a date
Either too early or too late."

THE FAITHFUL BIRD.*

HE greenhouse is my summer seat ;
My shrubs displaced from that retreat
 Enjoyed the open air ;
Two goldfinches, whose sprightly song
Had been their mutual solace long, 5
 Lived happy prisoners there.

They sang, as blithe as finches sing
That flutter loose on golden wing,
 And frolic where they list ;
Strangers to liberty, 'tis true, 10
But that delight they never knew,
 And therefore never missed.

But Nature works in every breast,
With force not easily suppressed ;†
 And Dick felt some desires, 15
That, after many an effort vain,
Instructed him at length to gain
 A pass between his wires.

The open windows seemed to invite
The freeman to a farewell flight ; 20

---

* Poems, Ed. 1794, vol. II. p. 359.
† All the Editions from 1794 to 1806 read " Instinct is
never quite suppress'd." The alteration appears in the Eds.
1808, 1810, 1812, 1817, and has been universally adopted.
In the 16th line, " which" was altered to " that," at the
same time.

But Tom was still confined;
And Dick, although his way was clear,
Was much too generous and sincere
    To leave his friend behind.

So settling on his cage, by play,   25
And chirp, and kiss, he seemed to say,
    You must not live alone—
Nor would he quit that chosen stand
Till I, with slow and cautious hand,
    Returned him to his own.*   30

O ye, who never taste† the joys
Of Friendship, satisfied with noise,
    Fandango, ball, and rout!
Blush when I tell you how a bird
A prison with a friend preferred   35
    To Liberty without.

---

* This stanza originally stood thus:—

> For, settling on his grated roof,
> He chirp'd and kiss'd him, giving proof
>   That he desired no more;
> Nor would forsake his cage at last,
> Till gently seiz'd, I shut him fast,
>   A prisoner as before.

The change is found in Ed. 1808.

† Originally " knew," altered in Ed. 1808.

THE NEEDLESS ALARM.*

A TALE.

HERE is a field, through which I often
pass,
Thick overspread with moss and silky
grass,
Adjoining close to Kilwick's echoing wood,
Where oft the bitch-fox hides her hapless brood,
Reserved to solace many a neighbouring squire, 5
That he may follow them through brake and brier,
Contusion hazarding of neck or spine,
Which rural gentlemen call sport divine.
A narrow brook, by rushy banks concealed,
Runs in a bottom, and divides the field; 10
Oaks intersperse it, that had once a head,
But now wear crests of oven-wood instead;
And where the land slopes to its watery bourn
Wide yawns a gulf beside a ragged thorn;
Bricks line the sides, but shivered long ago, 15
And horrid brambles intertwine below;
A hollow scooped, I judge, in ancient time,
For baking earth, or burning rock to lime.
 Not yet the hawthorn bore her berries red,
With which the fieldfare, wintry guest, is fed; 20
Nor Autumn yet had brushed from every spray,
With her chill hand, the mellow leaves away;

* Poems, Ed. 1794, vol. II. p. 365.

But corn was housed, and beans were in the stack,
Now therefore issued forth the spotted pack,
With tails high mounted, ears hung low, and throats
With a whole gamut filled of heavenly notes,   26
For which, alas! my destiny severe,
Though ears she gave me two, gave me no ear.
    The sun accomplishing his early march,
His lamp now planted on Heaven's topmost arch,
When, exercise and air my only aim,   31
And heedless whither, to that field I came,
Ere yet with ruthless joy the happy hound
Told hill and dale that Reynard's track was found,
Or with the high-raised horn's melodious clang 35
All Kilwick* and all Dinglederry* rang.
    Sheep grazed the field; some with soft bosom
        pressed
The herb as soft, while nibbling strayed the rest;
Nor noise was heard but of the hasty brook,
Struggling, detained in many a petty nook.   40
All seemed so peaceful, that from them conveyed,
To me their peace by kind contagion spread.
    But when the huntsman, with distended cheek,
'Gan make his instrument of music speak,
And from within the wood that crash was heard, 45
Though not a hound from whom it burst appeared,
The sheep recumbent, and the sheep that grazed,
All huddling into phalanx, stood and gazed,
Admiring, terrified, the novel strain,
Then coursed the field around, and coursed it round
        again;   50
But recollecting, with a sudden thought,
That flight in circles urged advanced them nought,

* Two woods belonging to John Throckmorton, Esq.—(C.)

They gathered close around the old pit's brink,
And thought again—but knew not what to think.
   The man to solitude accustomed long,   55
Perceives in every thing that lives a tongue;
Not animals alone, but shrubs and trees
Have speech for him, and understood with ease;
After long drought, when rains abundant fall,
He hears the herbs and flowers rejoicing all;   60
Knows what the freshness of their hue implies,
How glad they catch the largess* of the skies;
But, with precision nicer still, the mind
He scans of every locomotive kind;
Birds of all feather, beasts of every name,   65
That serve mankind, or shun them, wild or tame;
The looks and gestures of their griefs and fears
Have all articulation in his ears;
He spells them true by intuition's light,
And needs no glossary to set him right.   70
   This truth premised was needful as a text,
To win due credence to what follows next.
   Awhile they mused; surveying every face,
Thou hadst supposed them of superior race;
Their periwigs of wool and fears combined,   75
Stamped on each countenance such marks of mind,
That sage they seemed, as lawyers o'er a doubt,
Which, puzzling long, at last they puzzle out;
Or academic tutors, teaching youths,
Sure ne'er to want them, mathematic truths;   80
When thus a mutton statelier than the rest,
A ram, the ewes and wethers, sad, addressed.
   "Friends! we have lived too long. I never heard

* Ed. 1794 has "largeness." The mistake stands corrected
in Ed. 1798, vol. II. p. 235.

Sounds such as these, so worthy to be feared.
Could I believe, that winds for ages pent   85
In earth's dark womb have found at last a vent,
And from their prison-house below arise,
With all these hideous howlings to the skies,
I could be much composed, nor should appear,
For such a cause, to feel the slightest fear.   90
Yourselves have seen, what time the thunders rolled
All night, me resting quiet in the fold.
Or heard we that tremendous bray alone,
I could expound the melancholy tone;
Should deem it by our old companion made,   95
The ass; for he, we know, has lately strayed,
And being lost, perhaps, and wandering wide,
Might be supposed to clamour for a guide.
But ah! those dreadful yells what soul can hear,
That owns a carcass, and not quake for fear?   100
Demons produce them doubtless, brazen-clawed,
And fanged with brass the demons are abroad;
I hold it therefore wisest and most fit
That, life to save, we leap into the pit."
    Him answered then his loving mate and true,   105
But more discreet than he, a Cambrian ewe.
    " How! leap into the pit our life to save!
To save our life leap all into the grave!
For can we find it less? Contemplate first
The depth, how awful! falling there, we burst: 110
Or should the brambles, interposed, our fall
In part abate, that happiness were small;
For with a race like theirs no chance I see
Of peace or ease to creatures clad as we.
Meantime, noise kills not. Be it Dapple's bray, 115
Or be it not, or be it whose it may,

And rush those other sounds, that seem by tongues
Of demons uttered, from whatever lungs,
Sounds are but sounds, and till the cause appear,
We have at least commodious standing here.   120
Come fiend, come fury, giant, monster, blast
From earth or hell, we can but plunge at last."
   While thus she spake, I fainter heard the peals,
For Reynard, close attended at his heels
By panting dog, tired man, and spattered horse, 125
Through mere good fortune, took a diffcrent course.
The flock grew calm again, and I, the road
Following, that led me to my own abode,
Much wondered that the silly sheep had found
Such cause of terror in an empty sound   130
So sweet to huntsman, gentleman, and hound.

MORAL.

Beware of desperate steps.   The darkest day,
Live till to-morrow, will have passed away.

BOADICEA.*

AN ODE.

WHEN the British warrior queen,
    Bleeding from the Roman rods,
Sought, with an indignant mien,
    Counsel of her country's gods,

* Poems, Ed. 1782, p. 354.

Sage beneath the spreading oak   5
  Sat the Druid, hoary chief;
Every burning word he spoke,
  Full of rage and full of grief.

" Princess! if our aged eyes
  Weep upon thy matchless wrongs,   10
'Tis because resentment ties
  All the terrors of our tongues.

" Rome shall perish—write that word
  In the blood that she has spilt;
Perish, hopeless and abhorred,   15
  Deep in ruin as in guilt.

" Rome, for empire far renowned,
  Tramples on a thousand states;
Soon her pride shall kiss the ground—
  Hark! the Gaul is at her gates!   20

" Other Romans shall arise,
  Heedless of a soldier's name;
Sounds, not arms, shall win the prize,
  Harmony the path to fame.

" Then the progeny that springs   25
  From the forests of our land,
Armed with thunder, clad with wings,
  Shall a wider world command.

" Regions Cæsar never knew,
  Thy posterity shall sway;   30
Where his eagles never flew,
  None invincible as they."

Such the Bard's prophetic words,
    Pregnant with celestial fire,
Bending as he swept the chords   35
    Of his sweet but awful lyre.

She, with all a monarch's pride,
    Felt them in her bosom glow:
Rushed to battle, fought, and died;
    Dying, hurled them at the foe.   40

" Ruffians, pitiless as proud,
    Heaven awards the vengeance due;
Empire is on us bestowed,
    Shame and ruin wait for you!"

HEROISM.*

HERE was a time when Ætna's silent
          fire
    Slept unperceived, the mountain yet
          entire;
When, conscious of no danger from below,
She towered a cloud-capped pyramid of snow.
No thunders shook with deep intestine sound   5
The blooming groves that girdled her around,
Her unctuous olives, and her purple vines,.

* Poems, Ed. 1782, p. 357.   See Cowper's observations
upon a presumed geological inaccuracy in this poem, in his
letter to Newton, of 17th Dec., 1781. The lines seem to
have originally gone under the titles of the " Burning Mountain" and " Ætna."

(Unfelt the fury of those bursting mines)
The peasant's hopes, and not in vain, assured,
In peace upon her sloping sides matured.   10
When on a day, like that of the last doom,
A conflagration labouring in her womb,
She teemed and heaved with an infernal birth,
That shook the circling seas and solid earth.
Dark and voluminous the vapours rise,   15
And hang their horrors in the neighbouring skies,
While through the Stygian veil that blots the day,
In dazzling streaks the vivid lightnings play.
But oh! what Muse, and in what powers of song,
Can trace the torrent as it burns along?   20
Havoc and devastation in the van,
It marches o'er the prostrate works of man—
Vines, olives, herbage, forests disappear,
And all the charms of a Sicilian year.

  Revolving seasons, fruitless as they pass,   25
See it an uninformed and idle mass;
Without a soil to invite the tiller's care,
Or blade that might redeem it from Despair.
Yet Time at length (what will not Time achieve?)
Clothes it with earth, and bids the produce live. 30
Once more the spiry myrtle crowns the glade,
And ruminating flocks enjoy the shade.
O bliss precarious, and unsafe retreats!
O charming Paradise of shortlived sweets!
The self-same gale that wafts the fragrance round,
Brings to the distant ear a sullen sound: 36
Again the mountain feels the imprisoned foe,
Again pours ruin on the vale below,
Ten thousand swains the wasted scene deplore,
That only future ages can restore.   40

Ye monarchs, whom the lure of honour draws,
Who write in blood the merits of your cause,
Who strike the blow, then plead your own defence,
Glory your aim, but Justice your pretence;
Behold in Ætna's emblematic fires   45
The mischiefs your ambitious Pride inspires!

Fast by the stream that bounds your just domain,
And tells you where ye have a right to reign,
A nation dwells, not envious of your throne,
Studious of peace, their neighbours' and their own.
Ill fated race! how deeply must they rue   51
Their only crime, vicinity to you!
The trumpet sounds, your legions swarm abroad,
Through the ripe harvest lies their destined road;
At every step beneath their feet they tread   55
The life of multitudes, a nation's bread!
Earth seems a garden in its loveliest dress
Before them, and behind a wilderness;
Famine, and Pestilence, her firstborn son,
Attend to finish what the sword begun;   60
And echoing praises, such as fiends might earn,
And Folly pays, resound at your return.
A calm succeeds—but Plenty, with her train
Of heartfelt joys, succeeds not soon again;
And years of pining indigence must show   65
What scourges are the gods that rule below.

Yet man, laborious man, by slow degrees,
(Such is his thirst of opulence and ease)
Plies all the sinews of industrious toil,
Gleans up the refuse of the general spoil,   70
Rebuilds the towers that smoked upon the plain,
And the sun gilds the shining spires again.
Increasing commerce and reviving art

Renew the quarrel on the conqueror's part;
And the sad lesson must be learned once more, 75
That wealth within is ruin at the door.
What are ye, monarchs, laurelled heroes, say,
But Ætnas of the suffering world ye sway?
Sweet Nature, stripped of her embroidered robe,
Deplores the wasted regions of her globe,   80
And stands a witness at Truth's awful bar,
To prove you there destroyers, as ye are.
   O place me in some Heaven-protected isle,
Where Peace, and Equity, and Freedom smile;
Where no volcano pours his fiery flood,   85
No crested warrior dips his plume in blood;
Where Power secures what Industry has won;
Where to succeed is not to be undone;
A land that distant tyrants hate in vain,
In Britain's isle, beneath a George's reign!   90

ON

THE RECEIPT OF MY MOTHER'S PICTURE

OUT OF NORFOLK,

THE GIFT OF MY COUSIN, ANN BODHAM.*

H that those lips had language! Life
     has passed
With me but roughly since I heard thee
     last.

---

* The gift which called forth these lines was acknowledged
with great delight by Cowper, in a letter to Mrs. Bodham,

Those lips are thine—thy own sweet smile* I see,
The same that oft in childhood solaced me ;
Voice only fails, else how distinct they say,   5
" Grieve not, my child, chase all thy fears away !"
The meek intelligence of those dear eyes
(Blest be the Art that can immortalize,—
The Art that baffles Time's tyrannic claim
To quench it) here shines on me still the same. 10
   Faithful remembrancer of one so dear,
O welcome guest, though unexpected, here !
Who bidst me honour with an artless song,
Affectionate, a mother lost so long.
I will obey, not willingly alone,   15
But gladly, as the precept were her own :
And while that face renews my filial grief,
Fancy shall weave a charm for my relief,—
Shall steep me in Elysian reverie,
A momentary dream, that thou art she.   20
   My mother ! when I learned that thou wast dead,
Say, wast thou conscious of the tears I shed ?
Hovered thy spirit o'er thy sorrowing son,
Wretch even then, life's journey just begun ?
Perhaps thou gavest me, though unfelt,† a kiss ; 25
Perhaps a tear, if souls can weep in bliss—

dated the 27th Feb., 1790. The lines were printed in 1798, in two separate forms; one in 8vo. intended to range with the previous editions of the author's poems. and entitled, " Poems. I. On the Receipt of my Mother's Picture ; II. The Dog and the Water Lily. By William Cowper, of the Inner Temple, Esq." (London, J. Johnson, 1798, pp. 14) ; the other in a new edition of the Poems, 12mo. 1798, vol. I. p. 244.
   * " Smiles;" Ed. 1798, and subsequent editions down to 1806. In Ed. 1808 it was altered to " smile," which has been followed by all subsequent editors.
   † " Unseen;" in Eds. 1798 to 1806, altered in Ed. 1808.

Ah, that maternal smile! it answers—" Yes."
I heard the bell tolled on thy burial day,
I saw the hearse that bore thee slow away,
And, turning from my nursery window, drew   30
A long, long sigh, and wept a last adieu!
But was it such?—It was.—Where thou art gone
Adieus and farewells are a sound unknown;
May I but meet thee on that peaceful shore,
The parting word* shall pass my lips no more! 35
Thy maidens grieved themselves at my concern,
Oft gave me promise of thy† quick return.
What ardently I wished, I long believed,
And, disappointed still, was still deceived;
By expectation‡ every day beguiled,   40
Dupe of to-morrow even from a child.
Thus many a sad to-morrow came and went,
Till, all my stock of infant sorrow§ spent,
I learned at last submission to my lot,
But, though I less deplored thee, ne'er forgot. 45
     Where once we dwelt our name is heard no more,
Children not thine have trod my nursery floor;
And where the gardener Robin, day by day,
Drew me to school along the public way,
Delighted with my bauble coach, and wrapped 50
In scarlet mantle warm, and velvet capped,‖
'Tis now become a history little known,

* " Sound;" in Eds. 1798 to 1806, altered in Ed. 1808.
† " A;" the like.
‡ " Disappointment;" the like.
§ " Sorrow;" all Eds., except those of 1799, Southey,
Grimshawe, Dale, and Bell, which have " sorrows."
‖ Printed "cap" in 12mo. Ed. 1798, and "capt" in 8vo.
Ed. 1798, the last word of the preceding line being then
spelled in both editions "wrapt." " Capt" was continued
down to 1808, when "cap" was again adopted and continued

That once we called the pastoral house* our own.
Shortlived possession! but the record fair,
That memory keeps of all thy kindness there,   55
Still outlives many a storm that has effaced
A thousand other themes less deeply traced.
Thy nightly visits to my chamber made,
That thou mightest know me safe and warmly laid;
Thy morning bounties ere I left my home,   60
The biscuit, or confectionary plum;
The fragrant waters on my cheeks bestowed
By thy own hand, till fresh they shone and glowed:
All this, and more endearing still than all,
Thy constant flow of love, that knew no fall,   65
Ne'er roughened by those cataracts and breaks,
That humour interposed too often makes;
All this still legible in Memory's page,
- And still to be so to my latest age,
Adds joy to duty, makes me glad to pay   70
Such honours to thee as my numbers may;
Perhaps a frail memorial, but sincere,
Not scorned in Heaven, though little noticed here.
    Could Time, his flight reversed, restore the hours
When, playing with thy vesture's tissued flowers,
The violet, the pink, and jessamine,   76
I pricked them into paper with a pin,
(And thou wast happier than myself the while,
Wouldst softly speak, and stroke my head and smile),
Could those few pleasant days† again appear,   80
Might one wish bring them, would I wish them here?

in all Eds. down to 1825, and also by Grimshawe and Dale.
Southey having "wrapt" has "capt;" Bell having "wrapped"
has " capped."
    * Of Berkhamstead.
    † " Hours;" Eds. 1798 to 1806, altered in 1808.

I would not trust my heart—the dear delight
Seems so to be desired, perhaps I might.—
But no—what here we call our life is such,
So little to be loved, and thou so much,   85
That I should ill requite thee, to constrain
Thy unbound spirit into bonds again.

    Thou, as a gallant bark from Albion's coast
(The storms all weathered and the ocean crossed)
Shoots into port at some well-havened isle,   90
Where spices breathe, and brighter seasons smile.
There sits quiescent on the floods that show
Her beauteous form reflected clear below,
While airs impregnated with incense play
Around her, fanning light her streamers gay;— 95
So thou, with sails how swift! hast reached the
     shore,
" Where tempests never beat nor billows roar;"*
And thy loved consort on the dangerous tide
Of life, long since has anchored by† thy side.
But me, scarce hoping to attain that rest,   100
Always from port withheld, always distressed—
Me howling blasts‡ drive devious, tempest-tossed,
Sails ripped, seams opening wide, and compass lost,
And day by day some current's thwarting force
Sets me more distant from a prosperous course. 105
Yet§ oh the thought, that thou art safe, and he !
That thought is joy, arrive what may to me.
My boast is not that I deduce my birth

  * Garth (C.). But Garth's line (which is in the third
canto of the " Dispensary ") runs thus :—
     " Where billows never break nor tempests roar."
  † " At;" Eds. 1798 to 1806, altered in 1808.
  ‡ " Winds;" the like.
  § "But;" the like. Grimshawe alone, since 1808, has "but."

From loins enthroned, and rulers of the earth;
But higher far my proud pretensions rise—   110
The son of parents passed into the skies.
And now, Farewell.—Time unrevoked has run
His wonted course, yet what I wished is done.
By Contemplation's help, not sought in vain,
I seem to have lived my childhood o'er again;   115
To have renewed the joys that once were mine,
Without the sin of violating thine;
And while the wings of Fancy still are free,
And I can view this mimic show of thee,
Time has but half succeeded in his theft—   120
Thyself removed, thy power to soothe me left.

FRIENDSHIP.*

HAT Virtue, or what mental grace,
    But men unqualified and base
        Will boast it their possession?
    Profusion apes the noble part
Of Liberality of heart,   5
    And Dullness of Discretion.

* There are three versions of this poem, all differing in ways which curiously exemplify the results of the " poetic pains" which Cowper has celebrated in the Task.   The lines were written in November, 1782, (see Letter to Unwin of 30th November in that year,) but not printed until 1801, when Mr. Bull added them to the " Poems translated from the French of Madame de la Mothe Guion," published in a 12mo. volume at Newport Pagnel, (p. 104). In 1803 (i. 211) Hayley printed another version, and added the various readings between his copy and that of Mr. Bull in foot-notes.   Dr. John Johnson reprinted Hayley's copy in his volume of posthumous poetry published in 1815, but without the

If every polished gem we find
Illuminating heart or mind,
　　Provoke to imitation ;

---

various readings, and both Hayley's copy and Bull's have
been published in many editions since 1815, and occasionally
printed in different volumes of the same work, without any
indication of their connection.　Among the Unwin Papers,
now in the British Museum, there is a third version, a manuscript in the handwriting of the poet, (Addl. MS. No. 24,155,
fol. 143).　The differences are so considerable that it is
impossible to indicate them in notes only.　We have therefore printed Bull's version in the text, with notes of the
variations between it and the Unwin MS., and have given
Hayley's copy entire at the foot of the page.

ON FRIENDSHIP.

Amicitia nisi inter bonos esse non potest.—CICERO [LÆLIUS, sec. v.]

[1782.]

WHAT virtue can we name, or grace,
But men unqualified and base
　　Will boast it their possession ?
Profusion apes the noble part
Of Liberality of heart,　　　　　　　　　　　　5
　　And Dulness of Discretion.

But, as the gem of richest cost
Is ever counterfeited most,
　　So, always, Imitation
Employs the utmost skill she can　　　　　　　10
To counterfeit the faithful man,
　　The friend of long duration.

Some will pronounce me too severe—
But long experience speaks me clear ;
　　Therefore, that censure scorning,　　　　　15
I will proceed to mark the shelves,
On which so many dash themselves,
　　And give the simple warning.

Youth, unadmonished by a guide,
Will trust to any fair outside ;　　　　　　　20
　　An error soon corrected ;

No wonder Friendship does the same, 10
That jewel of the purest flame,
  Or rather constellation.

For who but learns with riper years
That man, when smoothest he appears,
  Is most to be suspected?
But here again a danger lies; 25
Lest, thus deluded by our eyes,
  And taking trash for treasure,
We should, when undeceived, conclude
Friendship, imaginary good,
  A mere Utopian pleasure. 30

An acquisition, rather rare,
Is yet no subject of despair;
  Nor should it seem distressful,
If either on forbidden ground,
Or where it was not to be found, 35
  We sought it unsuccessful.

No Friendship will abide the test
That stands on sordid interest
  And mean self-love erected;
Nor such as may awhile subsist 40
'Twixt sensualist and sensualist,
  For vicious ends connected.

Who hopes a friend, should have a heart
Himself well furnished for the part,
  And ready on occasion 45
To show the virtue that he seeks;
For 'tis an union that bespeaks
  A just reciprocation.

A fretful temper will divide
The closest knot that may be tied, 50
  By ceaseless sharp corrosion:
A temper passionate and fierce
May suddenly your joys disperse,
  At one immense explosion.

In vain the talkative unite 55
With hope of permanent delight:
  The secret just committed

No knave but boldly will pretend
The requisites that form a friend,
  A real and a sound one ;—   *15*

They drop through mere desire to prate,
Forgetting its important weight,
  And by themselves outwitted.   *60*

How bright soe'er the prospect seems,
All thoughts of Friendship are but dreams,
  If Envy chance to creep in;
An envious man, if you succeed,
May prove a dangerous foe indeed,   *65*
  But not a friend worth keeping.

As Envy pines at good possessed,
So Jealousy looks forth distressed
  On good that seems approaching;
And if Success his steps attend,   *70*
Discerns a rival in a friend,
  And hates him for encroaching.

Hence authors of illustrious name
(Unless belied by common fame)
  Are sadly prone to quarrel;   *75*
To deem the wit a friend displays,
So much of loss to their own praise,
  And pluck each other's laurel.

A man renowned for repartee,
Will seldom scruple to make free   *80*
  With Friendship's finest feeling;
Will thrust a dagger at your breast,
And tell you 'twas a special jest,
  By way of balm for healing.

Beware of tattlers; keep your ear   *85*
Close stopped against the tales they bear,*
  Fruits of their own invention;
The separation of chief friends
Is what their kindness most intends;
  Their sport is your dissension.   *90*

---

* "Hear;" Eds. 1815, Southey, Bell. "Bear;" Eds. Hayley (1803), 1817, Dale.

Nor any fool he would deceive,
But prove* as ready to believe,
    And dream that he had† found one.

Friendship that wantonly admits
A joco-serious play of wits
    In brilliant altercation,
Is union such as indicates,
Like Hand-in-Hand insurance-plates,   95
    Danger of conflagration.

Some fickle creatures boast a soul
True as the needle to the pole;
    Yet shifting, like the weather,
The needle's constancy forego   100
For any novelty, and show
    Its variations rather.

Insensibility makes some
Unseasonably deaf and dumb,
    When most you need their pity;   105
'Tis waiting till the tears shall fall
From Gog and Magog in Guildhall,
    Those playthings of the city.

The great and small but rarely meet
On terms of amity complete: 110
    The attempt would scarce be madder,
Should any, from the bottom, hope
At one huge stride, to reach the top
    Of an erected ladder.

Courtier and Patriot cannot mix   115
Their heterogeneous politics
    Without an effervescence,
Such as of salts with lemon-juice,
But which is rarely known to induce,
    Like that, a coalescence.   120

Religion should extinguish strife,
And make a calm of human life:
    But even those who differ

---

* MS. " proves."   † MS. " has."

Candid, and generous, and just,
Boys care but little whom they trust,—   20
   An error soon corrected ;

Only on topics left at large,
How fiercely will they meet and charge !   125
   No combatants are stiffer.

To prove, alas! my main intent,
Needs no great cost of argument,
   No cutting and contriving;
Seeking a real friend, we seem   130
To adopt the chymist's golden dream
   With still less hope of thriving.

Then judge or ere you choose your man,
As circumspectly as you can,
   And having made election,   135
See that no disrespect of yours,
Such as a friend but ill endures,
   Enfeeble his affection.

It is not timber, lead, and stone,
An architect requires alone,   140
   To finish a great building;
The palace were but half complete,
Could he by any chance forget
   The carving and the gilding.

As similarity of mind,   145
Or something not to be defined,
   First rivets our attention;
So manners decent and polite,
The same we practised at first sight,
   Must save it from declension.   150

The man who hails you Tom or Jack,
And proves by thumping on your back,
   His sense of your great merit,
Is such a friend, that one had need
Be very much his friend indeed,   155
   To pardon, or to bear it.

Some friends make this their prudent plan—
" Say little, and hear all you can ; "
   Safe policy, but hateful.

For who but learns in* riper years
That man, when smoothest he appears,
   Is most to be suspected?

But here again a danger lies,   25
Lest, having misapplied† our eyes,
   And taken trash for treasure,

So barren sands imbibe the shower,   160
But render neither fruit nor flower,—
   Unpleasant and ungrateful.

They whisper trivial things, and small;
But to communicate at all
   Things serious, deem improper;   165
Their feculence and froth they show,
But keep the best contents below,
   Just like a simmering copper.

These samples (for, alas! at last
These are but samples, and a taste   170
   Of evils yet unmentioned)
May prove the task a task indeed,
In which 'tis much if we succeed,
   However well intentioned.

Pursue the theme, and you shall find   175
A disciplined and furnished mind
   To be at least expedient,
And, after summing all the rest,
Religion ruling in the breast
   A principal ingredient.   180

True Friendship has, in short, a grace
More than terrestrial in its face,
   That proves it heaven-descended:
Man's love of woman not so pure,
Nor, when sincerest, so secure   185
   To last till life is ended.

---

* MS. " with."   † MS. " misemployed."

We should unwarily conclude
Friendship a false ideal good,
   A mere Utopian pleasure.   30

An acquisition rather rare
Is yet no subject of despair,
   Nor is it wise complaining,
If either on forbidden ground,
Or where it was not to be found,   35
   We sought without attaining.

No Friendship will abide the test
That stands on sordid interest,
   Or mean self-love erected;
Nor such as may awhile subsist   40
Between the sot and sensualist,
   For vicious ends connected.

Who seeks a friend should come disposed
To exhibit, in full bloom disclosed,
   The graces and the beauties   45
That form the character he seeks,
For 'tis a union that bespeaks
   Reciprocated duties.*

Mutual attention † is implied,
And equal truth on either side,   50
   And constantly supported;
'Tis senseless arrogance to accuse
Another of sinister views,
   Our ‡ own as much distorted.

* MS. " A just exchange of duties."
† MS. " Reciprocation."   ‡ MS. " your."

But will Sincerity suffice?   55
It is indeed above* all price,
   And must be made the basis;
But every virtue of the soul
Must constitute the charming whole,
   All shining in their places.   60

A fretful temper will divide
The closest knot that may† be tied
   By ceaseless sharp corrosion:
A temper passionate and fierce
May suddenly your joys disperse   65
   At one immense explosion.

In vain the talkative unite
In hopes of permanent delight—
   The secret just committed,
Forgetting its important weight,   70
They drop through mere desire to prate,
   And by themselves outwitted.

How bright soe'er the prospect seems,
All thoughts of friendship are but dreams,
   If Envy chance to creep in;   75
An envious man, if you succeed,
May prove a dangerous foe indeed,
   But not a friend worth keeping.

As Envy pines at good possessed,
So Jealousy looks forth distressed   80
   On good that seems approaching;

* MS. "I grant it is above."   † MS. "can."

And if success his steps attend,
Discerns a rival in a friend,
   And hates him for encroaching.

Hence authors of illustrious name,   85
Unless belied by common fame,
   Are sadly prone to quarrel,
To deem the wit a friend displays
A tax upon their own just praise,
   And pluck each other's laurel.   90

A man renowned for repartee
Will seldom scruple to make free
   With Friendship's finest feeling,
Will thrust a dagger at your breast,
And say he wounded you in jest,   95
   By way of balm for healing.

Whoever keeps an open ear
For tattlers, will be sure to hear
   The trumpet of contention ;
Aspersion is the babbler's trade,   100
To listen is to lend him aid,
   And rush into dissension.

A Friendship that in frequent fits
Of controversial rage emits
   The sparks of disputation,   105
Like Hand-in-Hand insurance plates,
Most unavoidably creates
   The thought of conflagration.

Some fickle creatures boast a soul
True as a* needle to the pole,   110
    Their humour yet so various—
They manifest their whole life through
The needle's deviations too,
    Their love is so precarious.

The great and small but rarely meet   115
On terms of amity complete;
    Plebeians must surrender,
And yield so much to noble folk,
It is combining fire with smoke,
    Obscurity with splendour.   120

Some are so placid and serene†
(As Irish bogs are always green)
    They sleep secure from waking;
And are indeed a bog, that bears
Your unparticipated cares,   125
    Unmoved and without quaking.

Courtier and Patriot cannot mix
Their heterogeneous politics
    Without an effervescence,
Like that of salts with lemon juice,   130
Which does not yet like that produce
    A friendly coalescence.

* MS. "the."
† In the MS. this and the preceding stanza are transposed, and the first three lines of this stanza stand as follows:—

    "As Irish bogs are always green,
    Some minds are sleepy and serene,
    Whose heart soe'er is aching."

Religion should* extinguish strife,
And make a calm of human life;
   But friends that chance to differ   135
On points which God has left at large,
How freely† will they meet and charge!
   No combatants are stiffer.

To prove at last‡ my main intent
Needs no expense of argument,   140
   No cutting and contriving—
Seeking a real friend, we seem
To adopt the chymists' golden dream,
   With still less hope of thriving.

Sometimes the fault is all our own,   145
Some blemish in due time§ made known
   By trespass or omission;
Sometimes occasion brings to light
Our friend's defect long hid from sight,
   And even from suspicion.   150

Then judge yourself, and prove your man,
As circumspectly as you can,
   And having made election,
Beware no negligence of yours,
Such as a friend but ill endures,   155
   Enfeeble his affection.

That secrets are a sacred trust,
That friends should be sincere and just,
   That constancy ‖ befits them,

---

* MS. "ought to."   † MS. "fiercely."   ‡ MS. "alas!"
   § MS. "suddenly."   ‖ MS. "sympathy."

Are observations on the case 160
That savour much of commonplace,
   And all the world admits them.

But 'tis not timber, lead, and stone,
An architect requires alone
   To finish a fine building— 165
The palace were but half complete,
If he could possibly forget
   The carving and the gilding.

The man that hails you Tom or Jack,*
And proves by thumps upon your back 170
   How he esteems your merit,†
Is such a friend that one had need
Be very much his friend indeed,
   To pardon or to bear it.

As similarity of mind, 175
Or something not to be defined,
   First fixes our attention;
So manners decent and polite,
The same we practised at first sight,
   Must save it from declension. 180

Some act upon this prudent plan,
" Say little, and hear all you can;"
   Safe policy, but hateful:
So barren sands imbibe the shower,
But render neither fruit nor flower,— 185
   Unpleasant and ungrateful.

---

* This and the following stanza are transposed in the MS.
† MS. " How well he knows your merit."

The man I trust, if shy to me,
Shall find me as reserved as he,
  No subterfuge, or pleading,*
Shall win my confidence again ;   190
I will by no means entertain
  A spy on my proceeding.

These samples—for alas ! at last
These are but samples, and a taste
  Of evils yet unmentioned—   195
May prove the task, a task indeed,
In which 'tis much if we succeed,
  However well-intentioned.

Pursue the search, and you will find
Good sense and knowledge of mankind   200
  To be at least expedient,
And, after summing all the rest,
Religion ruling in the breast
  A principal ingredient.

† The noblest Friendship ever shown   205
The Saviour's history makes known,
  Though some have turned and turned it ;

* MS.   "And deaf to all his pleading,
       ¶ I will withdraw my trust again,
       Determined not to entertain "

† This and the succeeding stanza do not appear in the MS.
In their place we find the following :—
      "There is a sober serious grace,
      A sanctity in Friendship's face,
        That proves it heaven-descended,
      The love of woman not so pure,
      Nor, even when truest, so secure
        To last till life is ended."

And whether being crazed or blind,
Or seeking with a biassed mind,
   Have not, it seems, discerned it.   210

O Friendship! if my soul forego
Thy dear delights while here below,
   To mortify and grieve me,
May I myself at last appear
Unworthy, base, and insincere,   215
   Or may my friend deceive me!

ON A MISCHIEVOUS BULL,

WHICH THE OWNER OF HIM SOLD AT THE AUTHOR'S

INSTANCE.*

O! thou art all unfit to share
   The pleasures of this place
With such as its old tenants are,
   Creatures of gentler race.

The squirrel here his hoard provides,   5
   Aware of wintry storms,
And woodpeckers explore the sides
   Of rugged oaks for worms.

The sheep here smooths the knotted thorn
   With frictions of her fleece;   10
And here I wander eve and morn,
   Like her, a friend to peace.

---

* Poems, Ed. 1808, vol. ii., p. 290.   The place alluded to
was doubtless the park at Weston.

Ah !—I could pity thee* exiled
　From this secure retreat—
I would not lose it to be styled　　　　15
　The happiest of the great.

But thou canst taste no calm delight;
　Thy pleasure is to show
Thy magnanimity in fight,
　Thy prowess—therefore, go !　　　　20

I care not whether east or north,
　So I no more may find thee;
The angry Muse thus sings thee forth,
　And claps the gate behind thee.

ANNUS MEMORABILIS, 1789.

WRITTEN IN COMMEMORATION OF HIS MAJESTY'S

HAPPY RECOVERY.†

RANSACKED, for a theme of song,
Much ancient chronicle, and long;
I read of bright embattled fields,
Of trophied helmets, spears, and shields,
Of chiefs whose single arm could boast　　　5

---

* One modern edition has " the."
† Written early in March, 1789, and sent to Lady Hesketh in a letter dated the 5th of that month; see also letter
to Mrs. King of the 12th of March, 1789. Printed in Poems,
Ed. 1808, vol. ii., p. 292.

Prowess to dissipate a host;
Through tomes of fable and of dream
I sought an eligible theme,
But none I found, or found them shared
Already by some happier bard.   10
    To modern times, with Truth to guide
My busy search, I next applied;
Here cities won, and fleets dispersed,
Urged loud a claim to be rehearsed,
Deeds of unperishing renown,   15
Our fathers' triumphs and our own.
    Thus as the bee, from bank to bower,
Assiduous sips at every flower,
But rests on none till that be found
Where most nectareous sweets abound,   20
So I, from theme to theme displayed
In many a page historic strayed,
Siege after siege, fight after fight,
Contemplating with small delight,
(For feats of sanguinary hue   25
Not always glitter in my view)
Till settling on the current year,
I found the far-sought treasure near;
A theme for poetry divine,
A theme to ennoble even mine,   30
In memorable Eighty-nine.
    The spring of Eighty-nine shall be
An era cherished long by me,
Which joyful I will oft record,
And thankful, at my frugal board;   35
For then the clouds of Eighty-eight,
That threatened England's trembling state
With loss of what she least could spare,

Her sovereign's tutelary care,
One breath of Heaven, that cried—"Restore!" 40
Chased, never to assemble more:
And far* the richest crown on earth,
If valued by its wearer's worth,
The symbol of a righteous reign,
Sat fast on George's brows again. 45
    Then peace and joy again possessed
Our Queen's long-agitated breast;
Such joy and peace as can be known
By sufferers like herself alone,
Who losing, or supposing lost, 50
The good on earth they valued most,
For that dear sorrow's sake forego
All† hope of happiness below,
Then suddenly regain the prize,
And flash thanksgivings to the skies! 55
    O Queen of Albion, queen of isles!
Since all thy tears were changed to smiles,
The eyes, that never saw thee, shine
With joy not unallied to thine,
Transports not chargeable with art 60
Illume the land's remotest part,
And strangers to the air of courts,
Both in their toils and at their sports,
The happiness of answered prayers,
That gilds thy features, show in theirs. 65
    If they who on thy state attend,
Awe-struck, before thy presence bend,

* "For;" Eds. 1809, 1810, 1812, 1817, Grimshawe,
Dale, Bell. "Far;" Eds. 1821, 1825, Southey.
† "Ill;" Ed. 1808, corrected in 1810 and subsequent
editions.

'Tis but the natural effect
Of grandeur that ensures respect;
But she is something more than Queen,   70
Who is beloved where never seen.

HYMN,

FOR THE USE OF THE SUNDAY SCHOOL AT OLNEY.*

HEAR, Lord, the song of praise and prayer,
   In Heaven thy dwelling place,
From infants made the public care,
   And taught to seek thy face.

Thanks for thy Word, and for thy Day,   5
   And grant us, we implore,
Never to waste in sinful play
   Thy holy Sabbaths more.

---

* On the 12th of August, 1789, Cowper wrote to his friend
Hill, " My friend, the vicar of the next parish [Mr. Bean],
engaged me the day before yesterday to furnish him by next
Sunday with a hymn to be sung on the occasion of his
preaching to the children of the Sunday School." The hymn
thus called forth was printed in Poems, Ed. 1808, vol. ii., p.
294, and again in vol. iii. (1815), p. 98. In the edition of
1817 the same repetition occurs in vol. ii., p. 339, and vol. iii.,
p. 111. Grimshawe printed half the little poem "for the benefit
of his younger readers," in vol. iv., p. 122, and the same half
again in vol. viii., p. 40, and the whole Hymn in vol. vii.,
p. 270. Dr. J. Johnson added a note to his copy in Ed. 1815,
8vo., p. 138, in which he assigned a little different date to
that given in Cowper's letter quoted above, but of course
Cowper himself was right.

Thanks that we hear,—but oh! impart
  To each desires sincere, 10
That we may listen with our heart,
  And learn as well as hear.

For if vain thoughts the minds engage
  Of older far than we,
What hope, that, at our heedless age, 15
  Our minds should e'er be free?

Much hope, if thou our spirits take,
  Under thy gracious sway,
Who canst the wisest wiser make,
  And babes as wise as they. 20

Wisdom and bliss thy word bestows,
  A sun that ne'er declines,
And be thy mercies showered on those
  Who placed us where it shines.

STANZAS

SUBJOINED TO THE YEARLY BILL OF MORTALITY OF

THE PARISH OF ALL-SAINTS, NORTHAMPTON,*

ANNO DOMINI 1787.

Pallida Mors æquo pulsat pede panperum tabernas,
Regumque turres.   HORACE [Ode iv., Lib. 1.]

Pale Death with equal foot strikes wide the door
Of royal halls and hovels of the poor.

WHILE thirteen moons saw smoothly run
The Nen's barge-laden wave,
All these, life's rambling journey done,
Have found their home, the grave.

Was man (frail always) made more frail   5
Than in foregoing years?
Did Famine or did Plague prevail,
That so much death appears?

No; these were vigorous as their sires,
Nor Plague nor Famine came;   10
This annual tribute Death requires,
And never waves his claim.

* Composed for John Cox, a parish clerk of Northampton,
under circumstances which Cowper stated in a letter to Lady
Hesketh of the 27th of November, 1787.   Mr. Bull printed
the lines at the end of his little volume of poems translated
from Madame Guion by Cowper, published at Newport
Pagnel, in 1801.   They will be found included in the edition
of Cowper's Poems, 1803, vol. ii., p. 335, and in all subsequent editions.

Like crowded forest-trees we stand,
  And some are marked to fall;
The axe will smite at God's command, 15
  And soon shall smite us all.

Green as the bay tree, ever green,
  With its new foliage on,
The gay, the thoughtless, have I* seen,
  I passed—and they were gone. 20

Read, ye that run, the awful truth
  With which I charge my page;
A worm is in the bud of youth,
  And at the root of age.

No present health can health insure 25
  For yet an hour to come;
No medicine, though it oft can† cure,
  Can always balk the tomb.

And oh! that humble as my lot,
  And scorned as is my strain, 30
These truths, though known, too much forgot,
  I may not teach in vain.

So prays your Clerk with all his heart,
  And, ere he quits the pen,
Begs *you* for once to take *his* part, 35
  And answer all—"Amen!"

  * "I have," Eds. 1801, 1806(2); "have I," Ed. 1808 and
subsequent editions.
  † "Often," the like; "oft can," in Ed. 1808.

ON A SIMILAR OCCASION.

FOR THE YEAR 1788.*

Quod adest, memento
Componere æquus.   Cætera fluminis
Ritu feruntur.   HORACE [Lib. III., Ode xxix.]

Improve the present hour, for all beside
Is a mere feather on a torrent's tide.

OULD I, from Heaven inspired, as sure
    presage
  To whom the rising year shall prove
    his last,
As I can number in my punctual page,
And item down the victims of the past;

How each would trembling wait the mournful sheet,
On which the press might stamp him next to die; 6
And reading here his sentence, how replete
With anxious meaning, Heavenward turn his eye!

Time then would seem more precious than the joys
In which he sports away the treasure now;   10
And prayer more seasonable than the noise
Of drunkards, or the music-drawing bow.

---

* Printed, like the preceding, by Bull, in 1801, also in the
general edition of Cowper's Poems in 1803, and in all subsequent editions.

Then doubtless many a trifler, on the brink
Of this world's hazardous and headlong shore,
Forced to a pause, would feel it good to think,   15
Told that his setting sun must rise no more.

Ah self-deceived! Could I, prophetic, say
Who next is fated, and who next to fall,
The rest might then seem privileged to play;
But, naming none, the Voice now speaks to all.   20

Observe the dappled foresters, how light
They bound, and airy, o'er the sunny glade—
One falls—the rest, wide-scattered with affright,
Vanish at once into the darkest shade.

Had we their wisdom, should we, often warned, 25
Still need repeated warnings, and at last,
A thousand awful admonitions scorned,
Die self-accused of life run all to waste?

Sad waste! for which no after-thrift atones:
The grave admits no cure for guilt or sin;   30
Dewdrops may deck the turf that hides the bones,
But tears of godly grief ne'er flow within.

Learn then, ye living! by the mouths be taught
Of all these sepulchres, instructors true,
That, soon or late, death also is your lot,   35
And the next opening grave may yawn for you.

ON A SIMILAR OCCASION.

—Placidâque ibi demum morte quievit.
VIRG. [Æn. IX., 445.]
There calm at length he breathed his soul away.

" MOST delightful hour by man
  Experienced here below,
The hour that terminates his span,
  His folly, and his woe!

" Worlds should not bribe me back to tread 5
  Again life's dreary waste,
To see again my day o'erspread
  With all the gloomy past.

" My home henceforth is in the skies,
  Earth, seas, and sun, adieu! 10
All Heaven unfolded to my eyes,
  I have no sight for you."

So spake Aspasio, firm possessed
  Of faith's supporting rod,
Then breathed his soul into its rest, 15
  The bosom of his God.

* Published, it is said, for the first time, in a memoir of
Cowper, in the work entitled " Public Characters, 1799-
1800," Lond. 8vo. 1799, p. 549. It was afterwards printed
in 1801, 1803, and subsequent editions, as the two preceding
similar poems.

He was a man among the few
   Sincere on Virtue's side;
And all his strength from Scripture drew,
   To hourly use applied.   20

That rule he prized, by that* he feared,
   He hated, hoped, and loved;
Nor ever frowned, or sad appeared,
   But when his heart had roved.

For he was frail as thou or I,   25
   And evil felt within:
But when he felt it, heaved a sigh,
   And loathed the thought† of sin.

Such lived Aspasio; and at last,
   Called up from Earth to Heaven,   30
The gulf of death triumphant passed,
   By gales of blessing driven.

" His joys be mine," each Reader cries,
   " When my last hour arrives:"
"They shall be yours," my Verse replies,   35
   " Such only be your lives."

* "What," Eds. 1801 to 1806(2); "that," Ed. 1808, and
subsequent editions.
   † "Thoughts," Eds. 1801 to 1806(2); "Thought," Ed.
1808, and subsequent editions.

ON A SIMILAR OCCASION.

FOR THE YEAR 1790.*

Ne commonentem recta sperne.
BUCHANAN. [Jephthes, 1. 782.]
Despise not my good counsel.

E who sits from day to day
    Where the prisoned lark is hung,
Heedless of his loudest lay,
    Hardly knows that he has sung.

Where the watchman in his round   5
    Nightly lifts his voice on high,
None, accustomed to the sound,
    Wakes the sooner for his cry.

So your Verse-man I, and Clerk,
    Yearly in my song proclaim   10
Death at hand—yourselves his mark—
    And the foe's unerring aim.

Duly at my time I come,
    Publishing to all aloud—
Soon the grave must be your home,   15
    And your only suit, a shroud.

* Printed in 1801, 1803, and subsequent editions, as the first of the preceding similar lines.

But the monitory strain,
   Oft repeated in your ears,
Seems to sound too much in vain,
   Wins no notice, wakes no fears.   20

Can a truth, by all confessed
 , Of such magnitude and weight,
Grow, by being oft expressed,*
   Trivial as a parrot's prate?

Pleasure's call attention wins,   25
   Hear it often as we may;
New as ever seem our sins,
   Though committed every day.

Death and Judgment, Heaven and Hell—
   These alone, so often heard,   30
No more move us than the bell
   When some stranger is interred.

Oh then, ere the turf or tomb
   Cover us from every eye,
Spirit of instruction! come,   35
   Make us learn that we must die.

* "Expressed," Eds. 1801 to 1806; "impressed," Ed. 1808, and all subsequent editions.

ON A SIMILAR OCCASION.

FOR THE YEAR 1792.*

Felix, qui potuit rerum cognoscere causas,
Atque metus omnes et inexorabile fatum
Subjecit pedibus, strepitumque Acherontis avari!
                              VIRG. [Georg. II., 490.]

Happy the mortal who has traced effects
To their first cause, cast fear beneath his feet,
And Death and roaring Hell's voracious fires!

THANKLESS for favours from on high,
　　Man thinks he fades too soon;
　Though 'tis his privilege to die,
　　Would he improve the boon.

But he, not wise enough to scan   5
　His best† concerns aright,
Would gladly stretch life's little span
　To ages, if he might.

To ages in a world of pain,
　To ages, where he goes   10
Galled by affliction's heavy chain,
　And hopeless of repose.

* Printed in 1801, 1803, and subsequent editions, as
the first of the preceding similar poems.
† "Best," Eds. 1801, 1803, one ed. of 1806, 1817, 1821,
1825, Dale; "blest," 1805, 1806, 1808, 1810, 1812, Southey,
Grimshawe, Bell.

Strange fondness of the human heart,
   Enamoured of its harm !
Strange world, that costs it so much smart,   15
   And still has power to charm.

Whence has the world her magic power ?
   Why deem we death a foe ?
Recoil from weary life's best hour,
   And covet longer woe ?   20

The cause is Conscience ;—Conscience oft
   Her tale of guilt renews :
Her voice is terrible though soft,
   And dread of Death ensues.

Then anxious to be longer spared   25
   Man mourns his fleeting breath :
All evils then seem light, compared
   With the approach of Death.

'Tis Judgment shakes him ; there's the fear
   That prompts the wish to stay :   30
He has incurred a long arrear,
   And must despair to pay.

Pay !—follow Christ, and all is paid ;
   His death your peace ensures ;
Think on the grave where *He* was laid,   35
   And calm descend to *yours*.

ON A SIMILAR OCCASION.

FOR THE YEAR 1793.*

De sacris autem hæc sit una sententia, ut conserventur.
CIC. DE LEG. [Lib II., sec. xix.]

But let us all concur in this one sentiment, that things
sacred be inviolate.

HE lives who lives to God, alone,
  And all are dead beside;
For other source than God is none,
  Whence life can be supplied.

To live to God is to requite   5
  His love as best we may:
To make his precepts our delight,
  His promises our stay.

But life, within a narrow ring
  Of giddy joys comprised,   10
Is falsely named, and no such thing,
  But rather death disguised.

Can life in them deserve the name,
  Who only live to prove,
For what poor toys they can disclaim   15
  An endless life above?

---

* Printed in 1801, 1803, and subsequent editions, as the
last preceding similar lines.

Who much diseased, yet nothing feel;
   Much menaced, nothing dread;
Have wounds which only God can heal,
   Yet never ask his aid !   20

Who deem his house a useless place,
   Faith, want of common sense;
And ardour in the Christian race,′
   A hypocrite's pretence !

Who trample order; and the day   25
   Which God asserts his own,
Dishonour with unhallowed play,
   And worship Chance alone !

If scorn of God's commands, impressed
   On word and deed, imply   30
The better part of man unblessed
   With life that cannot die ;

Such want it;—and that want, uncured
   Till man resigns his breath,
Speaks him a criminal, assured   35
   Of everlasting death.

Sad period to a pleasant course !
   Yet so will God repay
Sabbaths profaned without remorse,
   And Mercy cast away.   40

ON A GOLDFINCH,

STARVED TO DEATH IN HIS CAGE.*

IME was when I was free as air,
   The thistle's downy seed my fare,
     My drink the morning dew;
   I perched at will on every spray,
My form genteel, my plumage gay,   5
     My strains for ever new. .

But gaudy plumage, sprightly strain,
And form genteel were all in vain,
     And of a transient date;
For caught and caged, and starved to death, 10
In dying sighs my little breath
     Soon passed the wiry grate.

Thanks, gentle swain, for all my woes,
And thanks for this effectual close
     And cure of every ill!   15
More cruelty could none express;
And I, if you had shown me less,
     Had been your prisoner still.

---

* Poems, Ed. 1782, p. 329. Written in the summer of 1780; see letter to Unwin, 9th November, 1780, containing a copy of these lines, Addit. MS. Brit. Mus. 24, 154, fol. 49.

THE PINEAPPLE AND THE BEE.*

THE Pineapples, in triple row,
   Were basking hot, and all in blow;
   A Bee of most discerning taste
   Perceived the fragrance as he passed,
On eager wing the spoiler came,   5
And searched for crannies in the frame,
Urged his attempt on every side,
To every pane his trunk applied,
But still in vain, the frame was tight,
And only pervious to the light: 10
Thus having wasted half the day,
He trimmed his flight another way.
   "Methinks," I said, "in thee I find
The sin and madness of mankind.
To joys forbidden man aspires,   15
Consumes his soul with vain desires;
Folly the spring of his pursuit,
And disappointment all the fruit.
While Cynthio ogles, as she passes,
The nymph between two chariot glasses,   20
She is the Pineapple, and he
The silly unsuccessful Bee.
The maid who views with pensive air
The show-glass fraught with glittering ware,
Sees watches, bracelets, rings, and lockets,   25

* Poems, Ed. 1782, p. 330. Written about September, 1779; see letter to Hill of 2nd October in that year.

But sighs at thought of empty pockets;
Like thine, her appetite is keen,
But ah, the cruel glass between!"
   Our dear delights are often such;
Exposed to view, but not to touch.   30
The sight our foolish heart inflames,
We long for pineapples in frames;
With hopeless wish one looks and lingers;
One breaks the glass, and cuts his fingers;
But they whom Truth and Wisdom lead   35
Can gather honey from a weed.

HORACE, BOOK II. ODE X.*

ECEIVE, dear friend, the truths I teach,
   So shalt thou live beyond the reach
      Of adverse fortune's power;
Not always tempt the distant deep,
Nor always timorously creep   5
   Along the treacherous shore.

He that holds fast the golden mean,
And lives contentedly between
   The little and the great,
Feels not the wants that pinch the poor,   10
Nor plagues that haunt the rich man's door,
   Embittering all his state.

* Poems, Ed. 1782, p. 332.

The tallest pines feel most the power
Of wintry blasts;* the loftiest tower
    Comes heaviest to the ground;   15
The bolts that spare the mountain's side
His cloud-capped eminence divide,
    And spread the ruin round.

The well-informed philosopher
Rejoices with a wholesome fear,   20
    And hopes in spite of pain;
If Winter bellow from the north,
Soon the sweet Spring comes dancing forth,
    And Nature laughs again.

What if thine Heaven be overcast,   25
The dark appearance will not last;
    Expect a brighter sky.
The God that strings the silver bow
Awakes sometimes the Muses too,
    And lays his arrows by.   30

If hindrances obstruct thy way,
Thy magnanimity display,
    And let thy strength be seen;
But oh! if Fortune fill thy sail
With more than a propitious gale,   35
    Take half thy canvass in.

---

* "Blasts," Ed. 1782, altered to "blast" in Ed. 1786, but restored in the next edition, and printed "blasts" in subsequent editions, except Southey's.

A REFLECTION ON THE FOREGOING ODE.*

AND is this all? Can Reason do no more
    Than bid me shun the deep, and dread
       the shore?
    Sweet moralist! afloat on life's rough sea,
The Christian has an art unknown to thee:
He holds no parley with unmanly fears;   5
Where Duty bids he confidently steers,
Faces a thousand dangers at her call,
And trusting in his God, surmounts them all.

THE LILY AND THE ROSE.†

THE nymph must lose her female friend,
    If more admired than she—
But where will fierce contention end,
    If flowers can disagree?

Within the garden's peaceful scene   5
    Appeared two lovely foes,
Aspiring to the rank of Queen,
    The Lily and the Rose.

* Poems, Ed. 1782, p. 334.
† Ibid, p. 322. A copy in Cowper's handwriting is in
MS. Addit. Brit. Mus. 24,155, fol. 151.

The Rose soon reddened into rage,
   And swelling with disdain,   10
Appealed to many a poet's page
   To prove her right to reign.

The Lily's height bespoke command,
   A fair imperial flower;
She seemed designed for Flora's hand,   15
   The sceptre of her power.

This civil bickering and debate
   The Goddess chanced to hear,
And flew to save, ere yet too late,
   The pride of the parterre;   20

" Yours is," she said, " the nobler hue,
   And yours the statelier mien;
And till a third surpasses you,
Let each be deemed a Queen."

Thus soothed and reconciled, each seeks   25
   The fairest British fair;
The seat of empire is her cheeks,
   They reign united there.

IDEM LATINE REDDITUM.*

HEU inimicitias quoties parit æmula forma,
    Quam raro pulchræ pulchra placere
      potest !
    Sed fines ultra solitos discordia tendit,
Cum flores ipsos bilis et ira movent ?

Hortus ubi dulces præbet tacitosque recessus,   5
    Se rapit in partes gens animosa duas ;
Hic sibi regales Amaryllis candida cultus,
    Illic purpureo vindicat ore Rosa.

Ira Rosam et meritis quæsita superbia tangunt,
    Multaque ferventi vix cohibenda sinû,   10
Dum sibi fautorum ciet undique nomina vatum,
    Jusque suum, multo carmine fulta, probat.

Altior emicat illa, et celso vertice nutat,
    Ceu flores inter non habitura parem,
Fastiditque alios, et nata videtur in usus   15
    Imperii, sceptrum, Flora quod ipsa gerat.

Nec Dea non sensit civilis murmura rixæ,
    Cui curæ est pietas pandere ruris opes,
Deliciasque suas nunquam non prompta tueri,
    Dum licet et locus est, ut tueatur, adest.   20

* Poems, Ed. 1782, p. 324.

Et tibi forma datur procerior omnibus, inquit,
　Et tibi, principibus qui solet esse, color,
Et donec vincat quædam formosior ambas,
　Et tibi reginæ nomen, et esto tibi.

His ubi sedatus furor est, petit utraque nympham,
　Qualem inter Veneres Anglia sola parit;　　• 26
Hanc penes imperium est, nihil optant amplius,
　　hujus
Regnant in nitidis, et sine lite, genis.

THE POPLAR FIELD.*

THE poplars are felled;—farewell to the
　　shade,
And the whispering sound of the cool
　　colonnade !
The winds play no longer and sing in the leaves,
Nor Ouse on his bosom their image receives.

Twelve years have elapsed since I last took a view
Of my favourite field, and the bank where they
　　grew;　　　　　　　　　　　　　　　　6
And now in the grass behold they are laid,
And the tree is my seat, that once lent me a shade.

---

* Written about the close of 1784 (see letter to Unwin,
15th January, 1785), and first printed in the Gentleman's
Magazine for January, 1785, p. 53. The edition of the Poems
published in 1800 is the first in which it has been found
included, vol. II., p. 353.　The poplars alluded to stood near
Lavendon Mills, about a mile from Olney.

The blackbird has fled to another retreat,
Where the hazels afford him a screen from the
    heat,   10
And the scene where his melody charmed me before,
Resounds with his sweet-flowing ditty no more.

My fugitive years are all hasting away,
And I must ere long lie as lowly as they,
With a turf on my breast, and a stone at my head,
Ere another such grove shall arise in its stead. 16

'Tis a sight to engage me, if any thing can,
To muse on the perishing pleasures of man ;
Though his life be a dream, his enjoyments, I see,
Have a being less durable even than he.*   20

---

   * Cowper afterwards altered this stanza in the following
manner :—

> The change both my heart and my fancy employs,
> I reflect on the frailty of man, and his joys;
> Short-lived as we are, yet our pleasures, we see,
> Have a still shorter date, and die sooner than we.†

   † This note was added in the Edition of 1803, vol. I.
p. 332.

IDEM LATINE REDDITUM.*

OPULEÆ cccidit gratissima copia silvæ,
    Conticuêre susurri, omnisque evanuit
        umbra;
    Nullæ jam levibus se miscent frondibus
        auræ,
Et nulla in fluvio ramorum ludit imago.

Hei mihi! bis senos dum luctu torqueor annos, 5
His cogor silvis suetoque carere recessu,
Cum serò rediens, stratasque in gramine cernens,
Insedi arboribus, sub queîs errare solebam.

Ah ubi nunc merulæ cantus? Felicior illum
Silva tegit, duræ nondum permissa bipenni; 10
Scilicet exustos colles camposque patentes
Odit, et indignans et non rediturus abivit.

Sed qui succisas doleo succidar et ipse,
Et priùs huic parilis quàm creverit altera silva
Flebor, et, exequiis parvis donatus, habebo 15
Defixum lapidem tumulique cubantis acervum.

* Written probably in January, 1785, and sent to Nichols for the Gentleman's Magazine early in the succeeding month (see letter to Unwin, 7th February, 1785). It was printed in that magazine for the following August, p. 644, and in the Edition of the Poems, 1800, vol. II., p. 354.

Tam subitò periisse videns tam digna manere,
Agnosco humanas sortes et tristia fata—
Sit licèt ipse brevis, volucrique simillimus umbræ,
Est homini brevior citiùsque obitura voluptas.   20

VOTUM.*

MATUTINI rores, auræque salubres,
O nemora, et lætæ rivis felicibus herbæ,
Graminei colles, et amœnæ in vallibus
      umbræ !
Fata modò dederint quas olim in rure paterno
Delicias, procul arte, procul formidine novi,   5
Quam vellem ignotus, quod mens mea semper
      avebat,
Ante larem proprium placidam expectare senec-
      tam,
Tum demùm, exactis non infeliciter annis,
Sortiri tacitum lapidem, aut sub cespite, condi !

* Poems, Ed. 1782, p. 328.

TRANSLATIONS FROM VINCENT BOURNE.*

I. THE GLOWWORM.

ENEATH the hedge, or near the stream,
 A worm is known to stray,
That shows by night a lucid beam,
 Which disappears by day.

Disputes have been, and still prevail,   5
 From whence his rays proceed;
Some give that honour to his tail,
 And others to his head.

But this is sure—the hand of might,
 That kindles up the skies,   10
Gives him a modicum of light
 Proportioned to his size.

Perhaps indulgent Nature meant,
 By such a lamp bestowed,
To bid the traveller, as he went,   15
 Be careful where he trod:

---

* These four translations first appeared in Poems, Ed.
1782, pp. 335-343. The original Latin poems by Bourne
are to be found in all the editions of his " Poematia," and
also in the several editions of Cowper's Poems from 1803 to
1817. It is observable that these four translations by Cowper seem to have been overlooked in the beautiful edition of
Bourne's "Poematia" edited by Mitford (Pickering, 1840),
although those hereafter to be printed in our vol. III. were
all included in it.

Nor crush a worm, whose useful light
  Might serve, however small,
To show a stumbling stone by night,
  And save him from a fall.   20

Whate'er she meant, this truth divine
  Is legible and plain,
'Tis power almighty bids him shine,
  Nor bids him shine in vain.

Ye proud and wealthy, let this theme   25
  Teach humbler thoughts to you,
Since such a reptile has its gem,
  And boasts its splendour too.

II. THE JACKDAW.

THERE is a bird who, by his coat,
  And by the hoarseness of his note,
    Might be supposed a crow;
  A great frequenter of the church,
Where, bishop-like, he finds a perch,   5
  And dormitory too.

Above the steeple shines a plate,
That turns and turns, to indicate
  From what point blows the weather.
Look up—your brains begin to swim,   10
'Tis in the clouds—that pleases him,
  He chooses it the rather.

Fond of the speculative height,
Thither he wings his airy flight,
   And thence securely sees   15
The bustle and the raree-show,
That occupy mankind below,
   Secure and at his ease.

You think, no doubt, he sits and muses
On future broken bones and bruises,   20
   If he should chance to fall;
No; not a single thought like that
Employs his philosophic pate,
   Or troubles it at all.

He sees that this great roundabout,   25
The world, with all its motley rout,
   Church, army, physic, law,
Its customs and its businesses,
Is no concern at all of his,
   And says—what says he?—" Caw!"   30

Thrice happy bird! I too have seen
Much of the vanities of men;
   And sick of having seen 'em,
Would cheerfully these limbs resign
For such a pair of wings as thine,   35
   And such a head between 'em.

III. THE CRICKET.

ITTLE inmate, full of mirth,
Chirping on my kitchen hearth,
Wheresoe'er be thine abode,
Always harbinger of good,
Pay me for thy warm retreat,   5
With a song more soft and sweet;
In return thou shalt receive
Such a strain as I can give.

Thus thy praise shall be expressed,
Inoffensive, welcome guest!   10
While the rat is on the scout,
And the mouse with curious snout,
With what vermin else infest
Every dish, and spoil the best;
Frisking thus before the fire,   15
Thou hast all thine heart's desire.

Though in voice and shape they be
Formed as if akin to thee,
Thou surpassest, happier far,
Happiest grasshoppers that are;   20
Theirs is but a summer song,
Thine endures the winter long,
Unimpaired, and shrill, and clear,
Melody throughout the year.

Neither night nor dawn of day   25
Puts a period to thy play:
Sing, then—and extend thy span
Far beyond the date of man;
Wretched man, whose years are spent
In repining discontent,   30
Lives not, aged though he be,
Half a span, compared with thee.

IV. THE PARROT.

IN painted plumes superbly dressed,
  A native of the gorgeous east,
    By many a billow tossed;
  Poll gains at length the British shore,
Part of the captain's precious store,   5
  A present to his toast.

Belinda's maids are soon preferred,
To teach him now and then a word,
  As Poll can master it;
But 'tis her own important charge,   10
To qualify him more at large,
  And make him quite a wit.

" Sweet Poll!" his doting mistress cries,
" Sweet Poll!" the mimic bird replies,
  And calls aloud for sack.   15
She next instructs him in the kiss;
'Tis now a little one, like Miss,
  And now a hearty smack.

At first he aims at what he hears ;
And, listening close with both his ears,   20
   Just catches at the sound ;
But soon articulates aloud,
Much to the amusement of the crowd,
   And stuns the neighbours round.

A querulous old woman's voice   25
His humorous talent next employs,
   He scolds, and gives the lie.
And now he sings, and now is sick,
" Here, Sally, Susan, come, come quick !
   " Poor Poll is like to die !"   30

Belinda and her bird ! 'tis rare
To meet with such a well-matched pair,
   The language and the tone,
Each character in every part
Sustained with so much grace and art,   35
   And both in unison.

When children first begin to spell,
And stammer out a syllable,
   We think them tedious creatures ;
But difficulties soon abate,   40
When birds are to be taught to prate,
   And women are the teachers.

TRANSLATION OF PRIOR'S POEM

BEGINNING:—*

"The Merchant to conceal his treasure."

ERCATOR, vigiles oculos ut fallere
possit,
Nomine sub ficto trans mare mittit
opes:
Lene sonat liquidumque meis Euphelia chordis,
At solam exoptant te, mea vota, Chlöe.

Ad speculum ornabat nitidos Euphelia crines,   5
Cum dixit mea lux, Heus, cane, sume lyram.
Namque lyram juxtà positam cum carmine vidit,
Suave quidem carmen dulcisonamque lyram.

* Poems, Ed. 1782, p. 353. The original, under the title of " An Ode," will be found in Prior's Poems, vol. i., p. 49. Ed. 1725. A manuscript of the translation, in Cowper's hand-writing, is now in the British Museum (Add. MS. 24,154, fol. 8), and has been collated with our impression. On sending this manuscript to Unwin, Cowper accompanied it with the following explanation :—" Not having the poem, and not having seen it these twenty years, I had much ado to recollect it, which has obliged me to tear off the first copy, and write another. [Here follow the lines]. Your mother joins me in all you can wish us to say to yourself and all your family, by no means forgetting great John and little Marianne. May 1, —79."

Fila lyræ vocemque paro. Suspiria surgunt,
Et miscent numeris murmura mæsta meis, 10
Dumque tuæ memoro laudes, Euphelia, formæ,
Tota anima intereà pendet ab ore Chlöes.

Subrubet illa pudore, et contrahit altera frontem,
Me torquet mea mens conscia, psallo, tremo ;
Atque Cupidineâ dixit Dea cincta coronâ, 15
Heu ! fallendi artem quam didicere parum.

INSCRIPTION

FOR THE TOMB OF MR. T. A. HAMILTON.*

AUSE here, and think : a monitory
rhyme
Demands one moment of thy fleeting
time.
Consult Life's silent clock, thy bounding vein ;
Seems it to say—"Health here has long to reign?"
Hast thou the vigour of thy youth? an eye 5
That beams delight? a heart untaught to sigh?
Yet fear. Youth ofttimes, healthful and at ease,
Anticipates a day it never sees ;
And many a tomb, like Hamilton's, aloud
Exclaims " Prepare thee for an early shroud !"† 10

* Inscribed on a tombstone in the churchyard of Newport
Pagnel. It is to be hoped that it still remains there, legible.
Mr. Thomas Abbot Hamilton, a lace dealer in that town, of
Cowper's acquaintance, was connected with several families
at Olney. This inscription was printed in the collected
Poems, Ed. 1800, vol. II., p. 352.

† Mr. Hamilton died on the 7th July, 1788, in the 32nd
year of his age.

EPITAPH ON A HARE.*

ERE lies, whom hound did ne'er pursue,
Nor swifter greyhound follow,
Whose foot ne'er tainted morning dew,
Nor ear heard huntsman's halloo ;

Old Tiny, surliest of his kind,†   5
Who, nursed with tender care,
And to domestic bounds confined,
Was still a wild Jack hare.

Though duly from my hand he took
His pittance every night,   10
He did it with a jealous look,
And, when he could, would bite.

His diet was of wheaten bread,
And milk, and oats, and straw ;
Thistles, or lettuces instead,   15
With sand to scour his maw.

On twigs of hawthorn he regaled,
On pippins' russet peel,
And when his juicy salads failed,
Sliced carrot pleased him well.   20

---

* Poems, Ed. 1800, vol. II., p. 355. A manuscript copy which was sent by Cowper to Unwin on 30th March, 1783, is now in Addit. MS. Brit. Mus. No. 24,155, fol. 44. Another copy was sent to Bull, on the 7th March, 1783; see letter of that date.

† "Tiny, the surliest of his kind," is the reading of the Brit. Mus. manuscript.

A Turkey carpet was his lawn,
　　Whereon * he loved to bound,
To skip and gambol like a fawn,
　　And swing his rump around.

His frisking was at evening hours,   25
　　For then he lost his fear,
But most before approaching showers,
　　Or when a storm drew near.

Eight years and five round-rolling moons
　　He thus saw steal away,   30
Dozing out † all his idle noons,
　　And every night at play.

I kept him for his humour's ‡ sake,
　　For he would oft beguile
My heart of thoughts that made it ache,   35
　　And force me to a smile.

But now, beneath this § walnut shade,
　　He finds his long, last home,
And waits, in snug concealment laid,
　　Till gentler Puss shall come.   40

He, ‖ still more aged, ¶ feels the shocks,
　　From which no care can save,
And partner once of Tiny's box,
　　Must soon partake his grave.

---

* MS. "On which."　　　　† MS. "Slumbering."
‡ MS. "Old service."
§ All the modern Eds. have "his." We give the reading
of the MS. and of Ed. 1800, vol. ii., p. 357.
‖ MS. "She."　　　　¶ MS. "Ancient."

EPITAPHIUM ALTERUM.*

   Hic etiam jacet,
Qui totum novennium vixit,
      Puss.
   Siste paulisper,
  Qui præteriturus es,   5
  Et tecum sic reputa—
Hunc neque canis venaticus,
  Nec plumbum missile,
    Nec laqueus,
  Nec imbres nimii,   10
    Confecêre:
  Tamen mortuus est—
   Et moriar ego.

* Poems, Ed. 1800, vol. II., p. 358.

AN EPISTLE TO ROBERT LLOYD, ESQ.*

'TIS not that I design to rob
    Thee of thy birthright, gentle Bob,
    For thou art born sole heir, and single,
    Of dear Mat Prior's easy jingle;
Not that I mean, while thus I knit   5
My threadbare sentiments together,
To show my genius or my wit,
When God and you know I have neither;
Or such as might be better shown
By letting poetry alone.   10
'Tis not with either of these views
That I presume to address the Muse:
But to divert a fierce banditti,
(Sworn foes to every thing that's witty!)
That, with a black, infernal train,   15
Make cruel inroads in my brain,
And daily threaten to drive thence
My little garrison of sense:
The fierce banditti which I mean
Are gloomy thoughts, led on by Spleen.   20
Then there's another reason yet,
Which is, that I may fairly quit
The debt, which justly became due
The moment when I heard from you:
And you might grumble, crony mine,   25
If paid in any other coin;

* Hayley, 1803, vol. I. p. 15.

Since twenty sheets of lead, God knows,
(I would say twenty sheets of prose)
Can ne'er be deemed worth half so much
As one of gold, and yours was such.   30
Thus, the preliminaries settled,
I fairly find. myself pitchkettled,*
And cannot see, though few see better,
How I shall hammer out a letter.

    First, for a thought—since all agree—   35
A thought—I have it—let me see—
'Tis gone again—plague on't ! I thought
I had it—but I have it not.
Dame Gurton thus, and Hodge her son,
That useful thing, her needle, gone,   40
Rake well the cinders, sweep the floor,
And sift the dust behind the door ;
While eager Hodge beholds the prize
In old grimalkin's glaring eyes ;
And gammer finds it on her knees   45
In every shining straw she sees.
This simile were apt enough ;
But I have another, critic-proof !
The virtuoso thus, at noon,
Broiling beneath a July sun,   50
The gilded butterfly pursues,
O'er hedge and ditch, through gaps and mews ;
And, after many a vain essay,
To captivate the tempting prey,
Gives him at length the lucky pat,   55
And has him safe beneath his hat :

* Pitchkettled, a favourite phrase at the time when this
Epistle was written, expressive of being puzzled, or what in
the Spectator's time would have been called bamboozled.

Then lifts it gently from the ground;
But ah! 'tis lost as soon as found;
Culprit his liberty regains,
Flits out of sight, and mocks his pains.   60
The sense was dark; 'twas therefore fit
With simile to illustrate it;
But as too much obscures the sight,
As often as too little light,
We have our similes cut short,   65
For matters of more grave import.
That Matthew's numbers run with ease,
Each man of common sense agrees;
All men of common sense allow
That Robert's lines are easy too: 70
Where then the preference shall we place,
Or how do justice in this case?
" Matthew," says Fame, " with endless pains
" Smoothed and refined the meanest strains;
" Nor suffered one ill-chosen rhyme   75
" To escape him at the idlest time;
" And thus o'er all a lustre cast,
" That, while the language lives, shall last."
" An't please your ladyship," quoth I,
(For 'tis my business to reply)   80
" Sure so much labour, so much toil,
" Bespeak at least a stubborn soil:
" Theirs be the laurel-wreath decreed,
" Who both write well, and write full speed!
" Who throw their Helicon about   85
" As freely as a conduit spout!
" Friend Robert, thus like *chien savant*,
" Lets fall a poem *en passant*,
" Nor needs his genuine ore refine!
" 'Tis ready polished from the mine."   90

LINES

ADDRESSED TO MISS —— ON READING " THE
PRAYER FOR INDIFFERENCE."*

AND dwells there in a female heart,
　　By bounteous heaven designed,
The choicest raptures to impart,
　　To feel the most refined—

Dwells there a wish in such a breast　　　5
　　Its nature to forego,
To smother in ignoble rest
　　At once both bliss and woe !

Far be the thought, and far the strain,
　　Which breathes the low desire,　　　10
How sweet soe'er the verse complain,
　　Though Phœbus string the lyre.

Come, then, fair maid (in nature wise)
　　Who, knowing them, can tell
From generous sympathy what joys　　　15
　　The glowing bosom swell :

* Mrs. Greville's Ode, thus entitled, is printed in the
Annual Register, vol. v. p. 202, and also in the St. James's
Magazine, edited by Lloyd, vol. IV. p. 371. It is a prayer to
Oberon for some spell, "sovereign as juice of western flower,"
which should calm an over-excited mind. Cowper's lines
were printed by Dr. John Johnson, in vol. iii. of the Poems,
1815, p. 32; 12mo. p. 23.

In justice to the various powers
  Of pleasing, which you share,
Join me, amid your silent hours,
  To form the better prayer.   20

With lenient balm may 'Oberon hence
  To fairy land be driven,
With every herb that blunts the sense
  Mankind received from heaven.

" Oh ! if my Sovereign Author please,   25
  Far be it from my fate
To live, unblessed, in torpid ease,
  And slumber on in state.

" Each tender tie of life defied
  Whence social pleasures spring,   30
Unmoved with all the world beside,
  A solitary thing—"

Some Alpine mountain, wrapped in snow,
  Thus braves the whirling blast,
Eternal winter doomed to know,   35
  No genial spring to taste.

In vain warm suns their influence shed,
  The Zephyrs sport in vain,
He rears unchanged his barren head,
  Whilst beauty decks the plain.   40

What though in scaly armour dressed,
  Indifference may repel
The shafts of woe—in such a breast
  No joy can ever dwell.

'Tis woven in the world's great plan,   45
    And fixed by Heaven's decree,
That all the true delights of man
    Should spring from Sympathy.

'Tis Nature bids, and whilst the laws
    Of Nature we retain,   50
Our self-approving bosom draws
    A pleasure from its pain.

Thus grief itself has comforts dear
    The sordid never know ;
And ecstasy attends the tear   55
    When virtue bids it flow.

For when it streams from that pure source
    No bribes the heart can win,
To check, or alter from its course,
    The luxury within.   60

Peace to the phlegm of sullen elves,
    Who, if from labour eased,
Extend no care beyond themselves,
    Unpleasing and unpleased.

Let no low thought suggest the prayer ;—   65
    " Oh ! grant, kind Heaven, to me,
" Long as I draw ethereal air,
    " Sweet Sensibility."

Where'er the heavenly Nymph is seen,
    With lustre-beaming eye,   70
A train, attendant on their queen,
    (Her rosy chorus) fly.

The jocund Loves in Hymen's band,
   With torches ever bright,
And generous Friendship hand in hand,   75
   With Pity's watery sight.

The gentler Virtues too are join'd
   In youth immortal warm ;
The soft relations, which, combined,
   Give life her every charm.   80

The Arts come smiling in the close,
   And lend celestial fire ;
The marble breathes, the canvass glows,
   The Muses sweep the lyre.

" Still may my melting bosom cleave   85
   " To sufferings not my own,
" And still the sigh responsive heave
   " Where'er is heard a groan.

" So Pity shall take Virtue's part,
   " Her natural ally,   90
" And fashioning my softened heart,
   " Prepare it for the sky."

This artless vow may Heaven receive,
   And you, fond maid, approve :
So may your guiding angel give   95
   Whate'er you wish or love.

So may the rosy-fingered hours
   Lead on the various year,
And every joy, which now is yours,
   Extend a larger sphere.   100

And suns to come, as round they wheel,
  Your golden moments bless,
With all a tender heart can feel,
  Or lively fancy guess.

ANTI-THELYPTHORA.

A TALE IN VERSE.*

Ah miser,
Quantâ laboras in Charybdi!
HORACE, *Lib.* i. *Ode* 27.

IRY del Castro was as bold a knight,
As ever earned a lady's love in fight.
Many he sought, but one above the
  rest
His tender heart victoriously impressed.
In fairy land was born the matchless dame,   5
The land of dreams, Hypothesis her name,
There Fancy nursed her in ideal bowers,
And laid her soft in amaranthine flowers;

---

* Published in 1781, 4to. We have not been able to find a copy of the original edition and have therefore printed it from Southey (who had the merit of establishing it to be a work by Cowper), vol. VIII. p. 112. Cowper evidently felt very warmly on the subject of his relative Martin Madan's extraordinary and most pernicious Thelypthora; but, considering their previous acquaintance, it would have been better if Cowper had allowed it to pass with silent regret. Anonymous opposition to a man strangely led astray, but who had been kind to Cowper in a peculiar degree, was not commendable.

Delighted with her babe, the enchantress smiled,
And graced with all her gifts the favourite child.
Her wooed Sir Airy, by meandering streams,   11
In daily musings and in nightly dreams;
With all the flowers he found, he wove in haste
Wreaths for her brow, and girdles for her waist;
His time, his talents, and his ceaseless care,   15
All consecrated to adorn the fair;
No pastime but with her he deigned to take,
And if he studied, studied for her sake.
And for Hypothesis was somewhat long,
Nor soft enough to suit a lover's tongue,   20
He called her Posy, with an amorous art,
And graved it on a gem, and wore it next his heart.
   But she, inconstant as the beams that play
On rippling waters in an April day,
With many a freakish trick deceived his pains,   25
To pathless wilds and unfrequented plains,
Enticed him from his oaths of knighthood far,
Forgetful of the glorious toils of war.
'Tis thus the tenderness that Love inspires
Too oft betrays the votaries of his fires;   30
Borne far away on elevated wings,
They sport like wanton doves in airy rings,
And laws and duties are neglected things.
   Nor he alone addressed the wayward fair,
Full many a knight had been entangled there;   35
But still, whoever wooed her, or embraced,
On every mind some mighty spell she cast.
Some she would teach (for she was wondrous wise,
And make her dupes see all things with her eyes)
That forms material, whatsoe'er we dream,   40
Are not at all, or are not what they seem;

That substances, and modes of every kind,
Are mere impressions on the passive mind,
And he that splits his cranium, breaks at most
A fancied head against a fancied post ;   45
Others, that earth, ere Sin had drowned it all,
Was smooth and even as an ivory ball,
That all the various beauties we survey,
Hills, valleys, rivers, and the boundless sea,
Are but departures from the first design,   50
Effects of punishment and wrath divine.
She tutored some in Dœdalus's art,
And promised they should act the wild goose part,
On waxen pinions soar without a fall,
Swift as the proudest gander of them all.   55
    But Fate reserved Sir Airy to maintain
The wildest project of her teeming brain ;—
That wedlock is not rigorous, as supposed,
But man, within a wider pale enclosed,
May rove at will, where appetite shall lead,   60
Free as the lordly bull that ranges o'er the mead ;
That forms and rites are tricks of human law,
As idle as the chattering of a daw ;
That lewd incontinence, and lawless rape,
Are marriage in its true and proper shape ;   65
That man by Faith and Truth is made a slave,
The ring a bauble, and the priest a knave.
    " Fair fall the deed ! " the knight exulting cried,
" Now is the time to make the maid a bride ! "
    'Twas on the noon of an autumnal day,   70
October hight, but mild and fair as May ;
When scarlet fruits the russet hedge adorn,
And floating films envelope every thorn ;   .
When gently, as in June, the rivers glide,

And only miss the flowers that graced their side;
The linnet twittered out his parting song,   76
With many a chorister the woods among;
On southern banks the ruminating sheep,
Lay snug and warm;—'twas Summer's farewell
      peep!
Propitious to his fond intent there grew   80
An arbour near at hand of thickest yew,
With many a boxen bush, close-clipped, between,
And *phillyrea** of a gilded green.
  But what old Chaucer's merry page befits,
The chaster Muse of modern days omits.   85
Suffice it then in decent terms to say,
She saw, and turned her rosy cheek away.
Small need of Prayer Book, or of priest, I ween,
Where parties are agreed, retired the scene,
Occasion prompt, and appetite so keen.   90
Hypothesis (for with such magic power
Fancy endued her in her natal hour,)
From many a steaming lake and recking bog,
Bade rise in haste a dank and drizzling fog,
That curtained round the scene where they reposed,
And wood and lawn in dusky folds enclosed.   96
  Fear seized the trembling sex; in every grove
They wept the wrongs of honourable love.
" In vain," they cried, " are hymeneal rites,
" Vain our delusive hope of constant knights;   100
" The marriage bond has lost its power to bind,
'" And flutters loose, the sport of every wind.
" The bride, while yet her bride's attire is on,
" Shall mourn her absent lord, for he is gone,

---

* An evergreen shrub which bears a fruit like an olive.

" Satiate of her, and weary of the same,   105
" To distant wilds in quest of other game.
" Ye fair Circassians ! all your lutes employ,
" Seraglios sing, and harems dance for joy !
" For British nymphs, whose lords were lately true,
" Nymphs quite as fair, and happier once than you,
" Honour, esteem and confidence forgot,   111
" Feel all the meanness of your slavish lot.
" O cursed Hypothesis ! your hellish arts
" Seduce our husbands, and estrange their hearts,—
" Will none arise, no knight who still retains   115
" The blood of ancient worthies in his veins,
" To assert the charter of the chaste and fair,
" Find out her treacherous heart, and plant a dagger
          there ?
" A knight—(can he that serves the fair do less)
" Starts at the call of beauty in distress ;   120
" And he that does not, whatsoe'er occurs,
" Is recreant, and unworthy of his spurs." *
    Full many a champion, bent on daring deed,
Called for his arms, and for his princely steed ;
So swarmed the Sabine youth, and grasped the
          shield,   125
When Roman rapine, by no laws withheld,
Lest Rome should end with her first founders' lives,
Made half their maids, sans ceremony, wives.
But not the mitred few, the soul their charge,
They left these bodily concerns at large ;   130
Forms or no forms, pluralities or pairs,
Right reverend sirs ! was no concern of theirs.
The rest, alert and active, as became
A courteous knighthood, caught the generous flame ;

    * When a knight was degraded, his spurs were chopped
off. (C.)

One was accoutred when the cry began, 135
Knight of the Silver Moon, Sir Marmadan.*
Oft as his patroness who rules the night,
Hangs out her lamp in yon cærulean height,
His vow was (and he well performed his vow)
Armed at all points, with terror on his brow, 140
To judge the lands, to purge atrocious crimes,
And quell the shapeless monsters of the times.
For cedars famed, fair Lebanon supplied
The well-poised lance that quivered at his side,
Truth armed it with a point so keen, so just, 145
No spell or charm was proof against the thrust.
He couched it firm upon his puissant thigh,
And darting through his helm an eagle's eye,
On all the wings of chivalry advanced,
To where the fond Sir Airy lay entranced. 150
He dreamed not of a foe, or if his fear
Foretold one, dreamed not of a foe so near.
Far other dreams his feverish mind employed,
Of rights restored, variety enjoyed;
Of virtue too well fenced to fear a flaw; 155
Vice passing current by the stamp of law;
Large population on a liberal plan,
And woman trembling at the foot of man,
How simple wedlock fornication works, 159
And Christians marrying may convert the Turks.
The trumpet now spoke Marmadan at hand,
A trumpet that was heard through all the land;
His high-bred steed expands his nostrils wide,
And snorts aloud to cast the mist aside;
But he, the virtues of his lance to show, 165
Struck thrice the point upon his saddle bow:

* Monthly Review for October, 1781. (C.)

Three sparks ensued that chased it all away,
And set the unseemly pair in open day.
" To horse ! " he cried, "or by this good right hand,
" And better spear, I smite you where you stand."
　　Sir Airy, not a whit dismayed or scared,　171
Buckled his helm, and to his steed repaired,
Whose bridle, while he cropped the grass below,
Hung not far off upon a myrtle bough.
He mounts at once—such confidence infused　175
The insidious witch that had his wits abused ;
And she regardless of her softer kind,
Seized fast the saddle and sprang up behind.
" Oh, shame to knighthood ! " his assailant cried,
" Oh, shame ! " ten thousand echoing nymphs
　　　　replied.　180
Placed with advantage at his listening ear,
She whispered still that he had naught to fear,
That he was cased in such enchanted steel,
So polished and compact from head to heel,　184
" Come ten, come twenty,—should an army call
" Thee to the field, thou shouldst withstand them all."
　　" By Dian's beams," Sir Marmadan exclaimed,
" The guiltiest still are ever least ashamed
" But guard thee well, expect no feigned attack ;
" And guard behind the sorceress at thy back ! "
　　He spoke indignant, and his spurs applied,　191
Though little need, to his good palfrey's side ;
The barb sprang forward, and his lord, whose force,
Was equal to the swiftness of his horse,
Rushed with a whirlwind's fury on the foe,　195
And, Phineas like, transfixed them at a blow.
　　Then sang the married and the maiden throng,
Love graced the theme, and harmony the song ;

The Fauns and Satyrs, a lascivious race,
Shrieked at the sight, and, conscious, fled the place :
And Hymen, trimming his dim torch anew,   201
His snowy mantle o'er his shoulders threw ;
He turned and viewed it oft on every side,
And reddening with a just and generous pride,
Blessed the glad beams of that propitious day, 205
The spot he loathed so much for ever cleansed
    away.

ON

MARTIN MADAN'S ANSWER TO JOHN NEWTON'S

COMMENTS ON THELYPTHORA.*

QUARRELS with N. because M. wrote
    a book,
And N. did not like it, which M. could
    not brook,
So he called him a bigot, a wrangler, a monk,
With as many hard names as would line a good
    trunk,
And set up his back, and clawed like a cat,   5
But N. liked it never the better for that.
  Now N. had a wife, and he wanted but one,
Which stuck in M.'s stomach as cross as a bone ;
It has always been reckoned a just cause of strife,
For a man to make free with another man's wife,
But the strife is the strangest that ever was known,
If a man must be scolded for loving his own.

* Sent to Newton, in a letter dated 13th May, 1781, and
printed by Southey in his vol. IV. p. 91.

IMPROMPTU ON READING THE CHAPTER OF POLYGAMY IN MADAN'S THELYPTHORA.*

F John marries Mary, and Mary alone,
'Tis a very good match between Mary
    and John.
Should John wed a score, Oh, the claws,
    and the scratches !
It can't be a match—'tis a bundle of matches.

ON A REVIEW OF MADAN'S THELYPTHORA.†

HAVE read the Review ; it is learned
    and wise,
Clean, candid, and witty—Thelypthora
    dies.

* " One of those bagatelles which sometimes spring up
like mushrooms in my imagination, either while I am writing
or just before I begin. I sent it to you because to you I send
anything that I think may raise a smile, but should never have
thought of multiplying the impression."—Letter to Newton,
27th November, 1781. It appeared however in the Gentleman's Magazine, vol. L. p. 582.

† The article alluded to appeared in the pages of the
Monthly Review, vol. LXIII. and was written by the Rev.
Mr. Badcock. Mr. Robert Bell has given an account of
Thelypthora and the disturbance which it created in the
world of theology and morals, to which inquirers may turn
with profit (Bell's Cowper, II. 76). Cowper and Newton
were merely sharers in the general excitement occasioned
by Madan's extraordinary speculations.

SONNET

TO A YOUNG LADY ON HER BIRTHDAY. *

EEM not, sweet rose, that bloomest
    midst many a thorn,
    Thy friend, though to a cloister's
    shade consigned,
Can e'er forget the charms he left behind,
Or pass unheeded this auspicious morn,
In happier days, to brighter prospects born!   5
  Oh, tell thy thoughtless sex, the virtuous
    mind,
  Like thee, content in every state may find,
And look on Folly's pageantry with scorn.
To steer with nicest art betwixt the extreme
  Of idle mirth and affectation coy,   10
To blend good sense with elegance and ease,
To bid Affliction's eye no longer stream,
  Is thine;—best gift, the unfailing source of
    joy,
The guide to pleasures which can never cease.

* Grimshawe, vol. VIII. p. 19.

A POETICAL EPISTLE TO LADY AUSTEN.*

DEAR ANNA—between friend and friend,
Prose answers every common end;
Serves, in a plain and homely way,
To express the occurrence of the day;
Our health, the weather, and the news,   5
What walks we take, what books we choose;
And all the floating thoughts we find
Upon the surface of the mind.
    But when a poet takes the pen,
Far more alive than other men,   10
He feels a gentle tingling come
Down to his finger and his thumb,
Derived from nature's noblest part,
The centre of a glowing heart:
And this is what the world, who knows   15
No flights above the pitch of prose,
His more sublime vagaries slighting,
Denominates an itch for writing.
No wonder I, who scribble rhyme
To catch the triflers of the time,   20
And tell them truths divine and clear,
Which, couched in prose, they will not hear;
Who labour hard to allure and draw
The loiterers I never saw,
Should feel that itching and that tingling,   25
With all my purpose intermingling,

* Hayley, 1803, vol. I. p. 116.

To your intrinsic merit true,
When called to address myself to you.
  Mysterious are his ways whose power
Brings forth that unexpected hour,   30
When minds, that never met before,
Shall meet, unite, and part no more:
It is the allotment of the skies,
The hand of the Supremely Wise,
That guides and governs our affections,   35
And plans and orders our connexions:
Directs us in our distant road,
And marks the bounds of our abode.
Thus we were settled when you found us,
Peasants and children all around us,   40
Not dreaming of so dear a friend,
Deep in the abyss of Silver-End.*
Thus Martha,† even against her will,
Perched on the top of yonder hill;
And you, though you must needs prefer   45
The fairer scenes of sweet Sancerre,‡
Are come from distant Loire to choose
A cottage on the banks of Ouse.
This page of providence quite new,
And now just opening to our view,   50
Employs our present thoughts and pains:
To guess and spell what it contains:
But day by day, and year by year,
Will make the dark enigma clear;

* An obscure part of Olney, adjoining to the residence of
Cowper, which faced the market-place.
† Mrs. Jones, Lady Austen's sister, wife of the Rev. Thomas
Jones, curate of Clifton Reynes, who was one of the six stu-
dents expelled from St. Edmund Hall in 1768.
‡ Lady Austen's residence in France.

And furnish us, perhaps, at last,   55
Like other scenes already past,
With proof, that we, and our affairs,
Are part of a Jehovah's cares :
For God unfolds by slow degrees
The purport of his deep decrees ;   60
Sheds every hour a clearer light
In aid of our defective sight ;
And spreads, at length, before the soul
A beautiful and perfect whole,
Which busy man's inventive brain   65
Toils to anticipate in vain.

    Say, Anna, had you never known
The beauties of a rose full blown,
Could you, though luminous your eye,
By looking on the bud, descry,   70
Or guess, with a prophetic power,
The future splendour of the flower ?
Just so the Omnipotent, who turns
The system of a world's concerns,
From mere minutiæ can educe   75
Events of most important use ;
And bid a dawning sky display
The blaze of a meridian day.
The works of man tend, one and all,
As needs they must, from great to small !   80
And vanity absorbs at length
The monuments of human strength.
But who can tell how vast the plan
Which this day's incident began ?
Too small, perhaps, the slight occasion   85
For our dim-sighted observation ;

It passed unnoticed, as the bird
That cleaves the yielding air unheard,
And yet may prove, when understood,
A harbinger of endless good.   90
    Not that I deem, or mean to call,
Friendship a blessing cheap or small:
But merely to remark, that ours,
Like some of Nature's sweetest flowers,   '
Rose from a seed of tiny size,   95
That seemed to promise no such prize;
A transient visit intervening,
And made almost without a meaning,
(Hardly the effect of inclination,
Much less of pleasing expectation)   100
Produced a friendship, then begun,
That has cemented us in one;
And placed it in our power to prove,
By long fidelity and love,
That Solomon has wisely spoken;   105
" A threefold cord is not soon broken." *

        17th Dec. 1781.

                * Eccles. iv. 12.

THE FLATTING MILL.

AN ILLUSTRATION.*

WHEN a bar of pure silver or ingot of
    gold
    Is sent to be flatted or wrought into
    length,
It is passed between cylinders often, and rolled
In an engine of utmost mechanical strength.

Thus tortured and squeezed, at last it appears   5
Like a loose heap of ribbon, a glittering show,
Like music it tinkles and rings in your ears,
And, warmed by the pressure, is all in a glow.

This process achieved, it is doomed to sustain
The thump after thump of a gold-beater's mallet,
And at last is of service in sickness or pain   11
To cover a pill for a delicate palate.

Alas for the poet! who dares undertake
To urge reformation of national ill—
His head and his heart are both likely to ache   15
With the double employment of mallet and mill.

* Written in December, 1781, with a view to insertion in
Cowper's first volume of Poems; but not being thought suit-
able by Newton, it stood over, and was never published
until 1815, when Dr. John Johnson included it in his vol.
III. of the Poems, 8vo. p. 111; 12mo. p. 79.

If he wish to instruct, he must learn to delight,
Smooth, ductile, and even his fancy must flow,
Must tinkle and glitter like gold to the sight,
And catch in its progress a sensible glow.   20

After all he must beat it as thin and as fine
As the leaf that enfolds what an invalid swallows;
For truth is unwelcome, however divine,
And unless you adorn it, a nausea follows.

ON THE LOSS OF THE ROYAL GEORGE,

WRITTEN WHEN THE NEWS ARRIVED, BY DESIRE
OF LADY AUSTEN, WHO WANTED WORDS
TO THE MARCH IN SCIPIO.[*]

OLL for the brave!
 The brave that are no more!
All sunk beneath the wave.
 Fast by their native shore!

Eight hundred of the brave,   5
 Whose courage well was tried,
Had made the vessel heel,
 And laid her on her side.

---

[*] Hayley, 1803, vol. I. p. 126. We have collated our
copy with Cowper's manuscript, which is now Additional MS.
British Museum, 24,155, folio 40. The incident commemorated in these solemn lines occurred on the 29th August,
1782.

A land-breeze shook the shrouds,
    And she was overset;   10
Down went the Royal George,
    With all her crew complete!

Toll for the brave!
    Brave Kempenfelt is gone;
His last sea-fight is fought;   15
    His work of glory done.

It was not in the battle;
    No tempest gave the shock;
She sprang no fatal leak;
    She ran upon no rock.   20

His sword was in the sheath;
    His fingers held the pen,
When Kempenfelt went down
    With twice four hundred men.

Weigh the vessel up,   25
    Once dreaded by our foes!
And mingle with our cup
    The tears that England owes.

Her timbers yet are sound,
    And she may float again,   30
Full charged with England's thunder,
    And plough the distant main.

But Kempenfelt is gone,
    His victories are o'er;
And He and his Eight Hundred   35
    Must plough the wave no more.

IN SUBMERSIONEM NAVIGII,
CUI GEORGIUS REGALE NOMEN INDITUM.*

[TRANSLATION OF THE PRECEDING.]

PLANGIMUS fortes. Periêre fortes,
Patrium propter periêre littus
Bis quatèr centum ; subitò sub alto
    Æquore mersi.

Navis, innitens lateri, jacebat,   5
Malus ad summas trepidabat undas,
Cùm levis, funes quatiens, ad imum
    Depulit aura.

Plangimus fortes. Nimis, heu, caducam
Fortibus vitam voluêre Parcæ,   10
Nec sinunt ultrà tibi nos recentes
    Nectere laurus.

Magne, qui nomen, licèt incanorum,
Traditum ex multis atavis tulisti !
At tuos olim memorabit ævum   15
    Omne triumphos.

Non hyems illos furibunda mersit,
Non mari in clauso scopuli latentes,
Non fissa rimis abies, nec atrox
    Abstulit ensis.   20

* Hayley, 1803, vol. III. p. 163. Cowper's manuscript is
Additional MS. British Museum, 24,155, folio 40a.

Navitæ sed tum nimium jocosi
Voce fallebant hilari laborem,
Et quiescebat, calamoque dextram im-
    pleverat heros.

Vos, quibus cordi est grave opus piumque, 25
Humidum ex alto spolium levate,
Et putrescentes sub aquis amicos
    Reddite amicis !

Hi quidem (sic Diis placuit) fuêre :
Sed ratis, nondùm putris, ire possit   30
Rursùs in bellum, Britonumque nomen
    Tollere ad astra.

THE VALEDICTION.*

FAREWELL, false hearts ! whose best
    affections fail,
Like shallow brooks which summer suns
    exhale !

* We have stated in our Memoir (vol. I. p. ci.) the circumstances under which Cowper gave vent to his disappointment at the culpable silence of his friends Thurlow and George
Colman, in these indignant lines. He sent them to his friend
Unwin in a letter dated 10th November, 1783, and commented
upon his remarks on them in another letter, dated the 24th
of the same month. Until lately the lines have not been
completely published. Hayley gave a harmless extract from
them, and other editors, not having access (except Dr. John
Johnson) to the omitted passages, necessarily followed in his
wake. The lines are now in the British Museum (Additional
MS. 24,155, folio 146), and, as Southey remarked, there is
no longer any reason for suppressing any portion of them.

Forgetful of the man whom once ye chose,
Cold in his cause, and careless of his woes,
I bid you both a long and last adieu,   5
Cold in my turn, and unconcerned like you.
    First, farewell Niger !* whom now duly proved,
I disregard as much as once I loved.
Your brain well furnished, and your tongue well
       taught
To press with energy your ardent thought,   10
Your senatorial dignity of face,
Sound sense, intrepid spirit, manly grace,
Have raised you high as talents can ascend,
Made you a Peer, but spoiled you for a friend !
Pretend to all that parts have e'er acquired,   15
Be great, be feared, be envied, be admired,
To fame as lasting as the earth pretend,
But not, hereafter, to the name of friend !
I sent you verse, and, as your Lordship knows,
Backed with modest sheet of humble prose,   20
Not to recall a promise to your mind,
Fulfilled with ease had you been so inclined,
But to comply with feelings, and to give
Proof of an old affection still alive—
Your sullen silence serves at least to tell   25
Your altered heart—and so, my Lord, farewell !
    Next, busy actor on a meaner stage,†
Amusement-monger of a trifling age,
Illustrious histrionic patentee,
Terentius, once my friend, farewell to thee !   30
In thee some virtuous qualities combine
To fit thee for a nobler post than thine,

---

  * Lord Thurlow, raised to the Peerage 3rd June, 1778.
  † George Colman, the elder.

Who, born a gentleman, hast stooped too low,
To live by buskin, sock, and raree-show.
Thy schoolfellow and partner of thy plays   35
Where Nichol swung the birch and twined the bays,
And having known thee bearded and full grown,
The weekly censor of a laughing Town,
I thought the volume I presumed to send,
Graced with the name of a long absent friend,   40
Might prove a welcome gift, and touch thine heart,
Not hard by nature, in a feeling part.
But thou, it seems (what cannot grandeur do,
Though but a dream!) art grown disdainful too,
And strutting in thy school of Queens and Kings,
Who fret their hour and are forgotten things,   46
Hast caught the cold distemper of the day,
And, like his Lordship, cast thy friend away.

    Oh friendship! cordial of the human breast!
So little felt, so fervently professed!   50
Thy blossoms deck our unsuspecting years;
The promise of delicious fruit appears:
We hug the hopes of constancy and truth,
Such is the folly of our dreaming youth;
But soon, alas! detect the rash mistake   55
That sanguine inexperience loves to make;
And view with tears the expected harvest lost,
Decayed by time, or withered by a frost.
Whoever undertakes a friend's great part
Should be renewed in nature, pure in heart,   60
Prepared for martyrdom, and strong to prove
A thousand ways the force of genuine love.
He may be called to give up health and gain,
To exchange content for trouble, ease for pain,
To echo sigh for sigh, and groan for groan,   65

And wet his cheeks with sorrows not his own.
The heart of man, for such a task too frail,
When most relied on is most sure to fail;
And, summoned to partake its fellow's woe,
Starts from its office like a broken bow.   70
   Votaries of business and of pleasure prove
Faithless alike in friendship and in love.
Retired from all the circles of the gay,
And all the crowds that bustle life away,
To scenes where competition, envy, strife,   75
Beget no thunder-clouds to trouble life,
Let me, the charge of some good angel, find
One who has known, and has escaped mankind;
Polite, yet virtuous, who has brought away
The manners, not the morals, of the day: 80
With him, perhaps with her (for men have known
No firmer friendships than the fair have shown),
Let me enjoy, in some unthought-of spot,
All former friends forgiven, and forgot,
Down to the close of life's fast fading scene,
Union of hearts without a flaw between.   85
   'Tis grace, 'tis bounty, and it calls for praise,
If God give health, that sunshine of our days!
And if he add, a blessing shared by few,
Content of heart, more praises still are due—
But if he grant a friend, that boon possessed   90
Indeed is treasure, and crowns all the rest;
And giving one, whose heart is in the skies,
Born from above and made divinely wise,
He gives, what bankrupt nature never can,
Whose noblest coin is light and brittle man,   95
Gold, purer far than Ophir ever knew,
A soul, an image of Himself, and therefore true.

   Nov. 1783.

334

GRATITUDE.

ADDRESSED TO LADY HESKETH.*

THIS cap, that so stately appears,
　　With ribbon-bound tassel on high,
　　Which seems by the crest that it rears
　　Ambitious of brushing the sky:
This cap to my cousin I owe,　　　　　　　5
　　She gave it, and gave me beside,
Wreathed into an elegant bow,
　　The ribbon with which it is tied.

This wheel-footed studying chair,
　　Contrived both for toil and repose,　　　10
Wide-elbowed, and wadded with hair,
　　In which I both scribble and dose,
Bright-studded to dazzle the eyes,
　　And rival in lustre of that
In which, or astronomy lies,　　　　　　　15
　　Fair Cassiopeïa sat:

These carpets, so soft to the foot,
　　Caledonia's traffic and pride!
Oh spare them, ye knights of the boot,
　　Escaped from a cross country ride!　　　20

* Hayley, 1803, vol. II. p. 266.

This table and mirror within,
　Secure from collision and dust,
At which I oft shave cheek and chin,
　And periwig nicely adjust:

This moveable structure of shelves,   25
　For its beauty admired and its use,
And charged with octavos and twelves,
　The gayest I had to produce;
Where, flaming in scarlet and gold,
　My poems enchanted I view,   30
And hope, in due time, to behold
　My Iliad and Odyssey too:

This china that decks the alcove,
　Which here people call a buffet,
But what the gods call it above   35
　Has ne'er been revealed to us yet:
These curtains, that keep the room warm
　Or cool, as the season demands,
These stoves that for pattern and form
　Seem the labour of Mulciber's hands.   40

All these are not half that I owe
　To one, from our earliest youth,
To me ever ready to show
　Benignity, friendship, and truth;
For Time, the destroyer declared   45
　And foe of our perishing kind,
If even her face he has spared,
　Much less could he alter her mind.

Thus compassed about with the goods
   And chattels of leisure and ease,   50
I indulge my poetical moods
   In many such fancies as these;
And fancies I fear they will seem—
   Poets' goods are not often so fine;
The poets will swear that I dream   55
   When I sing of the splendour of mine.

1786.

ON THE QUEEN'S VISIT TO LONDON.*

THE NIGHT OF THE SEVENTEENTH OF MARCH, 1789.

WHEN, long sequestered from his throne
   George took his seat again,
By right of worth, not blood alone,
   Entitled here to reign,

---

* Hayley, 1803, vol. i. p. 326.   The lines were written
shortly after the event they commemorate.   They are mentioned in a letter to Lady Hesketh of the 14th April, 1789;
and in letters to Mrs. King, of the 22nd April and 30th
May of the same year.   In the last letter, Cowper men-
tions that they had been presented to the Princess
Augusta, who had probably given them to the Queen;
"but of their reception I have heard nothing . . . . It
would, indeed, be unreasonable to expect that persons who
keep a Laureate in constant pay should have either praise
or emolument to spare for every volunteer scribbler who
may choose to make them his subject."

Then Loyalty, with all her* lamps   5
    New trimmed, a gallant show!
Chasing the darkness and the damps,
    Set London in a glow.

'Twas hard to tell, of streets or squares,
    Which formed the chief display,   10
These most resembling clustered stars,
    Those the long milky way.

Bright shone the roofs, the domes, the spires,
    And rockets flew, self-driven,
To hang their momentary fires   15
    Amid the vault of heaven.

So, fire with water to compare,
    The ocean serves, on high
Up-spouted by a whale in air,
    To express unwieldy joy.   20

Had all the pageants of the world
    In one procession joined,
And all the banners been unfurled
    That heralds ere designed,

For no such sight had England's Queen   25
    Forsaken her retreat,
Where George, recovered, made a scene
    Sweet always doubly sweet.

---

* Hayley has " her lamps," and is followed by Grimshawe.
Dr. John Johnson (vol. III. 1815, 8vo. p. 114, 12mo. p. 81)
has "his lamps," and is followed by Southey and Bell.
Cowper had, perhaps, in his mind the Goddess Fides.

Yet glad she came that night to prove,
    A witness undescried,   30
How much the object of her love
    Was loved by all beside.

Darkness the skies had mantled o'er
    In aid of her design—
Darkness, O Queen! ne'er called before   35
    To veil a deed of thine!

On borrowed wheels away she flies,
    Resolved to be unknown,
And gratify no curious eyes
    That night except her own.   40

Arrived, a night like noon she sees,
    And hears the million hum;
As all by instinct, like the bees,
    Had known their sovereign come.

Pleased she beheld aloft portrayed,   45
    On many a splendid wall,
Emblems of health and heavenly aid,
    And George the theme of all.

Unlike the enigmatic line,
    So difficult to spell,   50
Which shook Belshazzar at his wine
    The night his city fell.

Soon watery grew her eyes and dim,
    But with a joyful tear,
None else, except in prayer for him,   55
    George ever drew from her.

It was a scene in every part
  Like those* in fable feigned,
And seemed by some magician's art
  Created and sustained.   60

But other magic there, she knew,
  Had been exerted none,
To raise such wonders in her view,
  Save love of George alone.

That cordial thought her spirit cheered,   65
  And through the cumbrous throng,
Not else unworthy to be feared,
  Conveyed her calm along.

So, ancient poets say, serene
  The sea-maid rides the waves,   70
And fearless of the billowy scene
  Her peaceful bosom laves.

With more than astronomic eyes
  She viewed the sparkling show;
One Georgian star adorns the skies,   75
  She myriads found below.

Yet let the glories of a night
  Like that, once seen, suffice,
Heaven grant us no such future sight,
  Such previous woe the price !   80

    * Hayley, " that;" Johnson " those."

IN MEMORY OF THE LATE JOHN

THORNTON, ESQ.*

POETS attempt the noblest task they can,
  Praising the Author of all good in
   man,
  And, next, commemorating worthies
   lost,
The dead in whom that good abounded most.
 Thee, therefore, of commercial fame, but more 5
Famed for thy probity from shore to shore,
Thee, THORNTON! worthy in some page to shine,
As honest and more eloquent than mine,
I mourn; or, since thrice happy thou must be,
The world, no longer thy abode, not thee.   10
Thee to deplore were grief misspent indeed;
It were to weep that goodness has its meed,
That there is bliss prepared in yonder sky,
And glory for the virtuous when they die.
 What pleasure can the miser's fondled hoard, 15
Or spendthrift's prodigal excess afford,
Sweet as the privilege of healing woe
Suffered by virtue combating below?
That privilege was thine; Heaven gave thee means
To illumine with delight the saddest scenes,   20

* Hayley, 1803, vol. I. p. 68.

Till thy appearance chased the gloom, forlorn
As midnight, and despairing of a morn.
Thou hadst an industry in doing good,
Restless as his who toils and sweats for food;
Avarice in thee was the desire of wealth   25
By rust unperishable or by stealth,
And if the genuine worth of gold depend
On application to its noblest end,
Thine had a value in the scales of Heaven
Surpassing all that mine or mint had given.   30
And, though God made thee of a nature prone
To distribution boundless of thy own,
And still by motives of religious force
Impelled thee more to that heroic course,
Yet was thy liberality discreet,   35
Nice in its choice, and of a tempered heat;
And though in act unwearied, secret still,
As in some solitude the summer rill
Refreshes, where it winds, the faded green,
And cheers the drooping flowers, unheard, un-
    seen.   40
    Such was thy charity; no sudden start,
After long sleep, of passion in the heart,
But steadfast principle, and, in its kind,
Of close alliance* to the Eternal Mind,
Traced easily to its true source above,   45
To Him whose works bespeak his nature, Love.
    Thy bounties all were Christian, and I make
This record of thee for the Gospel's sake;
That the incredulous themselves may see
Its use and power exemplified in thee.   50
    Nov. 1790.
        * Hayley, " alliance;" Johnson, " relation."

THE FOUR AGES.

COULD be well content, allowed the
    use
Of passed experience, and the wisdom
    gleaned
From worn-out follies, now acknowledged such,
To recommence life's trial, in the hope
Of fewer errors, on a second proof!   5
   Thus, while gray evening lulled the wind, and
    called
Fresh odours from the shrubbery at my side,
Taking my lonely winding walk, I mused,
And held accustomed conference with my heart;
When from within it thus a voice replied: 10
   "Couldst thou in truth? and art thou taught
    at length
This wisdom, and but this, from all the past?
Is not the pardon of thy long arrear,
Time wasted, violated laws, abuse
Of talents, judgment, mercies, better far   15
Than opportunity vouchsafed to err
With less excuse, and, haply, worse effect?"
   I heard, and acquiesced: then to and fro

* Hayley, 1803, vol. II. p. 173.

Oft pacing, as the mariner his deck,
My gravelly bounds, from self to human kind   20
I passed, and next considered—what is man ?
  Knows he his origin ? can he ascend
By reminiscence to his earliest date ?
Slept he in Adam ?   And in those from him
Through numerous generations, till he found .   25
At length his destined moment to be born ?
Or was he not, till fashioned in the womb ?
Deep mysteries both ! which schoolmen must have
        toiled
To unriddle, and have left them mysteries still.
  It is an evil incident to man,   30
And of the worst, that unexplored he leaves
Truths useful and attainable with ease,
To search forbidden deeps, where mystery lies
Not to be solved, and useless if it might.
Mysteries are food for angels ; they digest   35
With ease, and find them nutriment ; but man,
While yet he dwells below, must stoop to glean
His manna from the ground, or starve and die.

    May, 1791.

THE RETIRED CAT.*

POET'S cat, sedate and grave
As poet well could wish to have,
Was much addicted to inquire
For nooks to which she might retire,

    * Hayley, 1803, vol. I. p. 253.

And where, secure as mouse in chink,   5
She might repose, or sit and think.
I know not where she caught the trick—
   Nature perhaps herself had cast her
In such a mould philosophique,
   Or else she learned it of her master.   10
Sometimes ascending, debonair,
An apple tree, or lofty pear,
Lodged with convenience in the fork,
She watched the gardener at his work;
Sometimes her ease and solace sought   15
In an old empty watering pot;
There, wanting nothing save a fan,
To seem some nymph in her sedan
Apparelled in exactest sort,
And ready to be borne to court.   20
   But love of change, it seems, has place,·
Not only in our wiser race;
Cats also feel, as well as we,
That passion's force, and so did she.
Her climbing, she began to find,   25
Exposed her too much to the wind,
And the old utensil of tin
Was cold and comfortless within:
She therefore wished instead of those
Some place of more serene repose,   30
Where neither cold might come, nor air
Too rudely wanton with her hair,
And sought it in the likeliest mode
Within her master's snug abode.
   A drawer, it chanced, at bottom lined   35
With linen of the softest kind,
With such as merchants introduce

From India, for the ladies' use,
A drawer impending o'er the rest,
Half open in the topmost chest,   40
Of depth enough, and none to spare,
Invited her to slumber there ;
Puss with delight beyond expression
Surveyed the scene, and took possession.
Recumbent at her ease, ere long,   45
And lulled by her own humdrum song,
She left the cares of life behind,
    And slept as she would sleep her last,
When in came, housewifely inclined,
    The chambermaid, and shut it fast ;   50
By no malignity impelled,
But all unconscious whom it held.
    Awakened by the shock (cried Puss)
" Was ever cat attended thus ?
" The open drawer was left, I see,   55
" Merely to prove a nest for me,
" For soon as I was well composed,
" Then came the maid, and it was closed,
" How smooth these 'kerchiefs, and how sweet!
" Oh what a delicate retreat !   60
" I will resign myself to rest
" Till Sol, declining in the west,
" Shall call to supper, when, no doubt,
" Susan will come and let me out."
    The evening came, the sun descended,   65
And Puss remained still unattended.
The night rolled tardily away,
(With her indeed 'twas never day),
The sprightly morn her course renewed,
The evening gray again ensued,   70

And puss came into mind no more
Than if entombed the day before.
With hunger pinched, and pinched for room,
She now presaged approaching doom,
Nor slept a single wink, or purred,   75
Conscious of jeopardy incurred.
    That night, by chance, the poet watching,
Heard an inexplicable scratching;
His noble heart went pit-a-pat,
And to himself he said—"What's that?"   80
He drew the curtain at his side,
And forth he peeped, but nothing spied.
Yet, by his ear directed, guessed
Something imprisoned in the chest,
And, doubtful what, with prudent care   85
Resolved it should continue there.
At length a voice which well he knew,
A long and melancholy mew,
Saluting his poetic ears,
Consoled him and dispelled his fears: 90
He left his bed, he trod the floor,
He 'gan in haste the drawers explore,
The lowest first, and without stop
The rest in order to the top.
For 'tis a truth well known to most,   95
That whatsoever thing is lost,
We seek it, ere it come to light,
In every cranny but the right.
Forth skipped the cat, not now replete
As erst with airy self-conceit,   100
Nor in her own fond apprehension
A theme for all the world's attention,
But modest, sober, cured of all

Her notions hyperbolical,
And wishing for a place of rest   105
Any thing rather than a chest.
Then stepped the poet into bed,
With this reflection in his head.

MORAL.

Beware of too sublime a sense
Of your own worth and consequence: 110
The man who dreams himself so great,
And his importance of such weight,
That all around, in all that's done,
Must move and act for him alone,
Will learn in school of tribulation   115
The folly of his expectation.

1791.

THE JUDGMENT OF THE POETS.*

WO Nymphs, both nearly of an age,
    Of numerous charms possessed,
A warm dispute once chanced to wage,
    Whose temper was the best.

The worth of each had been complete,   5
    Had both alike been mild:

---

* Hayley, 1803, vol. I. p. 405. The Poem was sent to
Dr. John Johnson in a letter, dated 23rd May, 1791, in which
Cowper remarked,—" Oh! what a month of May has this
been! Let never poet, English poet at least, give himself
to the praises of May again."

But one, although her smile was sweet,
    Frowned oftener than she smiled.

And in her humour, when she frowned,
    Would raise her voice, and roar,   10
And shake with fury to the ground,
    The garland that she wore.

The other was of gentler cast,
    From all such frenzy clear,
Her frowns were seldom known to last,   15
    And never proved severe.

To poets of renown in song
    The Nymphs referred the cause,
Who, strange to tell, all judged it wrong,
    And gave misplaced applause.   20

They gentle called, and kind and soft,
    The flippant and the scold,
And though she changed her mood so oft,
    That failing left untold.

No judges, sure, were e'er so mad,   25
    Or so resolved to err—
In short, the charms her sister had
    They lavished all on her.

Then thus the god whom fondly they
    Their great inspirer call,   30
Was heard, one genial summer's day,
    To reprimand them all.

" Since thus ye have combined," he said,
  " My favourite Nymph to slight,
" Adorning May, that peevish maid,   35
  " With June's undoubted right,

" The minx shall, for your folly's sake,
  " Still prove herself a shrew,
" Shall make your scribbling fingers ache,
  " And pinch your noses blue."   40

YARDLEY OAK.*

URVIVOR sole, and hardly such, of all
      That once lived here thy brethren ! At
      my birth
      (Since which I number threescore
      winters past),
A shattered veteran, hollow-trunked perhaps,
As now, and with excoriate forks deform,   5
Relics of ages ! Could a mind, imbued
With truth from heaven, created thing adore,
I might with reverence kneel, and worship thee.
    It seems idolatry with some excuse,
When our forefather Druids in their oaks   10
Imagined sanctity. The conscience, yet
Unpurified by an authentic act
Of amnesty, the meed of blood divine,
Loved not the light, but, gloomy, into gloom

* Hayley, 1803, vol. III. p. 409.

Of thickest shades, like Adam after taste   15
Of fruit proscribed, as to a refuge, fled.
    Thou wast a bauble once, a cup and ball
Which babes might play with; and the thievish
       jay,
Seeking her food, with ease might have purloined
The auburn nut that held thee, swallowing down
Thy yet close-folded latitude of boughs,   21
And all thine embryo vastness, at a gulp.
But Fate thy growth decreed; autumnal rains
Beneath thy parent tree mellowed the soil
Designed thy cradle; and a skipping deer,   25
With pointed hoof dibbling the glebe, prepared
The soft receptacle, in which, secure,
Thy rudiments should sleep the winter through.
    So Fancy dreams. Disprove it, if ye can,
Ye reasoners broad awake, whose busy search   30
Of argument, employed too oft amiss,
Sifts half the pleasures of short life away!
    Thou fellest mature; and, in the loamy clod,
Swelling with vegetative force instinct,   34
Didst burst thine egg, as theirs the fabled twins,
Now stars; two lobes, protruding, paired exact;
A leaf succeeded, and another leaf,
And, all the elements thy puny growth
Fostering propitious, thou becamest a twig.
    Who lived when thou wast such? Oh, couldst
       thou speak,   40
As in Dodona once thy kindred trees
Oracular, I would not curious ask
The future, best unknown, but, at thy mouth
Inquisitive, the less ambiguous past.
    By thee I might correct, erroneous oft,   45

The clock of history, facts and events
Timing more punctual, unrecorded facts
Recovering, and misstated setting right—
Desperate attempt, till trees shall speak again !
   Time made thee what thou wast, king of the
      woods ;   50
And Time hath made thee what thou art—a cave
For owls to roost in. ˙ Once thy spreading boughs
O'erhung the champaign ; and the numerous flock
That grazed it stood beneath that ample cope
Uncrowded, yet safe sheltered from the storm. 55
No flock frequents thee now. Thou hast outlived
Thy popularity, and art become
(Unless verse rescue thee awhile) a thing
Forgotten, as the foliage of thy youth.
   While thus through all the stages thou hast
      pushed   60
Of treeship—first a seedling, hid in grass ;
Then twig ; then sapling ; and, as century rolled
Slow after century, a giant bulk
Of girth enormous, with moss-cushioned root
Upheaved above the soil, and sides embossed 65
With prominent wens globose ; till at the last
The rottenness, which time is charged to inflict
On other mighty ones, found also thee.
   What exhibitions various hath the world
Witnessed, of mutability in all   70
That we account most durable below !
Change is the diet on which all subsist,
Created changeable, and change at last
Destroys them—skies uncertain, now the heat
Transmitting cloudless, and the solar beam 75
Now quenching in a boundless sea of clouds—

Calm and alternate storm, moisture, and drought,
Invigorate by turns the springs of life
In all that live, plant, animal, and man,
And in conclusion mar them. Nature's threads, 80
Fine passing thought, e'en in her coarsest works,
Delight in agitation, yet sustain
The force that agitates not unimpaired ;
But worn by frequent impulse, to the cause
Of their best tone their dissolution owe.   85
   Thought cannot spend itself, comparing still
The great and little of thy lot, thy growth
From almost nullity into a state
Of matchless grandeur, and declension thence,
Slow, into such magnificent decay.   90
Time was when, settling on thy leaf, a fly
Could shake thee to the root—and time has been
When tempests could not. At thy firmest age
Thou hadst within thy bole solid contents
That might have ribbed the sides and planked the
        deck   95
Of some flagged admiral ; and tortuous arms,
The shipwright's darling treasure, didst present
To the four-quartered winds, robust and bold,
Warped into tough knee-timber, many a load !*
But the axe spared thee. In those thriftier days
Oaks fell not, hewn by thousands, to supply   101
The bottomless demands of contest waged
For senatorial honours. Thus to Time
The task was left to whittle thee away
With his sly scythe, whose ever-nibbling edge, 105

* Knee-timber is found in the crooked arms of oak, which,
by reason of their distortion, are easily adjusted to the angle
formed where the deck and the ship's sides meet.

Noiseless, an atom, and an atom more,
Disjoining from the rest, has unobserved,
Achieved a labour which had, far and wide,
By man performed, made all the forest ring.
    Embowelled now, and of thy ancient self   110
Possessing naught but the scooped rind that seems
A huge throat calling to the clouds for drink,
Which it would give in rivulets to thy root,
Thou temptest none, but rather much forbiddest
The feller's toil which thou couldst ill requite.   115
Yet is thy root sincere, sound as the rock,
A quarry of stout spurs and knotted fangs,
Which, crooked into a thousand whimsies, clasp
The stubborn soil, and hold thee still erect.
    So stands a kingdom, whose foundation yet   120
Fails not, in virtue and in wisdom laid,
Though all the superstructure, by the tooth
Pulverized of venality, a shell
Stands now, and semblance only of itself!
    Thine arms have left thee. Winds have rent
      them off   125
Long since, and rovers of the forest wild
With bow and shaft have burnt them. Some have
    left
A splintered stump bleached to a snowy white;
And some memorial none where once they grew.
Yet Life still lingers in thee, and puts forth   130
Proof not contemptible of what she can,
Even where Death predominates. The spring
Finds thee not less alive to her sweet force
Than yonder upstarts of the neighbouring wood,
So much thy juniors, who, their birth received   135
Half a millennium since the date of thine.

But since, although well qualified by age
To teach, no Spirit dwells in thee, nor voice
May be expected from thee, seated here
On thy distorted root, with hearers none,   140
Or prompter, save the scene, I will perform
Myself the oracle, and will discourse
In my own ear such matter as I may.
    One man alone, the father of us all,
Drew not his life from woman ; never gazed,   145
With mute unconsciousness of what he saw,
On all around him ; learned not by degrees,
Nor owed articulation to his ear ;
But moulded by his Maker into man
At once, upstood intelligent, surveyed   150
All creatures, with precision understood
Their purport, uses, properties, resigned
To each his name significant, and, filled
With love and wisdom, rendered back to Heaven
In praise harmonious the first air he drew.   155
He was excused the penalties of dull
Minority.   No tutor charged his hand
With the thought-tracing quill, or tasked his mind
With problems.   History, not wanted yet,
Leaned on her elbow, watching Time, whose course
Eventful, should supply her with a theme ; . . . 161

    1791.

A TALE.*

N Scotland's realm, where trees are few,
  Nor even shrubs abound;
But where, however bleak the view,
  Some better things are found.

For husband there and wife may boast 5
  Their union undefiled,
And false ones are as rare almost
  As hedgerows in the wild.

In Scotland's realm, forlorn and bare,
  This history chanced of late— 10
This history of a wedded pair,
  A chaffinch and his mate.

The spring drew near, each felt a breast
  With genial instinct filled;
They paired, and would have built a nest,† 15
  But found not where to build.

---

* This tale is founded on an article which appeared in the
Buckinghamshire Herald, for Saturday, June 1, 1793:—
"Glasgow, May 23. In a block, or pulley, near the head
of the mast of a gabert, now lying at the Broomielaw, there
is a chaffinch's nest and four eggs. The nest was built while
the vessel lay at Greenock, and was followed hither by both
birds. Though the block is occasionally lowered for the in-
spection of the curious, the birds have not forsaken the nest.
The cock, however, visits the nest but seldom, while the hen
never leaves it, but when she descends to the hull for food."
Hayley printed the lines in 1803, vol. II. p. 299.

† Hayley has "and only wished a nest." We have
adopted in preference the reading of Dr. John Johnson, in his
vol. III. of Cowper's Poems, 8vo. p. 307, 12mo. p. 224.

The heaths uncovered and the moors
  Except with snow and sleet,
Sea-beaten rocks and naked shores
  Could yield them no retreat.   20

Long-time a breeding-place they sought,
  Till both grew vexed and tired;
At length a ship arriving brought
  The good so long desired.

A ship!—Could such a restless thing   25
  Afford them place of rest?
Or was the merchant charged to bring
  The homeless birds a nest?

Hush—silent hearers profit most—
  This racer of the sea   30
Proved kinder to them than the coast,
  It served them with a tree.

But such a tree! 'twas shaven deal,
  The tree they call a mast,
And had a hollow with a wheel   35
  Through which the tackle passed.

Within that cavity aloft
  Their roofless home they fixed,
Formed with materials neat and soft,
  Bents, wool, and feathers mixed.   40

Four ivory eggs soon pave its floor
  With russet specks bedight—
The vessel weighs, forsakes the shore,
  And lessens to the sight.

The mother-bird is gone to sea,   45
    As she had changed her kind ;
But goes the male ?   Far wiser, he
    Is doubtless left behind.

No !   Soon as from ashore he saw
    The winged mansion move,   50
He flew to reach it, by a law
    Of never failing love.

Then, perching at his consort's side,
    Was briskly borne along,
The billows and the blast defied,   55
    And cheered her with a song.

The seaman, with sincere delight,
    His feathered shipmates eyes,
Scarce less exulting in the sight,
    Than when he tows a prize.   60

For seamen much believe in signs,
    And from a chance so new
Each some approaching good divines,
    And may his hopes be true !

Hail, honoured land ! a desert where   65
    Not even birds can hide ;
Yet parent of this loving pair,
    Whom nothing could divide.

And ye, who, rather than resign
    Your matrimonial plan,   70
Were not afraid to plough the brine,
    In company with man.

For whose lean country much disdain
  We English often show,
Yet from a richer nothing gain   75
  But wantonness and woe.

Be it your fortune, year by year,
  The same resource to prove,
And may ye, sometimes landing here,
  Instruct us how to love !   80

     June, 1793.

ON A SPANIEL, CALLED BEAU, KILLING
A YOUNG BIRD.*

A SPANIEL, Beau, that fares like you,
  Well fed, and at his ease,
Should wiser be, than to pursue
  Each trifle that he sees.

But you have killed a tiny bird,   5
  Which flew not till to-day,
Against my orders, whom you heard
  Forbidding you the prey.

Nor did you kill that you might eat,
  And ease a doggish pain,   10
For him, though chased with furious heat,
  You left where he was slain.

   * Hayley, 1803, vol. i. p. 316.

Nor was he of the thievish sort,
  Or one whom blood allures,
But innocent was all his sport   15
  Whom you have torn for yours.

My dog! what remedy remains,
  Since, teach you all I can,
I see you, after all my pains,
  So much resemble man?   20

BEAU'S REPLY.*

IR, when I flew to seize the bird
    In spite of your command,
  A louder voice than yours I heard,
    And harder to withstand.

You cried,—" Forbear!"—but in my breast
  A mightier cried—" Proceed!"—
'Twas Nature, Sir, whose strong behest
  Impelled me to the deed.

Yet, much as Nature I respect,
  I ventured once to break   10
(As you perhaps may recollect)
  Her precept, for your sake;

And when your linnet on a day,
  Passing his prison door,

* Hayley, 1803, vol. I. p. 317.

Had fluttered all his strength away,   15
And panting pressed the floor,

Well knowing him a sacred thing,
Not destined to my tooth,
I only kissed his ruffled wing,
And licked his feathers smooth.   20

Let my obedience then excuse
My disobedience now,
Nor some reproof yourself refuse
From your aggrieved Bow-wow:

If killing birds be such a crime   25
(Which I can hardly see)
What think you, Sir, of killing Time
With verse addressed to me?

July 15, 1793.

THE TREATMENT OF HIS HARES

MR. URBAN,   May 28.

CONVINCED that you despise no communications that may gratify curiosity, amuse rationally, or add, though but a little, to the stock of public knowledge, I send you a circumstantial account of an animal, which, though its general properties are pretty well known, is for the most part such a stranger to man that we are but little aware of its peculiarities. We know, indeed, that the hare is good to hunt and good to eat, but in all other respects poor Puss is a neglected subject.

In the year 1774, being much indisposed both in mind and body, incapable of diverting myself either with company or books, and yet in a condition that made some diversion necessary, I was glad of any thing that would engage my attention without fatiguing it. The children of a neighbour of mine had a leveret given them for a plaything; it was at that time about three months old. Understanding better how to tease the poor creature than to feed it, and soon becoming weary of their charge, they readily consented that their father, who saw it pining and growing leaner every day, should offer it to my acceptance. I was willing enough to

* For June, 1784, vol. liv., p. 412.

take the prisoner under my protection, perceiving that, in the management of such an animal, and in the attempt to tame it, I should find just that sort of employment which my case required. It was soon known among the neighbours that I was pleased with the present, and the consequence was, that in a short time I had as many leverets offered to me as would have stocked a paddock. I undertook the care of three, which it is necessary that I should here distinguish by the names I gave them—Puss, Tiny, and Bess. Notwithstanding the two feminine appellatives, I must inform you, that they were all males. Immediately commencing carpenter, I built them houses to sleep in; each had a separate apartment, so contrived that their ordure would pass through the bottom of it; an earthen pan placed under each received whatsoever fell, which being duly emptied and washed, they were thus kept perfectly sweet and clean. In the daytime they had the range of a hall, and at night retired each to his own bed, never intruding into that of another.

Puss grew presently familiar, would leap into my lap, raise himself upon his hinder feet, and bite the hair from my temples. He would suffer me to take him up, and to carry him about in my arms, and has more than once fallen fast asleep upon my knee. He was ill three days, during which time I nursed him, kept him apart from his fellows, that they might not molest him (for, like many other wild animals, they persecute one of their own species that is sick), and by constant care, and trying him with a variety of herbs, restored him to perfect health. No creature could be more grateful than my patient after his recovery; a sentiment which he most significantly expressed by licking my hand, first the back of it, then the palm, then every finger separately, then between all the fingers, as if anxious to leave no part of it unsaluted ; a ceremony which he never performed but once again upon a similar occasion. Finding him extremely tractable, I made it my custom to carry him always after breakfast into the garden, where he hid himself generally under the leaves of a cucumber vine, sleeping or chewing the cud till evening; in

the leaves also of that vine he found a favourite repast. I
had not long habituated him to this taste of liberty, before he
began to be impatient for the return of the time when he
might enjoy it. He would invite me to the garden by drumming upon my knee, and by a look of such expression, as it
was not possible to misinterpret. If this rhetoric did not immediately succeed, he would take the skirt of my coat between his teeth, and pull at it with all his force. Thus Puss
might be said to be perfectly tamed, the shyness of his nature
was done away, and on the whole it was visible by many
symptoms, which I have not room to enumerate, that he was
happier in human society than when shut up with his natural
companions.

Not so Tiny. Upon him the kindest treatment had not
the least effect. He too was sick, and in his sickness had an
equal share of my attention; but if after his recovery, I took
the liberty to stroke him, he would grunt, strike with his fore
feet, spring forward, and bite. He was however, very enter-
taining in his way; even his surliness was matter of mirth,
and in his play he preserved such an air of gravity, and performed his feats with such a solemnity of manner, that in
him too I had an agreeable companion.

Bess, who died soon after he was full grown, and whose
death was occasioned by his being turned into his box, which
had been washed, while it was yet damp, was a hare of great
humour and drollery. Puss was tamed by gentle usage;
Tiny was not to be tamed at all; and Bess had a courage
and confidence that made him tame from the beginning. I
always admitted them into the parlour after supper, when
the carpet affording their feet a firm hold, they would frisk,
and bound, and play a thousand gambols, in which Bess,
being remarkably strong and fearless, was always superior to
the rest, and proved himself the Vestris of the party. One
evening the cat, being in the room, had the hardiness to pat
Bess upon the cheek, an indignity which he resented by
drumming upon her back with such violence that the cat was
happy to escape from under his paws, and hide herself.

You observe, sir, that I describe these animals as having

each a character of his own. Such they were in fact, and their countenances were so expressive of that character, that, when I looked only on the face of either, I immediately knew which it was. It is said that a shepherd, however numerous his flock, soon becomes so familiar with their features, that he can, by that indication only, distinguish each from all the rest; and yet, to a common observer, the difference is hardly perceptible. I doubt not that the same discrimination in the cast of countenances would be discoverable in hares, and am persuaded that among a thousand of them no two could be found exactly similar: a circumstance little suspected by those who have not had opportunity to observe it. These creatures have a singular sagacity in discovering the minutest alteration that is made in the place to which they are accustomed, and instantly apply their nose to the examination of a new object. A small hole being burnt in the carpet, it was mended with a patch, and that patch in a moment underwent the strictest scrutiny. They seem too to be very much directed by the smell in the choice of their favourites: to some persons, though they saw them daily, they could never be reconciled, and would even scream when they attempted to touch them; but a miller coming in engaged their affections at once; his powdered coat had charms that were irrésistible. You will not wonder, sir, that my intimate acquaintance with these specimens of the kind has taught me to hold the sportsman's amusement in abhorrence; he little knows what amiable creatures he persecutes, of what gratitude they are capable, how cheerful they are in their spirits, what enjoyment they have of life, and that, impressed as they seem with a peculiar dread of man, it is only because man gives them peculiar cause for it.

That I may not be tedious, I will just give a short summary of those articles of diet that suit them best, and then retire to make room for some more important correspondent.

I take it to be a general opinion, that they graze, but it is an erroneous one, at least grass is not their staple; they seem rather to use it medicinally, soon quitting it for leaves of almost any kind. Sowthistle, dandelion, and lettuce, are their favourite vegetables, especially the last. I discovered by accident that fine white sand is in great estimation with them; I suppose as a digestive. It happened, that I was cleaning a birdcage when the hares were with me; I placed a pot filled with such sand upon the floor, to which being at once directed by a strong instinct, they devoured it voraciously; since that time I have generally taken care to see them well supplied with it. They account green corn a delicacy, both blade and stalk, but the ear they seldom eat; straw of any kind, especially wheat-straw, is another of their dainties; they will feed greedily upon oats, but if furnished with clean straw never want them; it serves them also for a bed, and, if shaken up daily, will be kept sweet and dry for a considerable time. They do not indeed require aromatic herbs, but will eat a small quantity of them with great relish, and are particularly fond of the plant called musk; they seem to resemble sheep in this, that, if their pasture be too succulent, they are very subject to the rot; to prevent which, I always made bread their principal nourishment, and, filling a pan with it, cut into small squares, placed it every evening in their chambers, for they feed only at evening and in the night; during the winter, when vegetables are not to be got, I mingled this mess of bread with shreds of carrot, adding to it the rind of apples cut extremely thin; for though they are fond of the paring, the apple itself disgusts them. These however not being a sufficient substitute for the juice of summer herbs, they must at this time be supplied with water; but so placed that they cannot overset it into their beds. I must not omit, that occasionally they are much pleased with twigs of hawthorn, and of the common brier, eating even the very wood when it is of considerable thickness.

Bess, I have said, died young; Tiny lived to be nine years old, and died at last, I have reason to think, of some hurt in his loins by a fall; Puss is still living, and has just completed his tenth year, discovering no signs of decay, nor even of age, except that he is grown more discreet and less frolicsome than he was. I cannot conclude without observing, that I have lately introduced a dog to his acquaintance, a spaniel that had never seen a hare to a hare that had never seen a spaniel. I did it with great caution, but there was no real need of it. Puss discovered no token of fear, nor Marquis the least symptom of hostility. There is, therefore, it should seem, no natural antipathy between dog and hare, but the pursuit of the one occasions the flight of the other, and the dog pursues because he is trained to it; they eat bread at the same time out of the same hand, and are in all respects sociable and friendly. Yours, &c.,

W. C.

P.S.—I should not do complete justice to my subject, did I not add, that they have no ill scent belonging to them, that they are indefatigably nice in keeping themselves clean, for which purpose nature has furnished them with a brush under each foot; and that they are never infested by any vermin.

MEMORANDUM FOUND AMONG MR. COWPER'S PAPERS.

Tuesday, March 9, 1786.

This day died poor Puss, aged eleven years eleven months. He died between twelve and one at noon, of mere old age, and apparently without pain.

END OF VOL II.